KU-747-552

macromedia®
DIRECTOR®8.5
SHOCKWAVE®
STUDIO

Using Director 8.5 Shockwave Studio

macromedia®

Trademarks

Afterburner, AppletAce, Attain, Attain Enterprise Learning System, Attain Essentials, Attain Objects for Dreamweaver, Authorware, Authorware Attain, Authorware Interactive Studio, Authorware Star, Authorware Synergy, Backstage, Backstage Designer, Backstage Desktop Studio, Backstage Enterprise Studio, Backstage Internet Studio, Design in Motion, Director, Director Multimedia Studio, Doc Around the Clock, Dreamweaver, Dreamweaver Attain, Drumbeat, Drumbeat 2000, Extreme 3D, Fireworks, Flash, Fontographer, FreeHand, FreeHand Graphics Studio, Generator, Generator Developer's Studio, Generator Dynamic Graphics Server, Knowledge Objects, Knowledge Stream, Knowledge Track, Lingo, Live Effects, Macromedia, Macromedia M Logo & Design, Macromedia Flash, Macromedia Xres, Macromind, Macromind Action, MAGIC, Mediamaker, Object Authoring, Power Applets, Priority Access, Roundtrip HTML, Scriptlets, SoundEdit, ShockRave, Shockmachine, Shockwave, Shockwave Remote, Shockwave Internet Studio, Showcase, Tools to Power Your Ideas, Universal Media, Virtuoso, Web Design 101, Whirlwind and Xtra are trademarks of Macromedia, Inc. and may be registered in the United States or in other jurisdictions including internationally. Other product names, logos, designs, titles, words or phrases mentioned within this publication may be trademarks, servicemarks, or tradenames of Macromedia, Inc. or other entities and may be registered in certain jurisdictions including internationally.

This guide contains links to third-party Web sites that are not under the control of Macromedia, and Macromedia is not responsible for the content on any linked site. If you access a third-party Web site mentioned in this guide, then you do so at your own risk. Macromedia provides these links only as a convenience, and the inclusion of the link does not imply that Macromedia endorses or accepts any responsibility for the content on those third-party sites.

Apple Disclaimer

APPLE COMPUTER, INC. MAKES NO WARRANTIES, EITHER EXPRESS OR IMPLIED, REGARDING THE ENCLOSED COMPUTER SOFTWARE PACKAGE, ITS MERCHANTABILITY OR ITS FITNESS FOR ANY PARTICULAR PURPOSE. THE EXCLUSION OF IMPLIED WARRANTIES IS NOT PERMITTED BY SOME STATES. THE ABOVE EXCLUSION MAY NOT APPLY TO YOU. THIS WARRANTY PROVIDES YOU WITH SPECIFIC LEGAL RIGHTS. THERE MAY BE OTHER RIGHTS THAT YOU MAY HAVE WHICH VARY FROM STATE TO STATE.

Copyright © 2001 Macromedia, Inc. All rights reserved. This manual may not be copied, photocopied, reproduced, translated, or converted to any electronic or machine-readable form in whole or in part without prior written approval of Macromedia, Inc. Part Number ZWD85M100

Acknowledgments

Writing: Jay Armstrong, Barbara Herbert, and Stephanie Gowin

Editing: Peter Fenczik, Rosana Francescato, and Anne Szabla

Multimedia Design and Production: John Lehnus and Noah Zilberberg

Print Design and Production: Chris Basmajian

Web Editing: Jane Dekoven and Jeff Harmon

Project Management: Joe Schmitz

Special Thanks: Sarah Allen, Chris Campbell, Margaret Dumas, Grace Gellerman, Lisa Gelobter, Tom Higgins, Buzz Kettles, Valerie Liberty, Dan Sadowski, Jake Sapirstein, and Ian Starr

Second Edition: March 2001

Macromedia, Inc.
600 Townsend St.
San Francisco, CA 94103

CONTENTS

CHAPTER 2

CHAPTER 3

CHAPTER 4
Sprites 119

CHAPTER 5
Behaviors 157

INTRODUCTION
Getting Started

. . . .

Macromedia Director 8 Shockwave Studio is the world's foremost authoring tool for creating interactive multimedia. Developers rely on Director to create attention-grabbing business presentations, advertising kiosks, interactive entertainment and educational products. To see some of the exciting and varied ways in which developers use Director, visit Macromedia's Gallery at www.macromedia.com. You can see great examples of Shockwave at www.shockwave.com.

Your users can view your completed Director movie over the Internet, either in a Web browser or independent of a browser, or as a stand-alone projector suitable for LANs and distribution through CD-ROM and DVD-ROM.

System requirements

The following hardware and software is the minimum required to author Director movies:

- For Microsoft Windows™: An Intel Pentium® II 200 processor running Windows 95/98 or NT version 4.0 or later; 32 MB of available RAM plus 100 MB of available disk space; a color monitor; and a CD-ROM drive.

- For the Macintosh®: A Power PC Macintosh180 running System 8.1 or later; 32 MB of available RAM plus 100 MB of available disk space; a color monitor; and a CD-ROM drive.

The following hardware and software is the minimum required to play back Director movies:

- For Microsoft Windows™: An Intel Pentium® 166 processor running Windows 95/98 or NT version 4.0 or later; 32 MB of installed RAM; Netscape Navigator 4.0, Microsoft Internet Explorer 4.0, or America Online 4.0 Web browser; and a color monitor.

- For the Macintosh®: A Power PC 120 Macintosh running System 8.1 or later; 32 MB of installed RAM; Netscape Navigator 4.0, Microsoft Internet Explorer 4.5, or America Online 4.0 Web browser; and a color monitor.

Installing Director

Follow these steps to install Director on either a Windows or a Macintosh computer.

To install Director on a Windows or a Macintosh computer:

1 Insert the Director CD into the computer's CD-ROM drive.

   In Windows, if the installation program doesn't start automatically, choose Run from the Windows Start menu, type **d:\setup.exe** (where **d** is your CD-ROM drive letter), and click OK.

2 On the Macintosh, double-click the Director Installer icon.

3 Follow the onscreen instructions.

4 If prompted, restart your computer.

What's new in Director 8

One of the most important changes in Director 8 is a Property Inspector that automatically switches context to match the current selection. The Property Inspector is referred to throughout this book. For basic information about it, see "The Property Inspector" on page 58.

Other new authoring features in Director 8 include the following:

Zoomable stage allows shrinking or expanding of the Stage window during authoring without affecting logical sprite sizes and positions. See "Increasing or decreasing your view of the Stage" on page 63.

Cast window List view provides a new way to display cast members, and provides the ability to sort and change member properties. See "Using Cast List view" on page 94.

Asset management fields on the Cast window, including a comments field and source control fields, are customizable for each cast member. See "Using Cast List view" on page 94

Linked scripts let you store scripts in external text files that can be edited separately from a Director movie. See "Using linked scripts" on page 217.

Bitmap compression allows JPEG compression for bitmap members in a DCR. You can specify compression for individual bitmaps, or at the movie level for all bitmaps in your DCR. An optimize in fireworks option lets you preview the JPEG image at various quality settings. Bitmap compression offers a compression strategy for 32-bit cast members with alpha channel data. See "Compressing bitmaps" on page 332.

Lockable sprites help prevent unintentional modifications during authoring. See "Locking and unlocking sprites" on page 132.

Guides on the Stage (in addition to the existing grid) help you place elements precisely. See "Positioning sprites using guides, the grid, or the Align window" on page 135.

Publish command lets you create a Shockwave movie, in your choice of HTML templates, by simply choosing File > Publish. A Publish Settings dialog box lets you configure how your want your Shockwave movie to appear in a browser. See "Creating Shockwave movies" on page 440.

Scalable Shockwave lets Shockwave movies stretch to fit the browser window while (optionally) preserving the original aspect ratio. See "Changing Publish settings" on page 441.

Multiple curve vectors offers the ability to create and edit vector cast members with more than one curve segment. See "Drawing vector shapes" on page 293.

Inline IME, available for Japanese operating systems, supports direct entry of double-byte Japanese text in Shockwave and projectors.

Enhanced Lingo performance and new parent-child scripting functionality. See "Parent script and child object basics" on page 280.

Imaging Lingo lets you create and manipulate bitmap images entirely in Lingo. See "Controlling bitmap images with Lingo" on page 319.

Sound control Lingo allows precise, professional quality control of sound playback. See "Playing sounds with Lingo" on page 365.

Resources for learning Director

The Director package contains a variety of media to help you learn the program quickly and become proficient in creating multimedia—including online help, a multimedia Guided Tour, a tutorial, integrated tooltips, printed books, and a regularly updated Web site.

Director includes the following main instructional components.

Director Help and the Guided Tour

Director Help is the comprehensive information source for all Director features. The help includes complete conceptual overviews of all features, animated examples, descriptions of all interface elements, and a reference of all Lingo commands and elements. They are extensively cross-referenced and indexed to make finding information and jumping to related topics quick and easy.

The best place to start learning Director is the Guided Tour included with Director Help. The Guided Tour provides a quick conceptual overview of how to use key features to create and distribute a movie.

Click the Help button in any dialog box to open the relevant help topic.

Director Tutorial

When you're ready to actually start working in Director, proceed to the Director Tutorial. The tutorial shows you how to create a basic movie with some of Director's most useful and powerful features. The tutorial appears in Director Help and in Chapter 1 of this book.

Using Director

This book is a printed excerpt of Director Help. It includes all the main topics in Director Help, but omits some topics that are less frequently used or becoming obsolete as Director evolves.

Lingo Dictionary

The *Lingo Dictionary* is a printed version of all the Lingo topics in Director Help.

Tooltips

When you place the pointer over a Director tool for a few seconds, a small tooltip appears that explains the function of the tool. When a keyboard shortcut is available, it is included in the tooltip.

In the following illustrations, Director is displaying tooltips for two different tools in the Cast window.

Keyboard shortcuts

Many commands that are available from Director menus are also accessible through the use of keyboard shortcuts. When you display a menu or submenu, the appropriate key combinations are shown next to the commands for which keyboard shortcuts are available.

The following illustration shows key board shortcuts for a variety of commands on the Control menu. (The illustration shows Director running on Windows. When Director is running on a Macintosh, the keyboard shortcuts reflect Macintosh keys.)

Director Support Center

The Director Support Center Web site (www.macromedia.com/support/director/) contains the latest information on Director, plus additional topics, examples, tips, and updates. Check the Web site often for the latest news on Director and how to get the most out of the program.

For example, you can visit the Director Support Center for additional information about these topics:

- Using Director 8 behaviors
- Working with Multiuser behaviors
- Using the Shockwave Multiuser Server
- XML parsing
- Troubleshooting Lingo
- Authoring from Lingo
- Controlling vector shapes with Lingo
- Specifying chunk expressions with dot syntax
- Optimizing bitmaps in Fireworks
- Creating Java applets with Director
- Creating dialog boxes from the MUI Xtra
- Director 8 keyboard shortcuts

Conventions used in Director Help and printed books

The help system and printed books use the following conventions:

- The terms *Lingo* and *Director* refer to version 8 of Director.

- Within the text and in Lingo examples, Lingo elements and parts of actual code are shown in this font. For example, set answer = 2 + 2 is a sample Lingo statement.

- Quotation marks that are part of Lingo statements are shown in the text and Lingo code examples as straight quotation marks (") rather than as curly quotation marks (").

- The continuation symbol (¬), which you enter by pressing Alt+Enter (Windows) or Option+Return (Macintosh), indicates that a long line of Lingo has been broken onto two or more lines. Lines of Lingo that are broken this way are not separate lines of code. When you see the continuation symbol in this book, type the lines as one line when you enter them in the Script window.

- Variables used to represent parameters in Lingo appear in *italics*. For example, *whichCastMember* is commonly used to indicate where you insert the name of a cast member in Lingo.

- Text that you should type is shown in **this** font.

Conventions used in Director Help and printed books

The Help system and printed books use the following conventions:

- The terms Stage and Score refer to Director's Stage and Score.

- Within the text, and in bigger examples, things that represent parts of actual code are shown in this font. For example, `on enterFrame`.

- Computer code is either part of a larger statement, in which case it's shown in the text, and in larger code examples, as syntax to be typed in, it's set off rather than as clarifying annotation marks.

- The continuation symbol (¬) when you enter code by pressing the Enter (Windows) or Return (Macintosh) keys, indicates that a long line of Lingo has been broken into two or more lines. Lines of Lingo that are too long to break sensibly wrap means a single line of code. When you see the continuation symbol at the break, type the lines as one line when you enter them in the Cast or Script window.

- Variable parts of text that represent in Lingo appear in italic. Italic text is information used to indicate where you insert the name of a movie. For the tutorial, you will create a movie that you will name Nov1.dir, and so on.

- The button you should type is shown in this font:

CHAPTER 1
Director 8 Tutorial

You're about to see how easy it is to master basic tasks necessary to create a movie in Director 8. With a few more simple steps, you can add multiuser functionality to a movie and export the entire project for distribution. By completing this tutorial, you'll learn Director fundamentals and acquire a basis for exploring more advanced Director features.

For the tutorial, you'll create a movie that plays in the Web page of an organization called GardenChat. You'll also take advantage of Director's multiuser behaviors to add chat functionality to the site, allowing members of the organization to discuss gardening tips with each other in real time.

The tutorial assumes no prior knowledge of Director other than the information provided in the Guided Tour. You should, however, be familiar with basic computer operations such as using menus and selecting and dragging objects. The tutorial takes approximately two hours to complete, and it focuses on many Director processes, including the following:

- Creating a new movie, cast members, and sprites

- Using inks

- Creating animation using tweening, frame-by-frame animation, and blends

- Importing media

- Synchronizing sound

- Attaching behaviors

- Controlling streaming over the Web

- Publishing your movie for Web playback

If you haven't watched the Guided Tour in Director Help, you should do so before starting this tutorial. The Guided Tour will introduce you to Director terminology and provide an overview of Director features.

View the completed Shockwave version of GardenChat

The tutorial takes you through the steps of creating an animated sequence that plays in a Web browser. When you publish a movie for Web playback, you create a Shockwave version of the movie with the .dcr extension. Your original Director movie remains unchanged.

1 Open your browser.

2 In your Director application folder, open the Learning folder and the Completed_Tutorials subfolder.

3 Drag the file Completed_Tutorial.html to your browser window.

The completed GardenChat movie plays in your browser in the Shockwave movie format.

View the completed DIR version of GardenChat

When you work on a Director movie, you use the authoring environment. Director movies saved in this environment have the .dir file extension. (These movies are not yet prepared for distribution.) Now view the completed DIR version of the tutorial movie to understand how the assets work together on the Stage and in the Score to create the movie.

Note: The DIR version of the completed tutorial movie does not include the chat component.

1 Launch Director and then choose File > Open.

2 Browse to your Director application folder, open the Learning folder and the Completed_Tutorials folder, and then open fun.dir.

3 To play the movie, click Play on the Control Panel or the toolbar along the top of the screen.

Stop

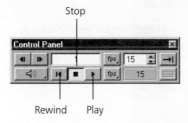

Rewind   Play

If the Control Panel and toolbar are not visible, you can select them from the Window menu.

4 After viewing the movie, click Stop and look at the Stage, Score, Cast window, and Property Inspector to get a sense of how the Director application and movie are organized.

If the Stage, Score, Cast window, and Property Inspector are not visible, you can select them from the Window menu.

Set up the movie

To begin your own version of GardenChat, you'll create a new movie and set the size of the Stage. You'll also select an appropriate color palette.

1 Choose File > New > Movie.

2 If you've made changes to the Fun.dir movie, Director prompts you to save them. Choose Don't Save.

Note that the default Stage is a different size than the Stage in the completed GardenChat movie.

3 To change your Stage size, click the Movie tab of the Property Inspector.

If the Property Inspector is not open, choose Window > Inspectors > Property. You should be in the default Graphical view, with the List View Mode icon deselected.

List View Mode

4 To specify a new Stage size in pixels, enter **450** in the first Stage Size field (width) and **500** in the second Stage Size field (height). After entering data in a field, click either the Stage or Property Inspector and the Stage resizes.

Because you are creating this movie for playback on the Web, you want to use a palette of Web-safe colors to ensure proper display. Director has a Web palette that you can select for your movie.

5 On the Movie tab of the Property Inspector, click the Movie Palette pop-up menu and select Web 216.

6 Choose File > Save. You can also press Control-S (Windows) or Command-S (Macintosh).

7 Name the movie **GardenChat1**.

8 Browse to the Learning folder within the Director application folder, and then open the My_Tutorial folder; then save your movie.

You must save your file in My_Tutorial; other tutorial files will point to your file in this location.

Note: As you complete the tutorial, remember to save your work frequently.

Create media in Director

You can create media in Director or import it from other programs. Simple media, such as text and backgrounds, are ideally suited for creation in Director.

Create a vector shape

Director lets you create multiple-curve vector shapes: mathematical descriptions of shapes filled with color or gradient colors. A vector shape uses much less memory than a comparable bitmap and downloads faster from the Internet.

You will create a vector shape filled with gradient colors to serve as your movie's background.

1 Choose Window > Vector Shape.

2 Click the Filled Rectangle tool and drag the cross hair from the upper left corner of the Vector Shape window to the lower right corner, creating a rectangle close to the size of your Stage.

   Exact size is not important; you can resize the image later.

 3 Click the rightmost Gradient Colors box and select a dark to medium shade of blue from the Color menu.

4 Click the leftmost color box and select a light sky blue.

 5 Click the Gradient button to create a smooth transition from light blue to dark blue.

6 From the Gradient Type pop-up menu at the top of the window, select Radial.

   Radial creates a circular, rather than linear, gradient effect.

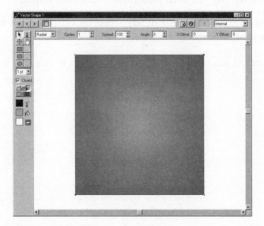

7 In the Y Offset box, type -70. (If you do not see the Y Offset box, make the window larger.)

This offsets the center of the gradient by moving it up 70 pixels, creating a sunlit sky effect.

You would use a positive number in the Y Offset box to move the gradient down.

8 In the Cast Member Name field at the top of the window, type **Sky** as the name.

Naming cast members makes it easier to identify them in the Score. If you don't enter a name, Director assigns a number to the cast member based on its position in the Cast window.

9 Close the Vector Shapes window.

Create a text cast member

The Text window offers standard text formatting controls in a window that resembles a word processing program.

1 Choose Window > Text.

2 If necessary, resize the window to see all of the controls along the top.

3 Use the various fields to set font attributes. To match the font attributes of the Completed_Tutorial movie, use Arial, 24-point bold.

4 Choose Modify > Font and click the Color box to select a shade of red.

5 In the Text window, type **Loading...**

6 Name the text cast member **Loading**.

7 Close the Text window.

View cast members in the Cast window

Notice how the cast members you've created appear in the Internal Cast window with the names you've entered.

Use the Cast View Style icon to toggle between Cast List view and Cast Thumbnail view. Note that each view offers different features that assist you in managing your cast members.

Cast View
Style icon

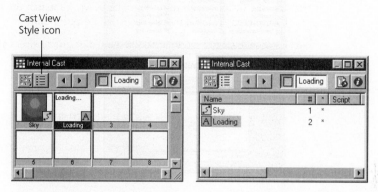

This movie only requires a single Cast window; it does not use many cast members or media types. For future projects, keep in mind that you can create as many Cast windows as necessary to organize your work.

Import cast members

The cast members you've worked with so far are typical of media that you create within Director. To use more complex media, you usually import from other applications.

Director can import many popular types of media, including bitmaps, text, digital video, Flash movies, and sounds. For this movie, you'll import bitmap cast members created in an image editing program, an audio file, and a Flash movie.

1 Choose File > Import.

2 Browse to the Learning folder within the Director application folder, and then open the Tutorial Media folder.

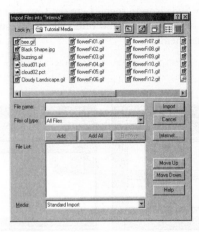

3 Click Add All.

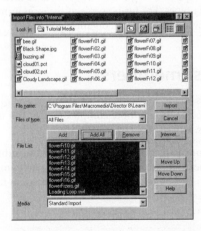

Files in the current folder appear on the list of files to import.

4 Verify that Standard Import appears in the bottom pop-up menu, and click Import.

Director begins importing the files. Depending on the type of computer you have and how many colors your system is set to display, Director may prompt you to confirm the type of media you are importing or to change the color depth (number of colors) in the current image.

5 In the Select Format dialog box, select Bitmap Image and Same Format for Remaining Files, and then click OK.

6 In the Image Options dialog box, select Same Settings for Remaining Images. Accept the other default settings, and then click OK.

7 If a Format dialog box prompts you for information about importing the buzzing.aif sound file, specify Sound rather than QuickTime as the format.

The files that you import appear in alphabetical order by file name as cast members in the Internal Cast window. The Cast window assigns the member a number, based on its position in Cast Thumbnail view.

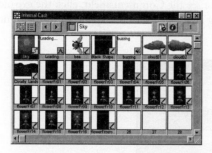

Note: If you change the cast member's position in the Cast window, the number assigned to the cast member also changes. In contrast, Cast List view offers a variety of list sorting options that do not affect the number assigned to the cast member.

Rename cast members

Although the cast member names are set to the file names of the imported files, you can change the names of cast members.

Notice that while most of the flower graphics in the tutorial follow the naming convention of flowerFr01, flowerFr02, flowerFr03, and so on, one flower is named flowerFrZero. You will rename flowerFrZero to make its name consistent with that of the other flowers.

1 In the Cast window, select flowerFrZero.

2 In the Cast Member Name field at the top of the Cast window, select the text and change the cast member name to **flowerFr00**.

Add cast member comments

Often you'll have comments that you'd like to include with a cast member. Director lets you add cast member comments on the Member tab of the Property Inspector. You can then view the comments in the Cast window (in List view).

For the tutorial, you'll make a note to yourself about the bee.

1   If the Cast window is not in List view, click the Cast View Style icon.

2   Click the bee cast member to select it.

3   On the Member tab of the Property Inspector, click the Comments field. (If you do not see the Comments field, click the expander arrow.) Type the following text: **Use a bombus spp (bumble bee), not an apis mellifera (honey bee).**

Expander arrow

4   Select the Cast window to see your comment in the Comments field.

To see the comment, you might have to scroll to the right or enlarge your Cast window.

Create sprites from cast members

You're now ready to start creating sprites—objects that control when, where, and how your cast members appear in your movie. For example, when you move a cast member to the Stage, you're creating a sprite to indicate where the cast member appears in your movie. When you move a sprite to the Score, you're creating a sprite to indicate when the cast member appears.

1 Make sure the Cast window, Score, Stage, and Property Inspector are visible. If they're not, choose them from the Window menu.

2 In the Score, click frame 10 of channel 1 to select it.

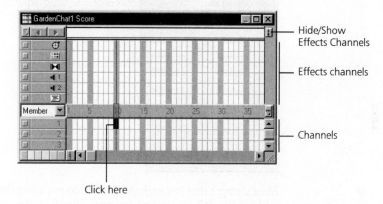

Hide/Show Effects Channels

Effects channels

Channels

Click here

It's a good idea to select the frame in the Score before creating a sprite to ensure that the cast member ends up in the desired frame.

3 In the Cast window, drag the Sky cast member to the center of the Stage.

You've created a sprite. Notice that the sprite starts on frame 10 in the Score, which is the frame you selected in the previous step.

Now you need to resize the Sky sprite to fit on the Stage. The most accurate method is to use the Property Inspector.

4 Click the Sky sprite to select it. On the Sprite tab of the Property Inspector, set the Left, Top, Right, and Bottom options to **0**, **0**, **450**, and **500**, respectively.

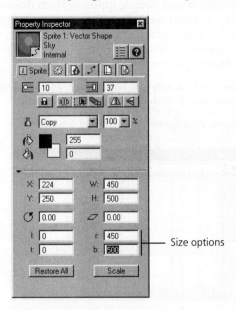

Size options

Most changes that you make to a sprite do not affect the cast member assigned to the sprite. When you resize a sprite, therefore, the cast member used to create the sprite does not resize.

Note: Sprites, by default, span 28 frames. You can change this default setting in the Sprite Preferences dialog box (Choose File > Preferences > Sprite.)

Change a sprite's ink

You can control the way a sprite's colors appear in Director by applying inks.

1 Drag the Sunny Landscape cast member to frame 10 of channel 2 in the Score.

The new sprite appears inside a white box—the sprite's bounding rectangle—in the center of the Stage.

2 Drag the Sunny Landscape sprite to the bottom of the Stage.

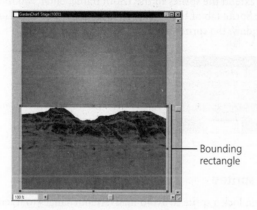

Bounding
rectangle

You can make the bounding rectangle transparent by applying Background Transparent ink, which takes the pixels of a specified color (the default is white) and makes them transparent.

3 Make sure the Sunny Landscape sprite is selected. In the Sprite tab of the Property Inspector, select Background Transparent from the Ink pop-up menu.

The landscape's bounding rectangle becomes transparent.

Change the duration of sprites

The Sky and Sunny Landscape sprites should be on the Stage while most of the movie plays, until frame 180.

1 Hold down Shift and click both sprites in the Score.

When you select multiple sprites, you can change settings for all selected sprites in the Property Inspector.

2 To extend the sprites to the 180th frame, enter 180 in the End Frame field on the Sprite tab of the Property Inspector. When you click anywhere in the window, the sprite spans extend to the 180th frame.

Lock sprites

You can lock a sprite to avoid inadvertent changes to it, either by you or by others working on the same project. Since you will be aligning one landscape over another, lock the Sunny Landscape in place.

After you lock a sprite, you cannot move it or change its settings until you unlock it.

1 Select the Sunny Landscape sprite either on the Stage or in the Score.

2 On the Sprite tab of the Property Inspector, click the Lock button.

Note: To unlock a sprite that is locked, you can select it in the Score and then click the Lock button.

Create additional sprites

Since the tutorial movie begins with a cloudy day, you'll create additional sprites on top of the sunny landscape background to produce the overcast effect.

1 Drag the Cloudy Landscape cast member to frame 10 of channel 3 in the Score. If necessary, click the sprite to select it and make the Score window active.

2 In the Sprite tab of the Property Inspector, select Background Transparent from the Ink pop-up menu.

3 To align the two landscapes accurately, select both landscape sprites in the Score and choose Modify > Align.

4 In the Vertical Alignment and Horizontal Alignment pop-up menus, select Align Reg. Point and then click Align.

5 Click OK when Director warns that the change will only apply to the unlocked sprite.

The two sprites align by their registration points. By default, the registration point of a bitmap cast member is its center.

6 On the Sprite tab of the Property Inspector, enter **130** in the End Frame field.

Again, click OK when Director warns that the change will affect only the unlocked sprite.

Remember to save your work frequently.

Zoom the Stage

Before you create an animated sequence that moves clouds across the sky, you will reduce the size of the Stage to make it easier to arrange the clouds.

In Director's authoring environment, you can use zooming to make the Stage either larger or smaller than your original movie. Zooming only affects your view of the Stage; it does not affect the Stage Size settings specified in the Property Inspector.

Director offers several different ways to zoom the Stage out, including the following method:

1   Click the Stage to make sure it's active.

2   Press Control-minus (Windows) or Command-minus (Macintosh) once to decrease the Stage size to 50%.

The percentage of the Stage size appears in the Stage title bar.

Notice that as you decrease the size of the Stage, you're increasing the size of the canvas area—the offstage area where you can drag cast members either before or after they appear on the Stage.

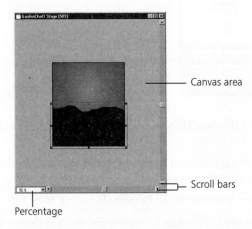

Canvas area

Scroll bars

Percentage

Add the cloud sprites

1   In the Score, select frame 10 of channel 4.

2 Drag the Cloud02 cast member to the Stage, placing it just above the mountain closest to the right edge of the Stage. It does not matter if the Cloud extends off the Stage into the canvas area.

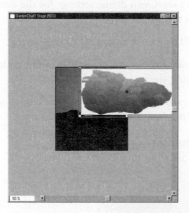

3 On the Sprite tab of the Property Inspector, type **120** in the End Frame field to extend the sprite's duration.

4 Set the sprite's ink to Background Transparent.

5 In the Score, create a sprite of the Cloud01 cast member in frame 10 of channel 5. Select the sprite and set its end frame to 95 and its ink to Background Transparent.

6 On the Stage, position the Cloud01 sprite to the left of the Cloud02 sprite.

7 Create another sprite of Cloud02 in frame 10 of channel 6. Select the sprite and set its end frame to 75 and its ink to Background Transparent.

8 Position the sprite on the Stage to cover as much of the visible blue sky as possible.

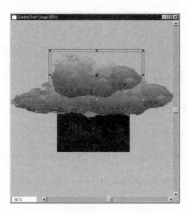

Create simple tweening animation

To make the clouds move across the sky, you'll use a simple animation technique called tweening. To tween, you define settings for the starting and ending frames, and Director fills in the frames in between.

1 Select the Cloud02 sprite in channel 4 of the Score.

2 On the Stage, locate the blue and red circle in the middle of Cloud02. This is a handle for tweening the path of a sprite.

3 Hold the Shift key and drag the handle to the left, all the way off the Stage and into the canvas area. Scroll to the left, if necessary.

As you drag, the tweening handle separates into different circles. A green circle indicates the starting location of the sprite, a blue circle shows the sprite in relation to the current frame, and a red circle represents the ending location. Holding the Shift key constrains the movement to a straight vertical or horizontal line.

4 Select the Cloud01 sprite and use the tweening handles to drag it all the way off the Stage, to the left, and into the canvas area.

5 Select the Cloud02 sprite in channel 6 and tween it off the Stage, to the left.

6 Return the Stage to 100% using one of these methods:

• With the Stage active, Press Control-plus (Windows) or Command-plus (Macintosh) once to increase the Stage size to 100%.

• Choose View > Zoom > 100%.

• Choose View > Zoom Stage In until the title bar indicates the Stage size is 100%.

- Click the Zoom menu and select 100%.

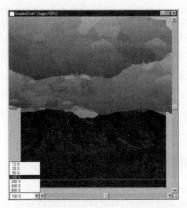

7 Organize your desktop to see both the Stage and the Score.

8 Click Rewind and Play on the toolbar along the top of the screen.

The clouds move between the starting and ending points you've defined.

Notice in the Score that the playback head (the red vertical bar) moves across each frame in the Score as the movie plays. The playback head indicates the current frame. You can drag the playback head across the Score to view the desired frame.

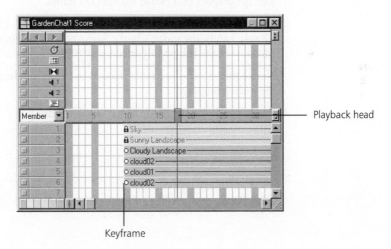

Keyframe

Playback head

9 Click Stop.

Note: In the Score, small circles now appear at the beginning and end of the three cloud sprites. These circles represent keyframes, and they indicate where the property of a sprite changes.

Stop the playback head from looping

When you play your movie, the playback head goes to the last frame in the movie and loops back to the first frame. In the tutorial movie, you want the playback head to stop on the last frame. Later in this tutorial, you will add a behavior to make the last frame play continuously.

To stop the playback head from looping, choose Control > Loop Playback to deselect it.

Now when you play your movie, the playback head stops on the last frame.

Blend sprites

In addition to tweening the path of a sprite, you can tween other sprite properties such as size, rotation, and blend. You tween blend settings to make a sprite fade in or out. In your tutorial movie, for example, after the clouds move off the Stage, you want the landscape to appear sunnier. You'll accomplish this with blend settings that fade the dark landscape out as the sunny one fades in.

You first want to indicate the frame in which the blend effect should start to take place.

1 In the Score, click frame 80 of the Cloudy Landscape sprite.

2 Choose Modify > Split Sprite.

The sprite splits into two at the selected frame.

3 Select the end keyframe (the small rectangle in frame 130) of the second Cloudy Landscape sprite. On the Sprite tab of the Property Inspector, select Blend from the Ink pop-up menu and 10% from the Blend pop-up menu.

Notice that the end keyframe changes to a small circle, indicating a change in the sprite's property.

4 Rewind and play the movie to see the blend effect.

Create frame-by-frame animation

A sprite is often an instance of a single cast member on the Stage or in the Score. However, one sprite can also include several cast members. In addition to using multiple sprites to create animation, you can use multiple cast members within a single sprite. Animation that uses multiple cast members is called frame-by-frame animation. This technique offers a way to create animation that is more complex than simple tweened animation.

Change the order of cast members

You can create frame-by-frame animation several different ways in Director. For this tutorial, you'll use the Cast to Time method, which lets you move a series of cast members to the Score as a single sprite.

To prepare for the Cast to Time method of animation, your cast members must appear in the Cast window in the same order that they'll appear in the animation. In the Cast Thumbnail view, notice that the first flower graphic, flowerFr00, is out of sequence.

1 If you are not already in the Cast Thumbnail window, click the Cast View Style icon.

2 Drag the thumbnail of flowerFr00 on top of flowerFr01.

   The flowerFr00 thumbnail takes the position flowerFr01 occupied, and flowerFr00 becomes the first flower in the group of flowers. The numbers the Cast window assigns to the cast members reflects the new order.

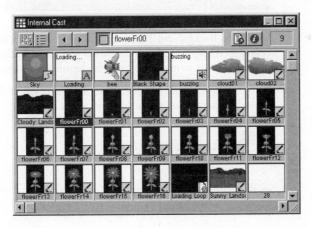

Create Cast to Time animation

1 Select frame 140 of channel 7 in the Score.

2 With the Cast window active, verify that the flower bitmaps are in order according to their title (flowerFr00, flowerFr01, flowerFr02...).

3 Select all of the flowers by Shift-clicking the first flower in the series, flowerFr00, and Shift-clicking the last flower (flowerFr16).

4 Choose Modify > Cast to Time, or press Alt (Windows) or Option (Macintosh) while dragging the cast members to the Stage.

The flowers appear as a single sprite in the selected Score frame.

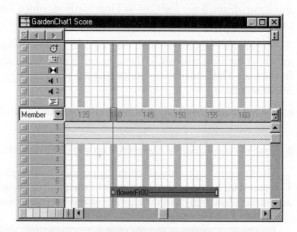

By default, Background Transparent ink is set to turn white bounding rectangles transparent. With the flower sprite, the background is black. You can set Director to make the black background transparent.

5 With the flower sprite selected, go to the Sprite tab of the Property Inspector. Click the Background Color box and select black.

— Background color box

6 Set the sprite's ink to Background Transparent.

7 In the Score, move the playback head to frame 155.

8 On the Stage, select and drag the flower sprite to the bottom center edge of the window.

9 Extend the flower sprite in the Score to frame 180.

10 Rewind and play the movie.

Attach behaviors to sprites

Director drag-and-drop behaviors offer functionality beyond what you can accomplish by simply dragging sprites to the Stage and Score. Behaviors also add intelligence and flexibility to a movie.

Instead of playing a series of frames exactly as the Score dictates, a behavior can control the movie in response to specific conditions and events.

In this tutorial, you will use behaviors to make a bee move randomly around a flower and also follow the movements of the user's mouse pointer.

When attaching behaviors to an entire sprite, rather than a frame, you can drag the behavior to the sprite in the Score or on the Stage.

1 Click frame 175 of channel 8 in the Score.

2 Drag the bee cast member to the Stage, close to the flower, and shorten the sprite to frame 180.

In addition to using the Property Inspector, you can drag a sprite's end frame to shorten or extend the sprite.

3 If the Library palette is not visible, choose Window > Library palette.

The Library palette displays categories containing all behaviors included with Director. The name of the active category appears in the Library List field at the top of the palette.

The name of each behavior appears next to an icon indicating its type.

4 Verify that you're in the Automatic category in the Library List field. Scroll down to the Random Movement and Rotation behavior. Hold the mouse pointer over the behavior icon to read the description of the behavior.

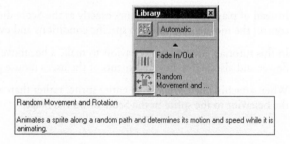

5 Drag the Random Movement and Rotation icon to the bee sprite in the Score. A Parameters dialog box appears, letting you specify how you want the behavior to perform. Accept the defaults by clicking OK.

Now you'll add another behavior to the bee, but you'll drag the behavior to the sprite on the Stage. You'll add the Turn Towards Mouse behavior, which will make the bee turn in response to the movement of your user's mouse pointer.

6 Select Animation > Interactive from the Library List pop-up menu.

7 Scroll down to the Turn Towards Mouse behavior. Hold the mouse pointer over the behavior and read the description that appears. Drag the behavior to the bee on the Stage.

Notice that a shaded rectangle appears around the selected sprite as you drag the behavior on top of it.

8 In the Parameters dialog box, from the middle pop-up menu, select Always and click OK.

You attach behaviors to frames for actions that affect how the movie, rather than a particular sprite, behaves. Now you'll attach a behavior that makes the last frame of the movie play repeatedly.

9 From the Library List pop-up menu, choose Navigation.

10 Scroll down to the Hold on Current Frame behavior and drag it to the script channel and the last frame of your movie. Hold on Current Frame is one of the few behaviors that does not require you to set additional parameters.

11 Rewind and play the movie.

Notice that when the movie reaches the last frame, it continues to play.

Remember to save your work frequently.

Add sound

Since a bee without its buzz seems less than adequate, you'll now add sound to the movie. Director offers many ways to add and synchronize sound, including use of cue points and Lingo. In this tutorial, you'll use a very simple procedure to control sound in the Score.

Controlling sounds in the Score is similar to controlling other sprites. Rather than using Score channels, however, you place the buzzing sound in a sound channel at the top of the Score. Next, you extend the sound so it's synchronized with the appearance of the bee.

1 If the sound channels are not visible along the top of the Score, click the expander arrow on the right side of the Score.

2 Drag the buzzing cast member to frame 175 of sound channel 1, and shorten the end keyframe to frame 180.

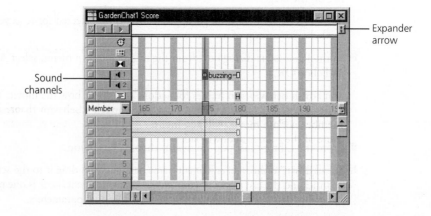

3 On the Sound tab of the Property Inspector, select Loop. This sets the sound so that it plays continuously while the bee is on the Stage.

4 Rewind and play the movie.

Control streaming

Streaming from the Internet causes a movie to play as soon as the content required for the first frame is downloaded to your user. The remaining content downloads in the background. Streaming dramatically shortens the perceived download time of a movie.

Create a looping introduction for a streaming movie

To create a movie that streams well, it's often a good idea to start with an introductory scene that downloads quickly and loops until the next scene has downloaded. In this tutorial, you'll add a loading Flash movie that lets your user know the rest of the movie is downloading.

1 Drag the Black Shape cast member to frame 1 of channel 1 in the Score. Rather than extending 28 frames, the sprite fits in the 10 available frames.

2 On the Sprite tab of the Property Inspector, resize the sprite by setting the Left, Top, Right, and Bottom options to **0, 0, 450,** and **500,** respectively.

3 In the Score, select frame 1 of channel 2, and drag the Loading text cast member to an area just above the middle of the Stage.

4 Select the Loading text sprite and set its ink to Background Transparent.

5 Drag the Loadloop cast member to frame 1 of channel 3 in the Score. This cast member, a Flash movie, will add interest to the movie while your user waits for more of the frames to download.

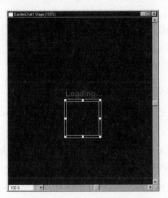

6 On the Stage, drag the Loadloop Flash movie so that it's centered underneath the text.

7 From the Library List pop-up menu, choose Internet > Streaming.

8 Drag the Loop Until Media in Frame is Available behavior to frame 1 of the script channel.

9 In the Parameters dialog box, type **10** in the Wait for Media in Frame field, then click OK.

You are telling Director to play the Flash movie until all of the media in frame 10 downloads. Once the sprites in frame 10 download, the looping behavior ends and the movie proceeds to play.

Note: You can view looping behaviors when you play the movie from a server.

Publish your movie for the Web in one step

Amazingly, Director can create a Web-friendly Shockwave version of your movie in one step.

To publish your move, save it and choose File > Publish.

Using the default Publish settings, Director creates a Shockwave version of your movie in the same directory as your original movie. Your browser window opens and your Shockwave movie plays.

Change Publish settings

When you use the Publish command, you take advantage of Director's default Publish settings, or you can modify them with the Publish Settings dialog box.

For the tutorial movie, rather than use the default HTML template specified in the Publish Settings dialog box, you'll use a special HTML page designed for GardenChat.

1 In Director, choose File > Publish Settings.

The Publish Settings dialog box appears.

2 On the Formats tab, choose No HTML Template from the HTML Template pop-up menu.

3 Save your movie and then choose File > Publish. Click OK at the prompt to overwrite your previous DCR file.

When you save your movie, Director also saves any changes you've made to the Publish Settings dialog box. The next time you want to publish your movie in the same way, you can simply choose File > Publish without having to modify Publish settings.

Add multiuser chat functionality to GardenChat

To add another layer of functionality to your Web site, you're going to use Director's multiuser behaviors to create chat capabilities. A group of your GardenChat users will then be able to discuss soil conditions, the best fertilizer, and the weather simultaneously and in real time.

If you've never used Director's multiuser behaviors, you'll see how simple it is to create a chat in about 5 minutes.

To build a chat, you launch a local server application that supports the chat, and you create a Director movie designed to communicate with the server. Then you create a Shockwave version of the movie.

Launch the Shockwave Multiuser Server and determine the server IP address

The Multiuser Server is included in the Director 8 default installation.

1 In your Director 8 application folder, open the Shockwave Multiuser Server 2.1 subfolder, and double-click the MultiuserServer icon.

   The server launches.

2 To determine the server's IP address and see additional information about the server, choose Status > Server.

3 Write down the server IP address or copy it to the Clipboard. You will need this information later.

Open the chat movie

1 In Director, choose File > Open.

2 Browse to your Director 8 application folder. Open the Learning folder and the My_Tutorial folder, and then open Chat.dir.

If you were to create this chat movie from scratch, you would place the text, fields, and artwork on the Stage. You could also use behaviors to add special effects. Most of this work is already completed for you. You will add the behaviors to your template to give the chat its multiuser functionality.

Use markers

In the Score, notice that six markers identify key scene changes.

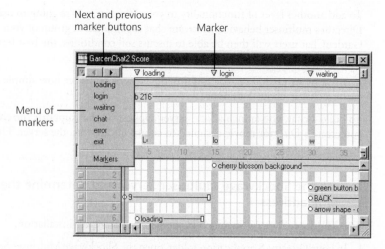

Next and previous marker buttons

Marker

Menu of markers

Markers can identify a specific frame, let you specify a frame to which to take your user, and so on. Now you will use markers to go to the beginning of a scene.

Click Next Marker twice to move the playback head to the login marker in frame 15.

Use the Sprite Overlay

The Sprite Overlay displays important information on the Stage about a selected sprite, including the sprite's name and the name of behaviors attached to the sprite. You can click the icons on the overlay to view different properties in the Property Inspector.

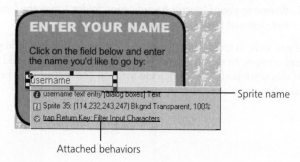

Sprite name

Attached behaviors

If the Sprite Overlay is not visible when you select a sprite, choose View > Sprite Overlay > Show Info.

Note: As you complete the following steps to attach behaviors, make sure you drag the behavior to the specified sprite and not to a background sprite, which would have a different name. Use the sprite name in the Sprite Overlay to assist you.

Add the Connect to Server behavior

The Connect to Server behavior connects your user to the Multiuser Server. You attach the Connect to Server behavior to the sprite your user will click to establish a server connection. In this tutorial, you will attach the Connect to Server behavior to the Enter sprite.

1 If the Library window is not open, choose Window > Library Palette.

2 From the Library List pop-up menu, choose Internet > Multiuser.

3 Drag the Connect to Server behavior to the Enter sprite on the Stage.

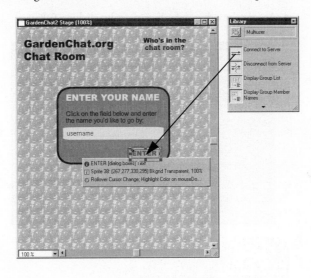

4 Set the following parameters:

- In the Which Member Holds the User Name pop-up menu, choose Username Text Entry.

- Accept the default setting of the Which Member Holds the User's Password pop-up menu.

- In the Which Marker to Go to When Connecting pop-up menu, choose Waiting.

- In the Which Marker to Go to When Connected pop-up menu, choose Chat.

- In the Which Marker to Go to If Connection Fails pop-up menu, choose Error.

- In the Server Address field, enter the server IP address that you recorded from the server application window.

- Verify that 1626 is in the Server Port Number field.

- Verify that the name of the movie is in the Movie ID String field.

- Accept the other default settings by clicking OK.

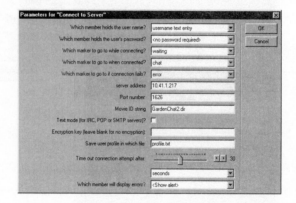

Add the Chat Input behavior

Now you can add the Chat Input behavior to the Chat Input text sprite. Chat Input is the behavior you attach to the text or field sprite in which your user enters information.

1 Click Next Marker twice to go to frame 45.

2 From the Library palette, drag the Chat Input behavior to the Chat Input text sprite on the Stage.

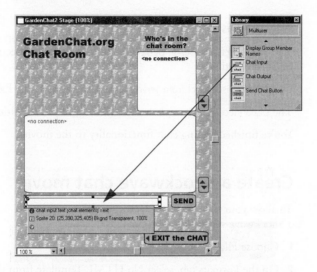

3 Accept the default parameters, and then click OK.

Add the Chat Output behavior

You attach the Chat Output behavior to the text or field sprite that will display the current chat text.

1 From the Library palette, drag the Chat Output behavior to the Chat Output sprite on the Stage.

2 Accept the default parameters by clicking OK.

Add the Send Chat Button behavior

You attach the Send Chat Button behavior to the sprite your user clicks to send the chat input text to the Multiuser Server, which then sends the text to chat participants. The Send Chat Button behavior includes a parameter that lets you select the sprite containing the information to send.

1 Drag the Send Chat Button behavior to the Send sprite on the Stage.

2 In the pop-up menu, select 20-Member 'Chat Input Text,' and then click OK.

Add the Disconnect from Server behavior

The Disconnect from Server behavior ends the server connection when your user has finished chatting.

To add the Disconnect from Server behavior, drag it to the Exit sprite on the Stage.

The Disconnect from Server behavior does not require additional parameters.

You've finished adding chat functionality to the movie.

Create a Shockwave chat movie

To allow your users to take advantage of the chat feature on the Web, you'll create a Shockwave version of your movie.

1 Choose File > Publish Settings.

2 On the Formats tab, select No HTML Template from the HTML Template pop-up menu and click OK.

3 Save Chat and choose File > Publish.

Chat appears in your Web browser.

4 Type your name in the Enter Your Name field and click Enter.

Remember, the Enter sprite is where you attached the Connect to Server behavior.

5 In the Chat Room, type a gardening question in the Chat Input area and click Send.

6 The text appears in the Chat Output field where other users, connected to the same server, can view and respond to the question.

Talk to yourself

Although the server and browser are on the same computer for this project, the server and chat room participants can be anywhere on the Internet. If no one else is connected to the server running your chat movie, you can chat with yourself using two different browser windows.

1 In your browser window, select the URL and copy it.

If you are using Netscape Navigator, you can find the URL in the Location field; if you are using Microsoft Internet Explorer, the URL is in the Address field.

2 Open a new browser window and paste the URL in the same field of the new browser. Press Enter (Windows) or Return (Macintosh).

A new version of Chat appears.

3 Resize the two browser windows to view both of them, side by side.

4 In the second version of GardenChat, log in by typing a new user name in the Enter Your Name field and click Enter.

You can now answer the gardening question that you posted, or you can post a new question.

Continue to switch from one browser to another, and type messages back and forth to yourself. View the conversation in the Chat Output field.

5 When you finish chatting, click Exit the Chat, which is where you attached the Disconnect from Server behavior.

6 Close one of the two open browser windows.

Set up other chat participants

If you have access to a Web server, you can place the HTML file and Shockwave movie on the server, then run your chat from any Internet location. For the chat to work, the Shockwave Multiuser Server application must be running at the IP address you specified for the movie.

View your GardenChat Web site

You're now ready to view both of your DCR files in the GardenChat Web site.

1 In your Director 8 application folder, open the Learning folder and the My_Tutorial folder, and drag the MyProject.html page to your browser window.

2 View the opening animation, and then click the Chat button to view your chat movie.

Continue learning about Director

By completing this tutorial, you've become familiar with Director features and procedures necessary to produce your own movie. You now know how to do the following:

- Create a new movie, cast members, and sprites
- Use inks
- Create animation using tweening, frame-by-frame animation, and blends
- Import media
- Synchronize sound
- Attach behaviors
- Control streaming over the Web
- Publish your movie for Web playback

Your final steps, outside the scope of this tutorial, would be to continue adding functionality to the HTML pages and to upload the HTML files to a server where they would be accessible to your users.

Continue learning about Director's many useful features by reading topics in *Using Director* and Director Help.

2

CHAPTER 2
Director basics

Macromedia Director 8 Shockwave Studio is the tool of choice for legions of Web and multimedia developers. With Director you can create movies for Web sites, kiosks, and presentations, as well as movies for education and entertainment. Movies can be as small and simple as an animated logo or as complex as an online chat room or game. Director movies can include a variety of media, such as sound, text, graphics, animation, and digital video. A Director movie can link to external media or be one of a series of movies that refer to one another.

Your users view completed Director movies in one of two ways:

- In the Shockwave movie format, which plays in Shockwave-enabled Web browsers. Millions of Web users already have the Shockwave player on their computers, browsers, or system software. Others have downloaded Shockwave, which is free, from Macromedia's Web site.

- In a projector, which plays on your user's computer as a stand-alone application.

Creating a new movie

Director is organized around a movie metaphor.

To create a new movie:

Choose File > New > Movie.

Introducing the Director workspace

When creating and editing a movie, you typically work in five key windows: the Stage, the Score, the Cast window, the Property Inspector, and the Control Panel.

The Stage

If the Stage is not open, choose Window > Stage.

The Stage is the visible portion of a movie on which you determine where your media elements appear.

During authoring you have the ability to define the properties of your Stage, such as its size and color. As you work on your movie, you can use zooming to make the Stage either larger or smaller than the original movie, while also scaling the coordinates for the Stage objects. To align objects on the Stage, you can choose to display guides and grids or use the Align window.

To scroll around the Stage, do one of the following:

- Use the scroll bars. (To show or hide Stage scroll bars, choose File > Preferences > General and select or deselect Show Stage Scrollbars.)

- Select the Hand tool from the Tool palette, then drag inside the Stage to reposition the visible portion.

- Bring the Stage to the front, hold down the Spacebar to temporarily switch to the Hand tool, then drag inside the Stage to reposition the visible portion.

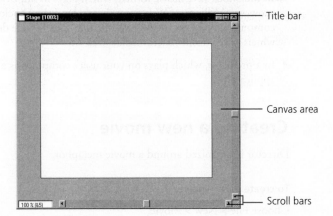

Title bar

Canvas area

Scroll bars

The Score

If the Score is not visible, choose Window > Score.

The Score organizes and controls a movie's content over time in rows that contain the media, called channels. The Score includes special channels that control the movie's tempo, sound, and color palettes. The Score also includes frames and the playback head. You use the Score to assign scripts—Lingo instructions that specify what the movie does when certain events occur in the movie.

You can control the Score by zooming to reduce or magnify your view and by displaying multiple Score windows. You can also control the Score's appearance by using File > Preferences > Score.

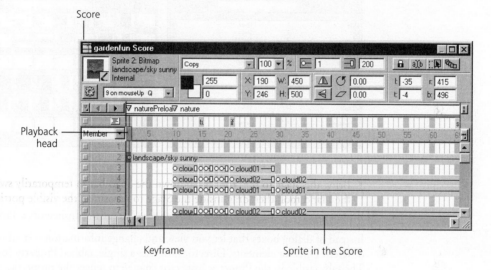

Score

Playback head

Keyframe

Sprite in the Score

The Cast window

If the Cast window is not visible, choose Window > Cast.

In the Cast window you can view your cast members, which are the media in your movie, such as sounds, text, graphics, and other movies. Cast members can also include assets that you use in your Score but not on the Stage, such as scripts, palettes, fonts, and transitions. You can create cast members in Director, and you can import existing media to include in your cast. The Cast window lets you view your cast members in either of two ways, depending on your preference: as a list or as thumbnails.

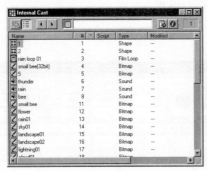

The Property Inspector

If the Property Inspector is not visible, choose Window > Inspectors > Property.

Instead of dialog boxes that let you view and change information related to different Director elements, Director now uses a single, tabbed Property Inspector. The tabs visible in the Property Inspector change to reflect the properties of the selected elements.

The Property Inspector provides a convenient way to view and change attributes of any selected object, or multiple objects, in your movie. Once you select an object, relevant category tabs and associated fields for it appear on the Property Inspector. If you select multiple objects, only the information common to all of the selected objects appears.

The List View Mode icon on the Property Inspector lets you toggle between a List and a Graphical view.

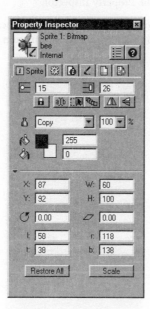

The following illustrations show different information appearing in the Property Inspector depending on what is selected. In the first illustration, a sprite is selected. In the second illustration, a cast member is selected.

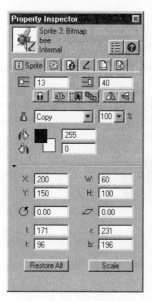 

To show more or less information in the Property Inspector:

Click the expander arrow in the Property Inspector.

The following illustrations show different information appearing in the Property Inspector depending on whether the expanded information is hidden or shown.

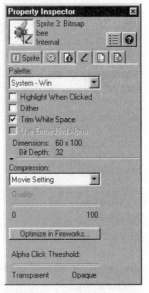

The Control Panel

If the Control Panel is not visible, choose Window > Control Panel.

The Control Panel governs how movies play back in the authoring environment only.

You can also use the toolbar buttons or keyboard shortcuts to play a movie. To go to a specific frame number, enter the number in the frame counter and press Enter (Windows) or Return (Macintosh).

Setting Stage and movie properties

You use the Property Inspector's Movie tab to specify settings that affect the entire movie, such as how colors are defined, the size and location of the Stage, the number of channels in the Score, copyright information, and font mapping. These settings apply only to the current movie, whereas the settings you choose from File > Preferences apply to every movie.

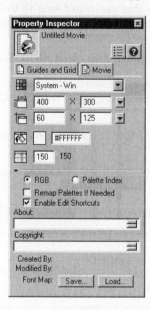

To set Stage and movie properties:

1 Click the Movie tab of the Property Inspector in Graphical view. (Note that the Movie tab appears only if you do not have an object selected on the Stage or in the Score.)

2 To choose a color palette for the movie, select a palette from the Movie Palette pop-up menu. This palette remains selected until Director encounters a different palette setting in the palette channel.

For a complete discussion of color palettes and using color in Director, see "Controlling color" on page 220.

3 To define the size of the Stage, choose a preset value from the Stage Size pop-up menu or manually enter values in the Width and Height fields.

4 To specify the location of the Stage during playback if the movie does not take up the full screen, choose an option from the Stage Location pop-up menu or enter values for Left and Top; these values specify the number of pixels the Stage is placed from the top left corner of the screen, and they apply only if the Stage is smaller than the current monitor's screen size.

- Centered places the Stage window in the center of your monitor. This option is useful if you play a movie that was created for a 13-inch screen on a larger screen, or if you're creating a movie on a larger screen that will be seen on smaller screens.

- Upper Left places the Stage in the upper left corner of the screen.

5 To set the color of the Stage for the movie, double-click the color box next to Stage Fill Color and select a color, or enter an RGB value in the box on the right.

6 To specify the number of channels in the Score, enter a value for Score Channels.

7 To determine how the movie assigns colors, choose either RGB or Palette Index.

- RGB makes the movie assign all color values as absolute RGB values.

- Palette Index makes the movie assign color according to its position in the current palette.

8 To remap colors in bitmaps with different color palettes to colors in the current palette, select Remap Palettes If Needed.

This option dynamically remaps bitmaps on the Stage without changing the cast members. For example, if a cast member uses a grayscale palette, it is drawn on the Stage using the grays available in the common palette.

9 To let users cut, copy, and paste Editable fields while a movie is playing, select Enable Edit Shortcuts.

10 To enter copyright and other information about the movie, enter text in the About and Copyright boxes.

This information is important if your movie is going to be downloaded from the Internet and saved on a user's system.

11 To save the current font map settings in a text file named Fontmap.txt, click Save. To load the font mapping assignments specified in the selected font map file, click Load. See "Mapping fonts between platforms for field cast members" on page 349.

Increasing or decreasing your view of the Stage

You can author in Director on a zoomed Stage—one that is either larger or smaller than the normal size of the movie. Additionally, the Stage includes an offstage canvas area within the Stage window but outside of the active movie area. This canvas area is useful for assembling your media either before or after they appear on the Stage.

The offstage canvas is also useful as a way to preload media in projectors. Sprites in a frame, but offstage, are loaded into memory so they are ready to play in the subsequent frame.

When you change the size of the Stage, any guides or grids you use to assist you with alignment will also scale to the zoomed size, and you can manipulate Stage objects just as you would on a Stage that is not zoomed.

The Stage window does not need to be in front when you zoom in or out.

To zoom the Stage, do one of the following:

- Press Control+the plus (+) key (Windows) or Command+the plus (+) key (Macintosh) to zoom in and increase the Stage size. Press Control+the minus (-) key (Windows) or Command+the minus (-) key (Macintosh) to zoom out and decrease the Stage size. (In Windows, if you want to use the keys on the numeric keypad, NumLock must be off.)

  You can press the keys repeatedly until the Stage is the desired size.

- Choose View > Zoom and select Zoom Stage In to increase the size of the Stage in increments, Zoom Stage Out to decrease Stage size, or a percentage to select a specific Stage size.

- If scroll bars are visible, click in the lower left corner of the scroll bar and choose a percentage. (To turn on scroll bars, choose File > Preferences > General and check Show Stage Scrollbars.)

- To zoom in while selecting an area of the Stage to center within the zoomed window, select the Magnifying Glass tool from the Tool palette. Click a point on the Stage to zoom and center.

- To zoom out while selecting an area of the Stage to center within the zoomed window, select the Magnifying Glass tool from the Tool palette. Press Alt (Windows) or Option (Macintosh) while clicking a point on the Stage to zoom and center.

The Stage's title bar indicates the zoom Stage size expressed as a percentage of the normal Stage size.

About Sprites

A sprite is an object that controls when, where, and how cast members appear in a movie. You create sprites by placing cast members on the Stage or in the Score. Creating a Director movie consists largely of defining where sprites appear, when they appear in the movie, how they behave, and what their properties are. Different sprites can be created from a single cast member. Each sprite can have its own values for different properties, and most changes to these properties do not affect the cast member. Most changes to a cast member, however, will change sprites created from that cast member.

For information on creating and changing sprites, see "Creating sprites" on page 120.

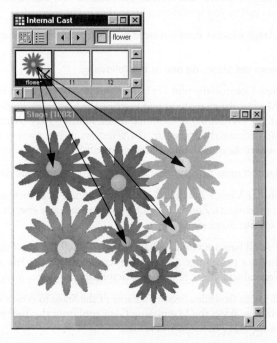

All these sprites display one bitmap image with different attributes.

About Channels in the Score

Channels are the rows in the Score that control your media. The Score contains sprite channels and special effects channels.

Sprite channels are numbered and contain sprites that control all visible media in the movie. Effects channels at the top of the Score contain behaviors as well as controls for the tempo, palettes, transitions, and sounds. The Score displays channels in the order shown here.

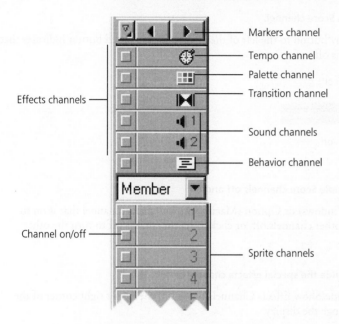

The first channel in the Score contains markers that identify places in the Score, such as the beginning of a new scene. Markers are useful for making quick jumps to specific locations in a movie. See "Using markers" on page 71.

While the Score can include up to 1000 channels, most movies use as few channels as possible to improve performance in the authoring environment and during playback. Sprites in higher channels appear on the Stage in front of sprites in lower channels. Use the Property Inspector's Movie tab to control the number of channels in the Score for the current movie. See "Setting Stage and movie properties" on page 61.

Turning on and off channels

To hide the contents of any channel on the Stage, or to disable the contents if they are not visible sprites, you use the button to the left of the channel. When you turn off a special effects channel, the channel's data has no effect on the movie. You should turn off Score channels when testing performance or working on complex overlapping animations. Turning off a channel has no effect on projectors or Shockwave.

To turn off a Score channel:

Click the gray button to the left of the channel. A darkened button indicates that the channel is off.

This channel is on

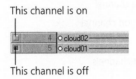

This channel is off

To turn multiple Score channels off and on:

Press Alt (Windows) or Option (Macintosh) and click a channel that is on to turn all the other channels off, or click a channel that is off to turn the other channels on.

To show or hide the special effects channels:

Click the Hide/Show Effects Channels button in the upper right corner of the Score to change the display.

Effects channels

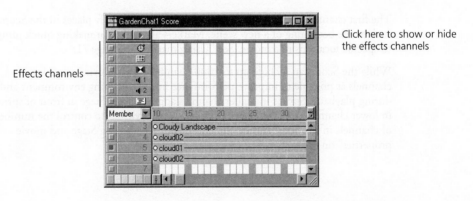

Click here to show or hide the effects channels

About Frames

A frame in a movie represents a single point in time, similar in theory to a frame in a celluloid film. Numbers listed horizontally in the sprite and special effects channels represent frames. Setting the number of frames displayed per second sets the movie's playback speed.

About the playback head

The playback head moves through the Score to show the frame currently displayed on the Stage. As you play your movie, the playback head automatically moves through your Score. You can also click any frame in the Score to move the playback head to that frame, and you can drag the playback head backward or forward through frames.

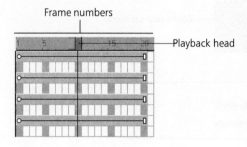

Frame numbers

Playback head

Changing your view of the Score

To narrow or widen the Score, you change the zoom percentage. Zooming in widens each frame, which lets you see more data in a frame. Zooming out shows more frames in less space, and is useful when moving large blocks of Score data.

To change the zoom setting, do one of the following:

- Choose View > Zoom and then choose an option.
- Choose an option on the Zoom pop-up menu to the right of the Score.

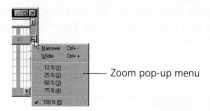

Zoom pop-up menu

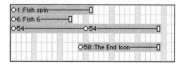

Score zoomed out to 50%

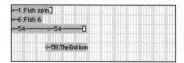

Score at 100%

Score zoomed in to 200%

You can also display more frames in a Score without changing the zoom setting. To do so, place a sprite in the rightmost frame of the score. Director will automatically display additional frames in the current view of the Score.

Using context menus

To let you quickly access certain commands, Director provides menus that display commands relevant to a particular element. These are called context menus because the commands on the menu vary depending on the context in which the menu is displayed.

In the following illustration, Director is displaying the context menu for a sprite.

To display a context menu:

Position your mouse over an element and then right-click (Windows) or Control-click (Macintosh).

Using many Score windows

You can view and work in different parts of a movie at the same time by opening additional Score windows. If your sprite bars occupy many frames in the Score, for example, you can open a second Score window to work on another place in the movie without scrolling. You can also drag sprites from one Score window to another.

To open a new Score window:

1 Activate the current Score window.

2 Choose Window > New Window to create a second Score window.

You can scroll in this window to a different location in the Score. Only the first Score window automatically scrolls to show the playback head location.

Changing Score settings

To control the appearance of the Score and the information displayed in numbered sprite channels, you set preferences for the Score. By doing so, you can display a script preview and cast member information. In addition, if you are accustomed to older versions of Director, you can make the Score work as it did in Director 5.

To change Score settings:

1   Chose File > Preferences > Score.

2   The Extended display option lets you display information within sprites in the Score. See "Displaying sprite labels in the Score" on page 130. To specify what cast member information appears in numbered sprite channels when Extended display is on, choose from the following options:

• Cast Member displays the cast member number, name, or both.

• Behaviors displays the behaviors attached to the sprite.

• Ink Mode displays the type of ink applied to the sprite.

• Blend displays the blend percentage applied to the sprite.

• Location shows the sprite's x and y screen coordinates.

• Change in Location shows the change in x and y coordinates relative to the previous cast member in that channel.

3   To display the first few lines of the selected script in a box at the top of the Score, select Script Preview.

4   To display the cast member's name and number when the pointer is over a sprite for a few seconds, check Show Data Tips.

5   To make Score features work like those in Director 5 and earlier versions, choose from the following options:

• Director 5 Style Score Display modifies the Director 8 Score window so it looks and behaves like the Director 5 Score window.

• Allow Drag and Drop makes sections of the Score moveable by dragging in the Director 5 style Score. To override this setting temporarily, press the Spacebar while the Score window is open.

• Allow Colored Cells displays a cell color selector at the left of the Score window so that you can choose a color for selected cells. Otherwise, the cell color selector is hidden, which improves performance when scrolling the Score window. If you've already applied color to cells, turning off this option hides cell colors but doesn't remove them.

Using markers

Markers identify fixed locations at a particular frame in a movie; you use markers when you're defining navigation. Using Lingo or draggable behaviors, you can instantly move the playback head to any marker frame. This is useful when jumping to new scenes from a menu or looping while cast members download from the Web. You can also use markers while authoring to advance quickly to the next scene.

Once you've marked a frame in the Score, you can use the marker name in your behaviors or scripts to refer to exact frames. Marker names remain constant no matter how you edit the Score. They are more reliable to use as navigation references than are frame numbers, which can change if you insert or delete frames in the Score.

You can use the Markers window to write comments associated with markers you set in the Score and to move the playback head to a particular marker.

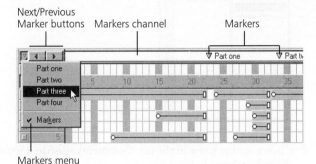

Next/Previous Marker buttons   Markers channel   Markers

Markers menu

To create a marker:

1 Click the markers channel.

  A text insertion point appears to the right of the marker.

2 Type a short name for the marker.

To delete a marker:

Drag the marker up or down and out of the markers channel.

To jump to markers while authoring, do any of the following:

- Click the Next Marker and Previous Marker buttons on the left side of the markers channel.

- Press the 4 and 6 keys on the numeric keypad to cycle backward and forward through markers.

- Choose the name of a marker from the Markers menu.

To move the playback head to a marker and enter marker comments:

1   Select a marker in the Score window and choose Window > Markers. The Markers window opens and displays comments associated with that frame.

2   Click a marker name in the list. Comments associated with markers appear in the right column.

   Note: Use Control+Left Arrow or Control+Right Arrow (Windows) or Command+Left Arrow or Command+Right Arrow (Macintosh) to move to the previous or next marker.

3   To enter or edit comments, begin typing at the insertion point that appears in the right column.

   By default, the marker name appears as the first line of text in the right column.

4   If you don't want to edit the marker name, press Enter (Windows) or Return (Macintosh) to start a new line.

Selecting and editing frames in the Score

You can select a range of frames in the Score and then copy, delete, or paste all the contents of the selected frames.

To move, copy, or delete all the contents of a range of frames:

1 Double-click in the frame channel to select frames.

Double-click here to select all sprites in a frame, including markers, special effects, and sounds. Double-click and drag to select a range of frames

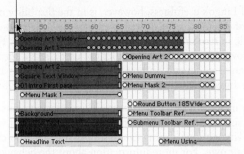

2 If you want to move or copy frames, choose Edit > Cut Frames or Edit > Copy Frames. If you want to delete frames, choose Edit > Clear Frames or press Delete.

If you cut, clear, or delete the selected frames, Director removes the frames and closes up the empty space.

Note: To delete a single frame, you can also choose Insert > Remove Frame.

3 To paste frames that you have cut or copied, select any frame and choose Edit > Paste Sprites.

If no frame is selected when you choose Edit > Paste Sprites, the Paste Options dialog box lets you decide how you want the frames to be pasted.

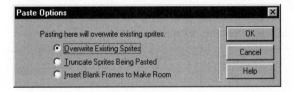

To add new frames:

1 Select a frame in the Score.

2 Choose Insert > Frames.

3 Enter the number of frames to insert.

The new frames appear to the right of the selected frame. Sprites in the frames you select are extended or tweened. For more information about tweening, see Chapter 12, "Animation."

About adding interactivity with Lingo

Lingo, Director's scripting language, adds interactivity to a movie. Lingo can accomplish many of the same tasks—such as moving sprites on the Stage or playing sounds—that you can accomplish using the Director interface.

Much of Lingo's usefulness, however, is in the flexibility it brings to a movie. Instead of playing a series of frames exactly as the Score dictates, Lingo can control the movie in response to specific conditions and events. For example, whether a sprite moves can depend on whether the user clicks a specific button; when a sound plays can depend on how much of the sound has already streamed from the Internet.

Director includes a set of prepackaged Lingo instructions, called behaviors, that you can simply drag to sprites and frames. Behaviors let you add Lingo's interactivity without writing Lingo scripts yourself. You can modify behaviors or create your own. For more information about the behaviors included with Director 8, see "Using Director 8 Behaviors" in the Director Support Center.

If you prefer writing scripts to using the Director interface and behaviors, Lingo provides an alternative way to implement common Director features; for example, you can use Lingo to create animation, stream movies from the Web, perform navigation, format text, and respond to user actions with the keyboard and mouse.

Writing Lingo also lets you do some things that the Score alone can't do. For example, Lingo's lists let you create and manage data arrays, and Lingo operators let you perform mathematical operations and combine strings of text.

For more general information about Lingo, see Chapter 6, "Writing Scripts with Lingo."

Converting movies created in previous versions of Director

Director 8 can convert movies from Director 6 and 7. You can also update movies to Director 8 by simply opening and saving them, but the Update Movies command is faster for converting large projects. It's also more effective for preserving links to external media. See "Processing movies with Update Movies" on page 453.

Note: The Director 8 Shockwave player can play Shockwave movies created with Director 5, 6, 7, and 8.

When you open a Director 6 or 7 movie in Director 8, or convert it to the new format with Update Movies, note the following:

- The data structure is changed to the latest file format.

- Shapes are not converted to the new Bézier shapes.

- Ink functionality is not updated unless you turn off Maintain Outdated Ink Mode Limitations in the Movie Properties dialog box.

- Old Score data, from versions of Director prior to Director 5, is converted to the new Score, combining adjacent frames in the old Score containing the same cast members into single sprites in the new Score. You may want to split or join sprites to make working in the Score more convenient.

Managing the Director authoring environment

While working on a movie, you can use several optional controls and features to increase your productivity. You can change preferences for Director interface functions and Internet connection features, you can print movies to see your work on paper, and you can monitor memory use with the Memory Inspector.

Setting general preferences

To control some of Director's default settings relating to the Stage and the user interface, you can use the General Preferences dialog box. These settings control the appearance of movies only in the authoring environment, not during playback.

To set Director default values:

1 Choose File > Preferences > General.

2 To specify the default size and location of the Stage and the way it animates when deactivated, choose Stage options.

   The Stage location settings affect the location of the Stage only in the authoring environment. To set the location of the Stage during playback, see "Setting Stage and movie properties" on page 61.

   - Use Movie Settings sets the Stage size to the movie's Stage size and location.

   - Match Current Movie opens a new movie in the Stage size of the movie that's currently open.

   - Center positions the Stage in the center of the screen by default, which is useful if the Stage size is smaller than the screen size. Otherwise, the movie plays using its original Stage position.

   - Reset Monitor to Movie's Color Depth (Macintosh only) automatically changes the color depth of your monitor to the color depth of a movie when it is opened in the authoring environment. See "Changing the color depth of a movie" on page 221.

   - Animate in Background runs animation in the background while you are working with other applications. When you are running animation in the background, the Stage remains on the screen, and the active application window appears in front of the Stage.

3 To set defaults for the Director user interface, choose User Interface options:

   - Dialogs Appear at Mouse Position displays dialog boxes at the mouse position. If this option is not selected, dialog boxes are centered on the monitor that contains the menu bar.

   - Save Window Positions on Exit saves the positions of all open windows every time you quit so they reappear in the same location when you start again.

   - Message Window Recompiles Scripts makes Director recompile all scripts when you press Enter (Windows) or Return (Macintosh) in the Message window. With this option off, Director recompiles scripts only when you choose Control > Recompile All Scripts.

   - Show Tooltips controls the definitions that appear when the pointer is over tools and buttons. Turn off this option to stop definitions from appearing.

   - Show Stage Scrollbars makes scroll bars appear in the Stage window.

4 To specify the unit of measure to use in the text ruler, choose inches, centimeters, or pixels from the Text Units pop-up menu. See "Formatting paragraphs" on page 342.

5 (Macintosh only) To allow Director to use available memory beyond the amount allocated to it, turn on Use System Temporary Memory.

Choosing Internet connection settings

Director can connect to the Internet to import cast members and retrieve data. It also launches a browser to preview movies and open those Director Help topics that are on www.macromedia.com. Use settings in the Network Preferences dialog box to control how the connection works and to define a preferred browser.

To choose Internet connection settings:

1 Choose File > Preferences > Network.

2 To specify the browser to launch when a movie running in the authoring environment encounters the gotoNetPage Lingo command, enter the path to the browser in the Preferred Browser field.

   To locate the browser, click the Browse button.

3 To enable or disable browser launching, select Launch When Needed.

4 To specify the amount of space that Director can use to cache data from the Internet on your hard disk, enter a value in the Disk Cache Size field.

5 To immediately empty the cache, click Clear.

6 To specify how often cached data is compared to the same data on the server, choose a Check Documents option:

• Once Per Session checks for data revisions only once from the time you start to the time you quit the application. This option improves performance but may not always display the most current version of a page.

• Every Time checks for changes whenever you request a page. This option slows performance but assures you are always viewing the most current version of a page.

7 To specify the configuration of your system's proxy server, choose a Proxies option.

   Browsers usually don't require proxy servers to interact with the network services of external sources, but in some network configurations, where a firewall blocks the connection between the browser software and a remote server, interaction with a proxy may be required.

   A firewall protects information in internal computer networks from external access, and in doing so, it may limit the ability to exchange information. To overcome this limitation, browser software can interact with proxy software. A proxy server interacts with the firewall and acts as a conduit, providing a specific connection for each network service protocol. If you are running browser software on an internal network from behind a firewall, you will need the name and associated port number for the server running proxy software for each network service.

• No Proxies specifies that you have a direct connection to the Internet.

• Manual Configuration controls proxy settings for your system. Enter the HTTP or FTP URL and port number.

Printing movies

You can print movie content to review it and mark changes, to distribute edits to a team, to make handouts from a presentation, or just to see your work on paper. You can print a movie while in authoring mode in a variety of ways. You can print an image of the Stage in standard or storyboard format, the Score, the cast member number and contents of text cast members in the Cast window, all scripts or a range of scripts (movie, cast, Score, and sprite scripts), the comments in the Markers window, the Cast window artwork, or the entire Cast window.

Note: Using Cast Text on the Print pop-up menu, you can print a table of text cast members at the resolution of your printer.

You can also use Lingo to control printing. See printFrom in the *Lingo Dictionary*.

To print part of a movie:

1 Choose File > Print.

2 To specify what part of the movie to print, choose an option from the Print pop-up menu.

You can print an image of the Stage, the Score, all scripts or a range of scripts (movie, cast, Score, and sprite scripts), cast text, cast art, cast thumbnails, and the comments in the Markers window.

The Scripts, Cast Text, Cast Art, and Cast Thumbnails print options specify a range of casts and cast members—internal or external. Information displayed in the Print dialog box depends on the selection to be printed.

3 To specify which frames of your movie are printed, choose a Frames option:

- Current Frame prints the frame that is currently on the Stage.

- Selected Frames prints the frames that are selected in the Score.

- All prints all the frames in your movie.

- Range prints the range of frames specified in the Begin and End boxes.

4 To specify which frames in the defined range to print, choose an Include option:

- Every Frame is the default setting and prints every frame specified in Range.

- One in Every _ Frames prints frames at the interval you specify in the box. For example, if you type 10, Director prints every tenth frame.

- Frames with Markers prints only the frames that have markers in the Score window.

- Frames with Artwork Changes in Channel _ prints the frames in which cast members move or in which new cast members are introduced in the Score. Specify the channel in the box.

5 To determine the layout of the items to print, click Options and choose from the following:

- Scale provides options to print at 100%, 50%, or 25% of the original size.

- Frame Borders creates a border around each frame.

- Frame Numbers prints the frame number with each frame.

- Registration Marks places marks on every page to align the page for reproduction.

- Storyboard Format is available only when you select 50% or 25% images to print. This option places marker comments next to the frame image.

- Date and Filename in Header prints a header on each page. The header consists of the name of the Director movie and the current date.

- Custom Footer prints a footer on each page. Type the footer in the field.

    The image at the left of the dialog box previews the layout options.

Monitoring memory use

The Memory Inspector displays information about how much memory is available to Director for your movie and indicates how much memory different parts of the current movie use and the total disk space the movie occupies. It also can purge all removable items from RAM if you are about to perform a memory-intensive operation.

To use the Memory Inspector:

1 Choose Window > Inspectors > Memory.

2 Observe the following memory use indicators:

- Total Memory displays the total system memory available, including the amount of RAM installed on your computer and any virtual memory available.

- Physical memory (Windows only) shows the amount of actual RAM installed in the system.

- Partition Size (Macintosh only) shows the amount of memory allocated to Director in the Get Info box, and is available only if Temporary Memory is enabled.

- Total Used indicates how much RAM is being used for a movie.

- Free Memory indicates how much more memory is currently available in your system.

- Other Memory indicates the amount of memory taken up by other applications.

- Used by Program indicates the amount of memory used by Director (excluding the amount of memory taken up by the Director application file itself).

- Cast and Score indicates the amount of memory used by the cast members in the Cast window and the notation in the Score window. Cast members include all the artwork in the Paint window, all the text in the Text windows, cast members that use the Matte ink in the Score, thumbnail images in the Cast window, and any sounds, palettes, buttons, digital video movies, or linked files imported into the cast and currently loaded into memory.

- Screen Buffer shows how much memory Director reserves for a working area while executing animation on the Stage.

3 To remove all purgeable items from RAM, including all thumbnail images in the Cast window, click Purge.

All cast members that have Unload (purge priority) set to a priority other than 0–Never (as specified in the Member tab of the Property Inspector) are removed from memory. This procedure is useful for gaining as much memory as possible before importing a large file. Edited cast members are not purged.

About using Xtras to extend Director functionality

Xtras are software components that extend Director functionality; some Xtras are installed with Director and others are available through third-party developers. Xtras provide capabilities such as importing filters and connecting to the Internet. You can use preexisting Xtras and, if you know the C programming language, you can create your own Xtras.

For information on creating Xtras, download the Xtras Developer's Kit from the Director Support Center.

You must distribute any Xtra that a movie requires along with the movie itself. Xtras can be packaged with projectors, or your user can download your required Xtras from the Internet. See "Managing Xtras for distributed movies" on page 437.

If your user is missing an Xtra that Director requires, an alert appears when the movie opens. For missing Xtra transition cast members, the movie performs a simple cut transition instead. For other missing Xtra cast members, Director displays a red X as a placeholder.

Types of Xtras

Five types of Xtras are supplied with Director: cast member Xtras, importing Xtras, scripting Xtras, transition Xtras, and tool Xtras.

- Cast member Xtras provide new media types to Director. They create or control a wide range of objects for use as cast members.

  Some of the cast member types built into Director, such as Shockwave Flash, Vector Shape, and Animated GIF, are provided as Xtras. Xtras provided by third-party developers can include databases, 3D graphics processors, special types of graphics, and so on. Cast member Xtras built into Director appear on the Insert > Media Element menu. Other cast member Xtras may not appear on this menu and may require Lingo implementation.

  When setting properties for an Xtra cast member, use the Property Inspector, which provides settings standard to all types of Xtra cast members. If there are settings that are unique to the current Xtra, you must click Option to open a second Properties dialog box that lets you change those settings.

  Some cast member Xtras have separate authoring and playback components. You should include only the playback components when distributing movies.

- Importing Xtras provide the code required to import various types of media into Director. When you link a movie to an external file, Director uses the importing Xtra to import the media every time the movie runs. To distribute a movie with external linked media, you must also include the Xtra required to import that type of media.

- Scripting Xtras add Lingo elements to predefined Lingo scripts. The NetLingo Xtra, for example, provides special Lingo elements for controlling Internet functions.

- Transition Xtras supply transitions in addition to the predefined transitions available in the Frame Properties: Transition dialog box.

- Tool Xtras provide useful functions in the authoring environment, but they don't do anything while a movie runs. They do not have to be distributed with movies.

Installing Xtras

To make custom Xtras available to Director, place them in the Xtras folder located in the same folder as the Director application. You must do this before you launch Director.

An Xtra can be in a folder within the Xtras folder up to five layers deep.

When you launch Director, you can use the openXlib command to open Scripting Xtras located in any folder. If you open an Xtra this way, you must use the closeXlib command to close it when Director has finished with it.

Copies of the same Xtra can have different file names or have the same file name but reside in different folders. If duplicate Xtras are available when Director launches, Director displays an alert. Delete any duplicate Xtras.

Director automatically closes Xtras when the application quits.

To make any Director movie appear on the Xtras menu and open as a movie in a window during authoring, place it in the Xtras folder.

About distributing movies

When you finish creating a movie, you have several choices about how to distribute it to users. You can distribute the movie as a Shockwave movie that plays within a Web page or as a projector that downloads to the user's computer or that you distribute on a disk.

- A Shockwave movie is a compressed version of the movie data only.

- A projector is a stand-alone version of a movie. You can include several movies in a single projector. Projectors appear on the system desktop as applications.

For more information about distributing movies, see Chapter 17, "Packaging Movies for Distribution."

Movies distributed from the Internet can begin playing as soon as the content for the first frame is downloaded. This is called streaming. You can control streaming with behaviors that make the movie wait for media at certain frames, or you can specify that a movie download completely before it begins playing. See "Setting movie playback options" on page 414.

To create a Shockwave movie that can play in a Web page, you use the Publish command. Director leaves your original movie in its DIR format. Director also creates a Shockwave movie in the DCR format.

If you use the default Publish settings, Director creates an HTML page completely configured with EMBED tags and everything else you need to run your movie in a browser. Director saves all of these new files, by default, in the same folder as your original Director movie. For more information about putting your Director movie on the Web, see "Creating Shockwave movies" on page 440.

For information on how to distribute Xtras with projectors, refer to TechNote 13965 in the Director Support Center. Although the note may refer to Director 7, the information is the same for Director 8.

CHAPTER 3
Cast members and Cast windows

. . . .

Cast members are the media and other assets in your movie. They can be bitmaps, vector shapes, text, scripts, sounds, Flash movies, QuickTime movies, AVI videos, and more. When you place a cast member on the Stage or in the Score, you create a sprite. For more information on sprites, see "Sprites" on page 119.

You use windows called casts to group and organize your cast members. To populate casts, you import and create cast members. You can create and use multiple casts in a movie.

You can create and edit cast members in Director using basic tools and media editors such as the Paint and Text windows, and you can also edit cast members using external editors. In addition, you can import cast members from nearly every popular media format into a movie file and link cast members to external files, for some media types, on a disk or the Internet for dynamic updating.

The Property Inspector contains asset management fields for cast members on the Member tab. These fields let you name your cast members, add comments about them, and view information such as creation and modification dates, and file size.

Casts can be internal—stored inside the movie file and exclusive to that movie—or external—stored outside the movie file and available for sharing with other movies. When you create a new movie, an empty internal cast is automatically created, and when you open the Cast window it is in the default List view.

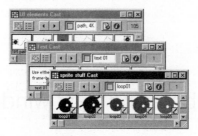

Internal casts

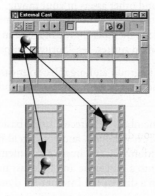

External casts

External casts are also useful for creating groups of commonly used cast members that you can switch while the movie plays, such as when you want to switch the language used in a movie. Using external casts can keep the movie size small for downloading; an external cast can download separately from the movie file if or when it is needed.

Creating new casts

Before assembling a large number of cast members, it's good practice to create the casts necessary to keep them organized. You can sort casts by type, edit cast properties, and use external casts for storing and sharing common media elements.

You can create as many casts as necessary; the number of casts does not affect the size of a movie for downloading.

You can include up to 32,000 cast members in a single cast, but it's usually best to group media such as text, buttons, and images logically in a few different casts for each movie.

To create a new cast:

1 Choose File > New > Cast.

2 Type a name for the new cast.

3 Specify how the cast is stored:

• Internal stores the cast within the movie file. This option makes the cast available only to the current movie.

• External stores the cast in a separate file outside the movie file. This option makes the cast available for sharing with other movies. For information about internal and external casts, see "Managing external casts" on page 114.

4 If you chose External and you don't want to use the cast in the current movie, deselect the Use in Current Movie option.

5 Click Create.

The cast is created, and a Cast window for the cast is opened in List view. See "Using the Cast window" on page 89.

6 If you created an external cast, choose File > Save while its Cast window is active, then save the cast in the desired directory.

Creating cast members

You can create several types of cast members in Director, which includes editors to create common media such as text, shapes, and bitmaps. You can also use Director for basic editing of media imported from other applications. You define external editors to launch from within Director when you double-click a cast member, and edit almost any type of supported media. See "Launching external editors" on page 112.

You can also import cast members. See "Importing cast members" on page 106.

To create a new cast member from the Insert menu:

1 Open the Cast window for the cast member you are creating.

   To place a cast member in a specific position, select the position in Thumbnail view. See "Using Cast Thumbnail view" on page 96. Otherwise, Director places the new cast member in the first empty position or after the current selection in the Cast window.

2 Choose Insert > Media Element and then choose the type of cast member to create.

   For more information on each choice, see the following sections:

   • "Using the Paint window" on page 304

   • "Using the Color Palettes window" on page 227

   • "Streaming linked Shockwave Audio and MP3 audio files" on page 369

   • "Creating text cast members" on page 338

   • "Embedding fonts in movies" on page 336

   • "Creating an animated color cursor cast member" on page 268

   • "Using animated GIFs" on page 303

   • "Drawing vector shapes" on page 293

   • "Using Flash Movies" on page 388

3 To create a control or button, choose from the following options:

   • Choose Insert > Control > Field to create a field cast member. Creating a field cast member also creates a sprite on the Stage. See "Working with fields" on page 347.

   • Choose Insert > Control > Push Button, Radio Button, or Check Box to create a button cast member and a sprite on the Stage. See "Using shapes" on page 331.

   • (Windows only) Choose Insert > Control > ActiveX to create an ActiveX cast member. See "Using ActiveX controls" on page 405.

To create a cast member in a media editing window:

1 Open a media editing window by choosing Window and then choosing the type of cast member you want to create (Paint, Text, Script, and so on).

2 Click the New Cast Member button to create a cast member of the corresponding type. The cast member is added to the most recently active Cast window.

New Cast Member button

Using the Cast window

In the Cast window, you can view the cast in either the default List view or the Thumbnail view. (You can change the default so that the Cast window opens in Thumbnail view. See "Setting Cast window preferences" on page 100.)

The Cast window lets you do the following:

- Organize and display all media in a movie.
- Move groups of cast members.
- Launch editors for cast members.
- Launch the Property Inspector to view, add, and change comments about your cast members, and to view and modify cast member properties.

To view the Cast window:

Choose Window > Cast or press Control+3 (Windows) or Command+3 (Macintosh). If there is more than one cast in the movie, you can choose which Cast window to open by choosing Window > Cast and then selecting a cast name from the Cast submenu.

Switching from one Cast window view to another

You can easily toggle between List and Thumbnail views of the Cast window.

To switch from one Cast window view to another, do one of the following:

- Click the Cast View Style icon on the Cast window to toggle between the two views.
- With the Cast window active, choose View > Cast and select either List or Thumbnail, as desired.
- Right-click (Windows) or Control-click (Macintosh) the Cast window and select either List or Thumbnail, as desired, from the context menu.

Using Cast window controls

The controls along the top of the Cast window are the same for both the Cast List and the Cast Thumbnail views. You use the controls to change the cast displayed in the Cast window, the cast member selection, or the name of a cast member. You can also use them to move cast members and to open a cast member's Script window or the Property Inspector.

To change the cast displayed in the current Cast window:

 Click the Cast button and choose a cast from the pop-up menu.

To open a cast in a new Cast window:

Right-click (Windows) or Control-click (Macintosh) the Cast button and choose a cast from the context menu.

To select the previous or next cast member:

◀ ▶ Click the Previous Cast Member or Next Cast Member button.

To move a selected cast member to a new position in the Cast window (Thumbnail view) or to the Stage:

 Drag from the Drag Cast Member button to the desired position in the Cast window or on the Stage.

This procedure is useful when the selected cast member has scrolled out of view.

To enter a cast member name:

Select a cast member and enter the name in the Cast Member Name box.

To edit a cast member script:

Select a cast member and click the Cast Member Script button.

To view cast member properties:

1 Select a cast member.

2 Do one of the following:

• Click the Cast Member Properties button.

• Right-click (Windows) or Control-click (Macintosh) and choose Cast Member Properties from the context menu.

• Choose Window > Inspectors > Property.

See "Viewing and setting cast member properties" on page 103.

To view the cast member number:

Refer to the Cast Member Number field.

Selecting cast members in the Cast window

Before changing, sorting, or moving cast members, you must select them in the Cast window.

To select a single cast member, do one of the following:

• In List view, click the name or icon (Windows) or click any part of the text or icon (Macintosh).

• In Thumbnail view, simply click the thumbnail image.

To select multiple adjacent cast members, do one of the following:

• In List view, Shift-click (Windows) or marquee-select the cast members (Macintosh)

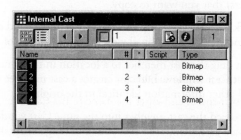

In Thumbnail view, click the first cast member in the range and then Shift-click the last cast member in the range.

To select multiple nonadjacent cast members:

In either List or Thumbnail view, Control-click (Windows) or Command-click (Macintosh) each cast member that you want to select.

Copying cast members

You can easily create multiple versions of a cast member in a single cast. For example, you may want several cast members to be identical except for color or size. You can also copy cast members from one Cast window to another.

To copy a cast member:

1 In either List or Thumbnail view, select the cast member (or multiple cast members) that you want to copy.

2 Alt-click (Windows) or Option-click (Macintosh) and drag the cast member to a new location in Thumbnail view or to the bottom of the list in List view.

   You can drag the cast member to a location in the same Cast window or to a different Cast window. Director creates a cast member with a new number but with all other information identical to the original.

3 If you copied the cast member into the same Cast window, change the name of the copied cast member so that you (and Lingo scripts) can distinguish it from the original. See "Naming cast members" on page 93.

Naming cast members

To avoid problems in Lingo when referring to cast members, you should name them and refer to them by name. Naming cast members doesn't affect Director performance. The name stays the same even if the cast member number changes.

Avoid duplicating cast member names. If more than one cast member has the same name, Lingo uses the cast member with the lowest number in the cast.

To name a cast member:

Select the cast member in either the List or the Thumbnail view of the Cast window and do one of the following:

- Enter a name in the Cast Member Name field at the top of the Cast window or in any of the editing windows.

Enter the cast member name here

- Enter a name in the Name field on the Cast or Member tab of the Property Inspector.

To name a cast member using Lingo:

Set the name cast member property. See name in the *Lingo Dictionary*.

Using Cast List view

Cast List view, the default view in which the Cast window opens, provides seven columns of information by default. They are as follows:

Column Title	Column Information
Name	The name of the cast member and an icon describing the cast member type. For more information on what the icons represent, see "Using Cast Thumbnail view" on page 96.
#	The number assigned to the cast member. Note that this number represents the order in which this cast member appears in Thumbnail view.
*	An asterisk in this column indicates the cast member has changed but you have not yet saved those changes.
Script	The word *Member* in this column means the cast member contains a script.
	The word *Movie* in this column means the cast member is a movie script.
	The word *Behavior* in this column means the cast member is a Behavior.
	You can use the Script icon to view the script or behavior.
Type	The cast member type
Modified	The date and time the cast member was changed
Comments	Displays text entered in the Property Inspector's Member tab, in the Comments field

Four additional columns are available via the Cast Window Preferences dialog box. See "Setting Cast window preferences" on page 100. The additional columns that you can display are as follows:

Column Title	Column Information
Size	The size in bytes, kilobytes, or megabytes
Created	The date and time the cast member was created
Modified By	Who modified the cast member. This value comes from the user login name (Windows) or the Sharing setup name (Macintosh).
Filename	The full path to the cast member if it is a linked asset

Resizing columns in Cast List view

You can resize the columns holding the pointer over the column boundary to activate the Resizing tool. Click and drag the column to the desired size.

Sorting Cast List view columns

You can sort the Cast List view columns in ascending and descending order by clicking the column title. When you sort the Cast List window by clicking the column title, you're only changing the way in which the information is displayed. You are not changing any cast member attributes.

About cast member order in Cast List view

Unlike the way in which cast members appear in Thumbnail view, in List view the cast member order does not always correspond to the member's physical location in the cast.

When working in List view, also keep in mind the following:

- In List view, Director places new cast members at the end of the list, and the cast member number becomes the first available number after the current selection.

- You can use Thumbnail view to reorder (and renumber) cast members by dragging them to different locations in the window; you cannot reorder cast members by dragging in List view.

Using Cast Thumbnail view

As the name suggests, the Cast Thumbnail view shows a very small (thumbnail) version of the cast member along with an icon that represents the cast member media type:

Icon	Cast member type	Icon	Cast member type
	Animated GIF		Behavior
	Bitmap		Button
	Check box		Custom Cursor
	Digital video		Field
	Film loop		Font
	Flash movie		Linked bitmap (all linked cast member icons are changed in the same way)
	OLE		Palette
	PICT		QuickTime video
	Radio button		Script
	Shape		Shockwave Audio
	Sound		Text
	Transition		Vector shape
	Xtra		

To turn off or on the display of cast member icons in Thumbnail view and change the Cast window display:

Choose File > Preferences > Cast; see "Setting Cast window preferences" on page 100.

Creating a custom cast member thumbnail

For most cast members, Director displays a scaled version as the thumbnail unless you define a custom thumbnail. Creating a custom thumbnail is most useful for behaviors that you want to identify in the Library palette, because behaviors have no identifying image.

To create a custom cast member thumbnail:

1 Select the bitmap image to use as the new thumbnail and copy it to your system's clipboard.

You can copy the image from any bitmap editor, including the Paint window. The image can be of any size, but smaller images look better because they require less scaling.

2 Using Thumbnail view, place the pointer over the cast member for which you are creating a custom thumbnail.

3 Right-click (Windows) or Control-click (Macintosh) and choose Paste Bitmap from the context menu.

The image from the clipboard replaces the current cast member thumbnail.

You can also use text as a thumbnail. Select text instead of a bitmap image in step 1, and then choose Paste Text from the context menu.

Moving cast members within the Cast window

To move a cast member to a new position within the Cast window, you can use Thumbnail view to see the representation of the cast member's position.

Note: When you move a cast member to a new position, Director assigns it a new number and updates all references to the cast member in the Score, but it doesn't automatically update references to cast member numbers in Lingo scripts. The best practice, therefore, is to always name cast members and refer to them by name in Lingo scripts.

To move a cast member to a new position or a different cast:

- Using Thumbnail view, drag the cast member to a new position in any open Cast window.

In Thumbnail view, a highlight bar indicates where the cast member will be placed. If you drag the cast member over a position that already contains a cast member, Director places your selected cast member in that position and moves the existing cast member one position to the right.

In List view, the cast member is added to the bottom of the list.

To cut, copy, and paste cast members to a new position or a different cast:

1 Select one or more cast members, then choose Cut or Copy from the Edit menu.

2 Do one of the following:

- In Thumbnail view, select an empty position in any open Cast window, and then choose Edit > Paste.

- In List view, deselect all cast members by clicking anywhere in the window except on a cast member name. Then choose Edit > Paste.

Note: In either Thumbnail or List view, if you paste cast members while other cast members are selected, you will overwrite the selected cast members.

To move a cast member to a position not currently visible in Thumbnail view:

1 Select the cast member you want to move.

2 Scroll the Cast window to display the destination position.

3 Drag from the Drag Cast Member button to the destination position.

Organizing cast members within the Cast window

The Sort command in the Modify menu helps clean up and organize the Cast window. Use Sort to order cast members by their media type, name, size, or usage in the Score. You can also use Sort to remove empty positions in a Cast window.

When you use the Sort command to sort a Cast window, Director can move cast members to new positions, with new cast member numbers.

Note: If you've written scripts that refer to cast members by number, Lingo won't be able to find cast members that have been moved. To avoid this problem, always name your cast members and refer to them by name in your scripts.

If you want to view the cast members in a different sort order without changing cast member numbers, click a column title in Cast List view. See "Sorting Cast List view columns" on page 95.

To sort the cast using the Modify menu:

1 With the Cast window active, select the cast members to sort or choose Edit > Select All.

2 Choose Modify > Sort.

3 In the Sort Cast Members dialog box, choose a sorting method.

- Usage in Score places selected cast members used in the Score at the beginning of the selection.

- Media Type groups all cast members according to their media type.

- Name groups the selection alphabetically by cast member name.

- Size arranges the selection with the largest files appearing first.

- Empty at End places all empty cast positions in the selection at the end.

4 Click Sort.

Director reorders the cast members according to the sorting method you selected. The Score automatically adjusts to the new cast member numbers.

Setting Cast window preferences

You use the Cast window preferences settings to control the appearance of the current Cast window or, if desired, all Cast windows. You can set different preferences for each Cast window. The title bar of the dialog box displays the name of the Cast window preferences you are changing.

To set Cast window preferences:

1 Select a Cast window to change.

2 Choose File > Preferences > Cast.

3 To set the Cast window to display in either List or Thumbnail view, select the appropriate Cast View option.

4 If you want your preferences to apply to all Cast windows, select Apply to All Casts.

5 To select the columns that appear in Cast List view, select the desired Columns in List options. See "Using Cast List view" on page 94.

6 To specify the maximum number of cast members displayed in the Cast window, choose a value from the Thumbnails Visible pop-up menu.

Note that this option does not limit the actual number of cast members that can exist in the cast. If you have a small number of cast members, you can hide the remaining unused cast positions to make better use of the vertical scroll bar. The default is 1000.

7 To specify the number of thumbnails in each row of the Cast window, choose an option from the Row Width pop-up menu.

The options for 8 Thumbnails, 10 Thumbnails, and 20 Thumbnails specify fixed-row widths that are independent of the window size; if the Cast window is smaller horizontally than the width of the cast row, you must use the horizontal scroll bar to reveal the rest of the cast. The Fit to Window option automatically adjusts the number of cast members per row to fit the current width of the Cast window. In this mode, the horizontal scroll bar is disabled since the entire width of the cast is always in view. The default is Fit to Window.

8 To set the size of each cast thumbnail image displayed in the Cast window, choose an option from the Thumbnail Size pop-up menu:

- Small 44 x 33 pixels
- Medium 56 x 42 pixels (default)
- Large 80 x 60 pixels

Thumbnails always maintain the standard 4:3 aspect ratio.

If the thumbnails appear fuzzy, they are probably displaying larger than their original size. To correct this, change the Cast window preferences thumbnail setting to a smaller size. Click OK when the alert message asks if thumbnails should be regenerated.

9 To select the display format of the cast member ID displayed below each cast thumbnail image in the Cast window, choose an option from the Label pop-up menu:

- Number displays the cast number.
- Name displays the cast name, if one exists; otherwise, this option displays the cast number in decimal format.
- Number:Name displays the cast number (in decimal format) and cast name, separated by a colon: for example, 340:Dancing Potato. If no name exists, this setting displays just the cast number in decimal format.

The chosen format is also used in other windows, including the Score, whenever a cast ID is displayed.

10 To specify whether Director displays an icon in the lower right corner of each cast member indicating the cast member's type, choose one of the following from the Media Type Icons pop-up menu: All Types, All but Text and Bitmap, or None.

11 To display a script indicator icon in the lower left corner of each cast member that has a script attached, select Script.

12 To make your preference settings the default settings, click Save as Default.

13 When you finish selecting your preferences, click OK.

Changing Cast properties

You use the Property Inspector to change the name of a Cast and to define how its cast members are loaded into memory.

To change Cast window properties:

1 With the Cast window as the active window, do one of the following:

- If the Property Inspector is not open, choose Window > Inspectors > Property, then click the Cast tab and display the Graphical view.

- If the Property Inspector is open, click the Cast tab and display the Graphical view.

- Choose Modify > Cast Properties.

- Right-click (Windows) or Control-click (Macintosh) in the Cast window and choose Cast Properties from the context menu.

2 To change the name of the current cast, enter the new name in the Name box.

3 Choose a Preload option to define how cast members are loaded into memory when the movie runs:

- When Needed loads each cast member into memory when it is required by the movie. This setting can slow down the movie while it plays, but it makes the movie begin playing sooner. This setting is the best choice when controlling cast members loading with Lingo.

- After Frame One loads all cast members (except those required for frame 1) when the movie exits frame 1. This setting can ensure that the first frame is displayed as quickly as possible, and it may be the best choice if the first frame of the movie is designed to remain onscreen for a number of seconds.

- Before Frame One loads all cast members before the movie plays frame 1. This setting makes the movie take longer to start playing, but it provides the best playback performance if there is enough memory to hold all cast members.

Viewing and setting cast member properties

You can display and set properties for individual cast members, or for multiple cast members at once, even if the cast members are different types. In both cases, you use the Property Inspector.

You can also set cast member properties by using Lingo (see "Setting cast member properties using Lingo" on page 116).

To view and set cast member properties:

1 Select one or more cast members.

2 Do one of the following:

• If the Property Inspector is open, click the Member tab.

• If the Property Inspector is not open, choose Window > Inspectors > Property, then click the Member tab.

As with all fields in the Property Inspector, if you've selected multiple cast members, the information common to all of the selected cast members appears. Any changes you make apply to all of the selected cast members.

3 Display the Graphical view on the Member tab.

The Member tab displays the following:

- Editable fields to view or change the cast member's name, a Comments field to enter text that appears in the Comments column of the Cast List window, and an Unload pop-up menu that lets you choose how to remove a cast member from memory. For more information on using the Unload pop-up menu, see "Controlling cast member unloading" on page 114.

- View-only fields that indicate the cast member's size, when the cast member was created and modified, and the name of the person who modified the cast member.

For an Xtra cast member, the information displayed in the Property Inspector is determined by the developer of the Xtra. Some Xtras have options in addition to those listed here. For non-Macromedia Xtras, refer to documentation supplied by the developer.

For information on specific cast member properties, see these topics

- "Using animated GIFs" on page 303"
- "Embedding fonts in movies" on page 336
- "Using Flash Movies" on page 388
- "Synchronizing media" on page 384
- "Setting sound cast member properties" on page 362
- "Setting text or field cast member properties" on page 350
- "Setting Xtra cast member properties" on page 117
- "Creating an animated color cursor cast member" on page 268
- "Streaming linked Shockwave Audio and MP3 audio files" on page 369

Finding cast members

You can search for cast members by name, type, and color palette. You can search for selected cast members used in the Score, such as when you are preparing a movie for distribution. You can also search for cast members not used in the Score—for example, to clean up a movie and reduce the space and memory required to save and run the movie.

Before releasing a movie, it's a good idea to remove unused cast members to make the movie as small as possible for downloading.

To find cast members:

1 Choose Edit > Find > Cast Member.

2 In the Find Cast Member dialog box, choose a Cast window to search from the Cast pop-up menu.

   To search every cast in the movie, select All Casts.

3 Choose a search option:

• Select Name and enter search text in the text box. For example, to search for a group of related cast members that share a common element in their names, you might enter the word **Bird** to search for cast members named Bird 1, Bird 2, and Bird 3.

• Select Type and choose an option from the pop-up menu to search for cast members by media type.

• Select Palette and choose an option from the pop-up menu. You can use this option to search for and resolve palette conflicts.

• Select Usage to locate all cast members that aren't used in the Score. Note that cast members found with this option may be used in the movie by a Lingo script.

   Director displays the found cast member.

4 Do one of the following:

• Choose a cast member on the list and click Select to close the dialog box and select the cast member in the Cast window.

• Click Select All to close the dialog box and select all listed cast members in the Cast window.

To find a cast member in the Score:

1 Select a cast member to search for in the cast or the Score. If you select a sprite that includes multiple cast members, Director searches for the first cast member in the sprite; to select a cast member other than the first, open the sprite to select the cast member. (For information on selecting sprites, see "Selecting sprites" on page 122.)

2 Choose Edit > Find > Selection or press Control-H (Windows) or Command-H (Macintosh).

   Director searches the Score and highlights the first Score cell it finds.

3 Choose Edit > Find Again to find the next occurrence of the cast member in the Score.

Importing cast members

Importing lets you create cast members from external media. You can either import data into a Director movie file or create a link to the external file and re-import the file each time the movie opens. Linked files let you display dynamic media from the Internet, such as sports scores, sounds, and weather pictures, which makes downloading movies faster. See "About linking to files" on page 110.

Director can import cast members from almost every popular media file format. .

You can import files by using the Import dialog box, dragging files from the desktop to a Cast window, or using Lingo.

To import cast members and specify import options:

1 In Thumbnail view, select an empty position in a cast.

   If no cast position is selected, Director places the new cast member in the first available position in the current cast in Thumbnail view. In List view, Director places the new cast member at the end of the list.

2 Choose File > Import.

3 To import a file from the Internet, click Internet and enter a URL.

4 To import local files, choose the type of media to import from the Files of Type (Windows) or Show (Macintosh) pop-up menu.

   All the files in the current directory appear unless you make a selection.

5 To select a file or files to import, do one of the following:

• Double-click a file.

• Select one or more files and click Add.

• Click Add All.

   You can switch folders and import files from different folders at the same time.

6   From the Media pop-up menu at the bottom of the dialog box, choose an
    option to specify how to treat imported media:

• Standard Import imports all selected files, storing them inside the movie file
  but not updating them when changes are made to the source material. If you
  selected the option to import from the Internet in step 3, Director retrieves the
  file immediately from the Internet if a connection is available.

  Note: AVI and QuickTime files are always linked to the original external file (see the next
  option), even if you select Standard Import.

• Link to External File creates a link to the selected files and imports the data
  each time the movie runs. If you choose to import from a URL via the Internet,
  the media is dynamically updated. See "About linking to files" on page 110.

  Note: Text and RTF files are always imported and stored inside the movie file (see the
  previous option), even if you select Link to External File.

• Include Original Data for Editing preserves the original data in the movie file
  for use with an external editor.

  When this option is selected, Director keeps a copy of the original cast member
  data and sends the original to the external editor when you edit the cast
  member. This option preserves all of the editor's capabilities. For example, if
  you specify Photoshop to edit PICT images, Director maintains all of the
  Photoshop object data. See "Launching external editors" on page 112.

• Import PICT File as PICT prevents PICT files from being converted to bitmaps.

7   If you selected a PICS or Scrapbook file to import, click Options to specify
    options for these files. See "Setting import options for PICS and Scrapbook
    files" on page 112.

8   When you've finished selecting the files, click Import.

    If you've imported a bitmap with a color depth or color palette that differs
    from the current movie, the Image Options dialog box appears, in which
    you must enter additional information. See "Choosing import image options"
    on page 111.

For information on importing specific media, see these sections:

- "About importing bitmaps" on page 302
- "Importing internal and linked sounds" on page 360
- "Using Director movies within Director movies" on page 399
- "Importing internal and linked sounds" on page 360
- Chapter 13, "Text"
- "Using animated GIFs" on page 303
- "Using Flash Movies" on page 388
- "Using linked scripts" on page 217

To import files by dragging:

1 In the Explorer (Windows) or on the system desktop (Macintosh), select a file or files to import.

2 Drag the files from the desktop to the desired position in the Cast window Thumbnail view, or to the Cast window List view.

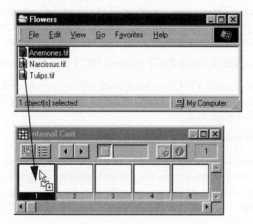

If you drag to List view, the imported files are added at the bottom of the list.

To import files with Lingo:

Use the importFileInto command to import a file. Set the fileName cast member property to assign a new file to a linked cast member. See importFileInto and fileName in the *Lingo Dictionary*.

About import file formats

Director can import files in all the formats listed in the following table. For information on additional file formats Director may support, see the Director Support Center Web site.

Type of file	Supported formats
Animation and multimedia	Flash movies, animated GIF, PowerPoint presentations, Director movies, Director external cast files
Image	BMP, GIF, JPEG, LRG (xRes), Photoshop 3.0 (or later), MacPaint, PNG, TIFF, PICT, Targa
Multiple-image file	Windows only: FLC, FLI
	Macintosh only: PICS, Scrapbook
Sound	AIFF, WAV, MP3 audio, Shockwave Audio, Sun AU, uncompressed and IMA compressed
	Macintosh only: System 7 sounds
Video	QuickTime 2, 3 and 4; AVI
Text	RTF, HTML, ASCII (often called Text Only), Lingo scripts
Palette	PAL, Photoshop CLUT

About linking to files

Director re-imports media every time a movie runs when Link to External File is selected in the Import dialog box (Choose File > Import). Linking makes it easier to use bulky media such as long sounds and is especially useful for showing media from the Internet that change frequently. Linking also makes downloading movies faster; users can choose whether to view linked files, so the files do not download unless they're needed.

When you link to an external file, Director creates a cast member that stores the name and location of the file. Saving a movie saves only the link to the linked cast member. Keep linked files in a folder that's close to the original movie file. Pathnames are restricted to 4096 characters by the system. URLs can be up to 260 characters. If you store a file too many folders away from the movie or using a very long URL, it may fail to link correctly.

When distributing movies with linked media, follow these guidelines:

- If you distribute a movie, you also must include all linked cast member files, and they must be in their expected locations. In addition, the Xtras used to import the media must be present when the movie runs (either on the user's computer or included in your movie). For more information, see "Setting Xtra cast member properties" on page 117.

- When you link to media on the Internet, the media must be present at the specified URL when the movie runs. Provide for link failure, because you can't guarantee that an Internet transaction will be successful.

- To retrieve media from the Internet during playback, Director requires that the projector include certain Xtras. To include these Xtras automatically, click Add Network in the Movie Xtras dialog box. (Movies playing in Web browsers do not require these Xtras.)

Note: Use File > Preferences > Network to define standard network settings for the Director authoring environment; see the Network Preferences topic in Director Help.

Choosing import image options

If you import a bitmap cast member with a color depth or color palette different from that of the Stage (the current movie), Director lets you choose the image's color depth and color palette. You can choose to import the bitmap at its original color depth or at the Stage color depth. (The Stage color depth is the same as the system color depth.) You can also choose to import the image's color palette or remap the image's colors to a palette in the movie.

In many cases, it's easiest to change the image's color depth to the depth of the movie and remap the image to the color palette used in the rest of the movie. For more on controlling color in Director, see Chapter 7, "Color, Tempo, and Transitions."

If you change 16-, 24-, or 32-bit cast members to 8 or fewer bits, you must remap the cast members to an existing color palette.

To choose bitmap image options for importing:

1 Import a bitmap image by choosing File > Import. (For more information on this procedure, see "Importing cast members" on page 106.)

2 If the Image Options dialog box appears while you are importing a bitmap image using File > Import, choose a Color Depth option:

- Image specifies the color depth and palette of the image.

- Stage specifies the color depth of the current Stage.

3 Choose a Palette option to change palette settings for 2-, 4- or 8-bit images:

- Import imports the image with its color palette. The palette appears as a new cast member immediately following the bitmap cast member.

- Remap To replaces the image's colors with the most similar solid colors in the palette you select from the pop-up menu.

4 Choose Image options:

- Trim White Space removes any white pixels from the edges of the image. Deselect this option to preserve the white canvas around an image.

- Dither blends the colors in the new palette in the Palette section to approximate the original colors in the graphic.

5 To apply the current settings to all the remaining files selected for importing, select Same Settings for Remaining Images.

Setting import options for PICS and Scrapbook files

You can import PICS and Scrapbook files several different ways. These file formats are available only on the Macintosh.

To set import options for PICS and Scrapbook files:

1 Import the PICS or Scrapbook cast member by choosing File > Import. (For more information on this procedure, see "Importing cast members" on page 106.)

2 If the PICS/Scrapbook Options dialog box appears while you are importing an image using File > Import, specify the range of images to import:

- All Frames imports up to 512 frames in a PICS file or from a Scrapbook file. Each frame will be imported as a separate cast member.

- From/To selects a range of cells. The imported PICS or Scrapbook frames are added to the Score beginning at the selected cell; any existing Score data will be replaced by the imported frames.

   If the PICS file was created using a previous version of Director, you must enter 1 as the starting frame to import.

3 To import only the image, not the surrounding white space, select Contract White Space.

4 To place the imported artwork in the Paint window in its original position relative to the other artwork in the series, select Original Position.

5 To center each piece of imported artwork relative to the rest of the artwork in the series, click Centered.

Launching external editors

You can specify external applications to edit many types of media. All the types of media for which you can define an external editor are listed in the Editors Preferences dialog box. Once you set up an external editor for a particular media type, Director launches the application when you edit a cast member of that type. When you finish editing a cast member in an external editor and then save and close the file, Director re-imports the cast member media.

If you want to use an external editor for a cast member you import, select Include Original Data for External Editing when you import the cast member. (For more information, see "Importing cast members" on page 106.)

It is not possible to define an external editor for any cast member created by an Xtra. These include text, vector shapes, Flash movies, and custom cursors.

To define an external editor:

1 Choose File > Preferences > Editors.

2 Choose a type of media for which you want to define an external editor.

3 Click Edit.

4 Click Browse or Scan to locate the application.

You can specify any application capable of editing the selected type of media.

5 To determine which editor appears when you double-click a cast member, choose Use Internal Editor or Use External Editor.

• If you usually want to make changes inside of Director and only occasionally want to use the external editor, choose Use Internal Editor.

• If you usually want to use the external editor to make changes to the cast member, choose Use External Editor.

To launch an external editor:

1 Select a cast member of a media type for which you have defined an external editor, then do one of the following:

• If you specified Use External Editor when you defined the external editor for this media type, double-click the cast member.

• Choose Edit > Launch External Editor.

• While the cast member is selected and the Cast window is active, right-click (Windows) or Control-click (Macintosh) and choose Launch External Editor from the context menu.

Director launches or switches to the application used to create the cast member, sending the original data to the external editor.

Note: If you've specified an external editor and you want to edit a cast member with Director's internal editors, select the cast member and choose Edit > Edit Cast Member.

2 Edit the cast member.

Note that if you change an image in the Paint window and then edit the image with an external editor, changes made in the Paint window, with the exception of registration points, are lost. Director warns you if this is a possibility.

3 Save and close the file. Director re-imports the cast member.

Controlling cast member unloading

When Director runs low on memory, it removes cast members from memory. You use the Property Inspector to specify the priority with which a cast member is removed from memory. When a cast member is available in memory, it appears almost instantly. When it needs to be loaded from disk, the loading can cause a delay. Set your cast members so that frequently used cast members remain in memory as long as possible.

These settings are the same for all types of cast members.

To specify the Unload setting:

1 Select the cast members in the Cast window.

2 In the Member tab of the Property Inspector, display the Graphical view and then choose an option from the Unload pop-up menu:

- 3—Normal sets the selected cast members to be removed from memory after any priority 2 cast members have been removed.

- 2—Next sets the selected cast members to be among the first removed from memory.

- 1—Last sets the selected cast members to be the last removed from memory.

- 0—Never sets the selected cast members to be retained in memory; these cast members are never unloaded.

Managing external casts

An external cast is a separate file that must be explicitly linked to a movie for the movie to use its cast members.

If you link an external cast to a movie, Director opens the cast every time it opens the movie. If you don't link an external cast to a movie, you must open and save the file separately. You can use unlinked external casts as libraries to store commonly used elements for authoring, such as scripts, buttons, and so on; see "Creating libraries" on page 116.

When you distribute a movie that uses an external cast, you must include the external cast file. For disk-based movies, the cast must be in the same relative path in your files as it was when the movie was created. For Shockwave movies on the Web, the cast must be at the specified URL.

To create an external cast:

1 Choose File > New > Cast.

2 Type a name for the new cast.

3 Specify that the cast be stored as an external cast.

If you don't want to use the cast in the current movie, deselect the Use in Current Movie option.

4 Click Create.

The cast is created, and a Cast window for the cast is opened in List view. See "Using the Cast window" on page 89.

5 Choose File > Save while the Cast window is active, then save the cast in the desired directory.

To link an external cast to a movie:

1 Choose Modify > Movie > Casts.

2 In the Movie Casts dialog box, click Link.

3 Locate and select the external cast you want and then click Open.

You can link to casts on your local disk or to casts stored at any URL. Click Internet to enter a URL for a linked external cast.

4 Click OK.

To unlink a cast from a movie:

1 Choose Modify > Movie > Casts.

2 In the Movie Casts dialog box, select the external cast.

3 Click Remove.

To save a movie and all open casts, linked or unlinked:

Choose File > Save All.

Note: To use a cast member from an external cast without creating a link to the external cast, first copy the cast member to an internal cast or to a (different) linked external cast.

Creating libraries

A library is a special type of unlinked external cast. When you drag a cast member from an external cast library to the Stage or Score, Director automatically copies the cast member to one of the movie's internal casts. Libraries are useful for storing any type of commonly used cast members, especially behaviors. A library cannot be linked to a movie. See "Attaching behaviors" on page 158.

When you create a library as explained in the following procedure, it appears on the Library pop-up menu in the Library palette.

To create a library:

1 Create an external cast file, following the procedure under "Creating new casts" on page 87. Do not select Use in Current Movie.

2 With the Cast window for the external cast active, choose File > Save and place the external cast in the Libs folder in the Director application folder.

Setting cast member properties using Lingo

Lingo lets you control and edit cast members by setting their properties. Some properties are available for every type of cast member. Other properties are available only for specific cast member types. See entries for individual properties in the *Lingo Dictionary*.

To specify the cast member's content:

Set the media cast member property.

To specify the cast member's name:

Set the name cast member property. .

To set the contents of the cast member's comments field:

Set the comments cast member property. You can store any text information in this field that you find useful and access it at runtime by getting the comments property.

To specify the cast member's purge priority:

Set the purgePriority cast member property.

To specify the content of the script, if any, attached to the cast member:

Set the scriptText cast member property.

To specify the file assigned to a linked cast member:

Set the fileName cast member property.

For additional cast member properties that Lingo can test and set, refer to the *Lingo Dictionary* sections that discuss the specific cast member type.

Setting Xtra cast member properties

Xtra cast members have the same Name and Unload properties as other cast members, but they may also contain an extra panel of options accessible from the Property Inspector. To set cast member properties, use the Member tab and the custom tab for the type of cast member you are working with. The Member tab contains an Edit button and may contain a More Options button. Use the Edit button to edit the cast member with its default editor. Use the More Options button to display the Cast Member Properties dialog box for the current cast member.

The custom tab for the type of cast member you are working with may also contain a More Options button. This button will display the Cast Member Properties dialog box for the current cast member.

The content of the Properties dialog box is determined by the developer of the Xtra. For non-Macromedia Xtras, refer to any documentation supplied by the developer.

To view or change Xtra cast member properties:

1 Select an Xtra cast member.

2 Open the Property Inspector and click the Member tab.

The Member tab displays information about the member:

- The cast member name
- The name of the cast that contains the cast member
- The size in kilobytes
- The creation date
- The date the cast member was last modified
- The name of the user who last modified the cast member

3 Use the Name field to view or edit the cast member name.

4 To specify how Director removes cast members from memory if memory is low, choose options from the Unload pop-up menu. See "Controlling cast member unloading" on page 114.

5 To set special options for the current Xtra cast member, click the custom tab for the cast member you are working with. Some types of Xtra cast members will also have a More Options button on this tab. Use it to set any properties of the cast member that are not displayed on the tab itself.

CHAPTER 4
Sprites

A sprite is an object that controls when, where, and how cast members appear in a movie. Multiple sprites can use the same cast member. You can also switch the cast member assigned to a sprite as the movie plays. You use the Stage to control *where* a sprite appears and you use the Score to control *when* it appears in your movie.

Sprites display on the Stage layered according to the channel in which they're in the Score. Sprites in higher-numbered channels appear in front of sprites in lower-numbered channels. A movie can include up to 1000 sprite channels. Use the Movie tab of the Property Inspector to control the number of channels. See "Setting Stage and movie properties" on page 61.

Sprite properties include the sprite's size and location, the cast member assigned to the sprite, and the frames in which the sprite occurs. Different properties can alter the appearance of a sprite. You can rotate, skew, flip, and change the color of sprites without affecting cast members. You can change sprite properties with the Property Inspector or Lingo.

In Lingo, some properties are available only for certain types of sprites. Such properties typically are characteristics related to the specific sprite type. For example, Lingo has several digital video properties that determine the contents of tracks in digital video sprites.

To control the way a sprite's colors appear on the Stage, you use sprite inks. By selecting Background Transparent ink in the Property Inspector, for example, you turn all white pixels transparent and remove the white border (the bounding rectangle) around bitmap images (assuming the sprite is over a white background). Other inks provide more complex and interesting effects such as reversed colors or colors that change in different ways depending on the background color.

For additional introductory information about sprites, see the Guided Tour in Director Help.

Creating sprites

You create a sprite by dragging a cast member to either the Stage or the Score; the sprite appears in both places. New sprites, by default, span 28 frames. To change the default sprite duration, choose File > Preferences > Sprite; see "Changing sprite preferences" on page 121.

To create a new sprite:

1 Click to select the frame in the Score where you want the sprite to begin.

2 From the Cast window, in either List or Thumbnail view, do one of the following:

- Drag a cast member to the position on the Stage where you wish to place the sprite.

- Drag a cast member to the Score. Director places the new sprite in the center of the Stage.

- To create a sprite one frame long, press Alt (Windows) or Option (Macintosh) and drag a cast member to the Stage or Score.

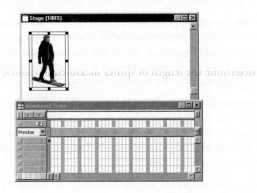

Changing sprite preferences

You use the Sprite Preferences dialog box to control the way sprites behave and appear in the Score window and on the Stage.

To change preferences for sprites:

1 Choose File > Preferences > Sprite.

2 To determine if selecting a sprite on the Stage selects the entire span of the sprite or only the current frame in the sprite, choose a Stage Selection option:

- Entire Sprite selects the sprite in all frames that it occupies.

- Current Frame Only selects only the current frame of the sprite.

3 To determine the appearance and behavior of sprites yet to be created, choose Span Defaults options. These options do not change settings for existing sprites.

- Display Sprite Frames turns on Edit Sprite Frames for all new sprites. See "Editing sprite frames" on page 248.

- Tweening turns on tweening for all tweenable properties. This option is on by default. With this option off, sprites must be manually tweened when new frames or keyframes are added to the sprite. For additional information on tweening, see Chapter 8, "Animation."

4 To determine the length of sprites measured in frames, choose Span Duration options.

- Frames defines the default number of frames for sprites.

- Width of Score Window sets the sprite span to the visible width of the Score window.

- Terminate at Markers makes new sprites end at the first marker. See "Using markers" on page 71.

Selecting sprites

To edit or move a sprite, you must select it. You can select sprites, frames within sprites, and groups of sprites in several different ways.

 You use the Arrow tool on the Tool palette to select sprites prior to most operations. You can also select sprites with the Rotate and Skew tool to enable rotation and skewing. See "Rotating and skewing sprites" on page 144.

When selecting sprites, you often want to select a certain frame or range of frames within the sprite instead of the entire sprite. When you make certain changes to a frame within a sprite, it becomes a selectable object called a keyframe. See "Editing sprite frames" on page 248.

A selected sprite appears on the Stage with a double border. When you select a single frame within a sprite, the sprite appears on the Stage with a single border.

Entire sprite selected

Single frame within sprite selected

To select sprites, do one of the following:

Note: The following techniques select an entire sprite only if Edit Sprite Frames is not enabled for the sprite(s) you select.

- On the Stage, click a sprite to select the entire sprite span.

  You can change sprite preferences so that selecting a sprite on the Stage selects only the current frame instead of the entire sprite. See "Changing sprite preferences" on page 121.

- In the Score, click the horizontal line within a sprite bar; do not click the keyframes, the start frame, or the end frame.

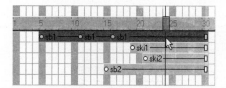

- To select a contiguous range of sprites either on the Stage or in the Score, select a sprite at one end of the range and then Shift-click a sprite at the other end of the range. You can also drag to select all the sprites in an area.

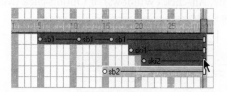

- To select discontiguous sprites, Control-click (Windows) or Command-click (Macintosh) the discontiguous sprites.

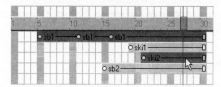

To select a keyframe, do one of the following:

- To select just a keyframe, click the keyframe indicator.

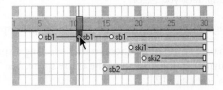

- To select a keyframe and sprites at the same time, Control-click (Windows) or Command-click (Macintosh) the keyframe and the sprites you want to select.

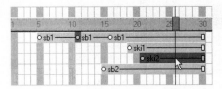

To select a frame within a sprite that isn't a keyframe, do one of the following:

- In the Score, Alt-click (Windows) or Option-click (Macintosh) the frame within the sprite.

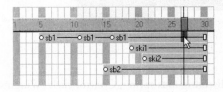

- On the Stage, Alt-click (Windows) or Option-click (Macintosh) to select only the current frame of the sprite. The sprite appears on the Stage with a single border.

To select all the sprites in a channel:

Click the channel number at the left side of the Score.

Layering sprites

A sprite appears in front of other sprites on the Stage according to its channel. Sprites in higher-numbered channels appear in front of sprites in lower-numbered channels.

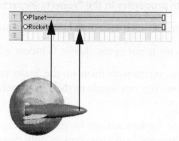

The rocket in channel 2 appears in front of the planet in channel 1.

To change a sprite's layer on the Stage:

1 Select the sprite. To select the contents of an entire channel, click the channel number at the left side of the Score.

2 Do one of the following:

- Choose Modify > Arrange and select a command from the submenu to change the order of sprites.

- Drag the sprite in the Score from one channel to another.

- If you selected a channel, drag its contents to another channel.

Displaying and editing sprite properties

As you work with sprites in your movie, you'll want to keep track of and possibly modify sprite properties. Director offers several methods of accomplishing this using one or more of the following:

- The Property Inspector

- The Sprite toolbar, which includes a subset of Sprite fields found on the Property Inspector

- The Sprite Overlay, which displays, directly on the Stage, the most commonly used properties for selected sprites

- Sprite labels, which appear within the sprite bars in the Score and let you view important sprite properties

- Lingo

Displaying and editing sprite properties in the Property Inspector

Depending on your preference, you can use either the Sprite toolbar or the Property Inspector to perform many of the same procedures.

To display and edit sprite properties in the Property Inspector:

1 Select one or more sprites on either the Stage or the Score.

2 If the Property Inspector is not open, choose Window > Inspectors > Property.

The Property Inspector opens with focus on the Sprite tab. The Graphical view is the default view. You can toggle to the List view by clicking the List View Mode icon.

The Property Inspector displays settings for the current sprite. If you select more than one sprite, the Property Inspector displays only their common settings.

Thumbnail —

A thumbnail image of the sprite's cast member appears in the upper left corner of the Property Inspector.

Note: To open a window in which you can edit the sprite's cast member, you can double-click the thumbnail image.

3 Edit any of the following sprite settings in the Property Inspector:

- Start Frame and End Frame display the start and end frame numbers of the sprite. Enter new values to adjust how long the sprite plays. See "Changing the duration of a sprite on the Stage" on page 140.

- Lock changes the sprite to a locked sprite so you or other users cannot change it. For additional information on locked sprites, see "Locking and unlocking sprites" on page 132.

- Editable applies only to text sprites, and lets you edit the selected text sprite on the Stage during playback. See "Selecting and editing text on the Stage" on page 340.

- Moveable lets you position the selected sprite on the Stage during playback. See "Visually positioning sprites on the Stage" on page 134.

- Trails makes the selected sprite remain on the Stage, leaving a trail of images along its path as the movie plays. If Trails is not selected, the selected sprite is erased from previous frames as the movie plays.

- Flip Horizontal and Flip Vertical reverse the sprite horizontally or vertically to form an inverted image. See "Flipping sprites" on page 147.

- The Ink pop-up menu displays the ink of the current sprite and lets you choose a new ink color. See "Using sprite inks" on page 150.

- Blend determines the blend percentage of the selected sprites. See "Setting blends" on page 149.

- Foreground and Background color boxes determine the colors of the selected sprite. See "Changing the color of a sprite" on page 148.

- Reg Point Horizontal (X) and Vertical (Y) display the location of the registration point in pixels from the top left corner of the Stage. See "Editing sprite properties with Lingo" on page 131.

- Width (W) and Height (H) show the size of the sprite's bounding rectangle in pixels.

- Rotation Angle rotates the sprite by the number of degrees you enter. See "Rotating and skewing sprites" on page 144.

- Skew Angle slants the sprite by the number of degrees you enter. See "Rotating and skewing sprites" on page 144.

- Left, Top, Right, and Bottom show the location of the edges of the sprite's bounding rectangle.

- Restore All reverts the height and width to that of the cast member.

- Scale opens the Scale Sprite dialog box, where you can resize the selected sprite. See "Resizing and scaling sprites" on page 142.

Displaying sprite properties in the Sprite toolbar

The Sprite toolbar displays a subset of the same information and fields found on the Sprite tab in the Property Inspector. You can use either the Sprite toolbar or the Property Inspector, depending on your preference, to perform many of the same procedures.

To show or hide the Sprite toolbar in the Score:

While the Score is active, choose View > Sprite Toolbar.

Using the Sprite Overlay

The Sprite Overlay displays important sprite properties directly on the Stage. You can open editors, inspectors, and dialog boxes to change sprite properties by clicking the corresponding icons in the Sprite Overlay.

To display the Sprite Overlay when a sprite is selected:

Choose View > Sprite Overlay > Show Info.

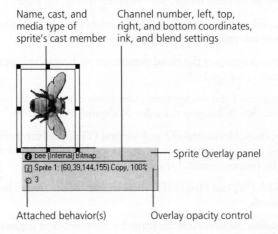

Name, cast, and media type of sprite's cast member

Channel number, left, top, right, and bottom coordinates, ink, and blend settings

Sprite Overlay panel

bee [Internal] Bitmap
Sprite 1: (60,39,144,155) Copy, 100%
3

Attached behavior(s)

Overlay opacity control

To use Sprite Overlay options to change how the overlay appears:

1 Click the Sprite on the Stage to select it.

2 In the Sprite Overlay panel, click the icon that represents the data you want to edit:

 • To edit the Sprite's cast member, click this icon to open the tab in the Property Inspector that applies to this type of sprite. For example, clicking this icon displays the Vector tab for a vector sprite, the Text tab for a text sprite, and so on.

 • To open the Sprite tab of the Property Inspector, click this icon.

• To open the Behavior tab of the Property Inspector, click this icon. See Chapter 5, "Behaviors."

To change the Sprite Overlay's appearance to suit your preferences:

1 Choose View > Sprite Overlay > Settings.

2 Choose a Display option to determine when sprite properties are visible and active:

• Roll Over displays sprite properties only when the pointer is over a single sprite.

• Selection displays sprite properties when a sprite is selected.

• All Sprites displays sprite properties for all sprites on the Stage.

3 Use the Text Color box to select the color for text displayed in the Sprite Overlay.

To change the opacity of the Sprite Overlay panel:

Drag up or down the small thin line that appears on the right edge of the Sprite Overlay panel.

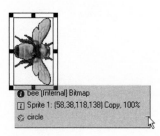

Displaying sprite labels in the Score

Sprite labels appear in the Score's sprite bars and display key information about the sprite in relation to the movie. For example, if you detect a strange blip caused by an ink effect, you can turn on Ink display and quickly locate the problem in a sprite label. You can change the information that appears in labels; for example, you can use the Extended display option to display the precise location of a sprite in every frame.

To display sprite labels:

1   With the Score as the active window, choose View > Sprite Labels.

2   Choose from the following options:

• Keyframes

• Changes Only (shown at 800%)

• Every frame (shown at 800%)

• First frame

Note that many options are useful only when the Score is zoomed to 400% or 800%.

To change sprite label options:

Choose a display option from the Display pop-up menu in the Score or from the View > Display menu.

- Member displays the name and number of the sprite's cast member.

`⊙1 :CM-Name—▯`

- Behavior displays the behavior assigned to the sprite.

`⊙8 :Beep——▯`

- Location displays the x and y coordinates of the sprite's registration point.

`⊙-160, 120——▯`

- Ink displays the ink effect applied to each sprite.

`⊙Matte———▯`

- Blend displays the blend percentage.

`⊙50———▯`

- Extended displays any combination of display options; choose options by choosing File > Preferences > Score.

Editing sprite properties with Lingo

You can use Lingo to check and edit sprite properties with scripts as the movie plays.

To check a property value:

Use the put command or check in the Watcher window. See put in the *Lingo Dictionary*.

To edit a property:

Use the equals (=) operator or the set command to assign a new value to the property. See = (equals) and set...to, set...= in the *Lingo Dictionary*

Locking and unlocking sprites

During authoring, you can lock sprites to avoid inadvertent changes to the sprite, either by you or by someone else working on the same project. When you lock a sprite, you can no longer change its settings, although you still see it represented on the Stage and in the Score. While preserving the settings of your locked sprites, you can continue to create and edit unlocked sprites.

Locking sprites is not supported during playback.

Note: If you try to perform an operation on a group of locked and unlocked sprites, a message appears that indicates the operation will affect only the unlocked sprites.

To lock a sprite:

In the Stage or the Score, select one or more sprites to lock and do one of the following:

- Choose Modify > Lock Sprite.

- In the Sprite tab of the Property Inspector, click the padlock icon.

- Right-click (Windows) or Option-click (Macintosh) and choose Lock Sprite from the context menu.

In the Score, a locked sprite appears with a padlock in front of its name. On the Stage, a locked sprite appears with a padlock in its upper right corner.

To select a locked sprite on the Stage:

Hold down the L key while selecting the sprite.

To unlock a sprite:

In the Score or on the Stage, select one or more sprites to unlock and do one of the following:

- Choose Modify > Unlock Sprite.

- In the Sprite tab of the Property Inspector, click the padlock icon.

- Right-click (Windows) or Option-click (Macintosh) and choose Unlock Sprite from the context menu.

Positioning sprites

The easiest way to position a sprite is to simply drag the sprite into place on the Stage. To position a sprite more precisely, you can do any of the following:

- Set a sprite's position on the Stage by entering coordinates in the Property Inspector.

- Use the Tweak window.

- Use guides or the grid.

- Use the Align window.

- Set the sprite's coordinates in Lingo.

The following diagram shows all of the sprite coordinates you can specify.

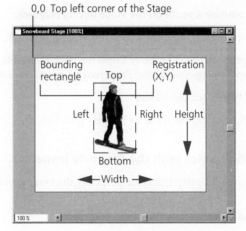

Director places the image of a cast member on the Stage by specifying the location of its registration point. For many cast members, such as bitmap or vector shapes, the registration point is in the center of the bounding rectangle by default. For other types of cast members, the registration point is at the upper left corner. (For instructions on changing the location of the registration point of bitmap cast members, see "Changing registration points" on page 315. For instructions on changing a vector shape cast member's registration point, see "Editing vector shapes" on page 298.)

Visually positioning sprites on the Stage

You can position sprites on the Stage by dragging them or by using the arrow keys.

To visually position a sprite on the Stage:

1 Choose Window > Stage to display the Stage.

2 Do one of the following on the Stage:

• Drag a sprite to a new position. Hold down Shift to constrain the movement to horizontal or vertical straight lines.

• Select a sprite and use the arrow keys to move the selected sprite 1 pixel at a time. Hold down Shift as you press an arrow key to move the selection 10 pixels at a time.

To visually position a sprite on the Stage during playback:

1 Select a sprite that you want to position during playback.

2 In the Sprite tab of the Property Inspector, click Moveable. See "Displaying and editing sprite properties in the Property Inspector" on page 126.

3 Begin playing back the movie.

4 On the Stage, drag the sprite to the new position.

Positioning sprites with the Property Inspector

You can use the Property Inspector to specify the exact coordinates of a sprite.

To set sprite coordinates in the Property Inspector:

1 With the Property Inspector open and in Graphical view, select a sprite to reposition.

2 On the Sprite tab of the Property Inspector, specify the sprite coordinates in pixels, with 0,0 at the upper left corner of the Stage, as follows:

• Specify attributes in the X and Y fields to change the horizontal and vertical coordinates of the registration point.

• Specify coordinates in the W and H fields to change the width and height of the sprite.

• Specify values for l, r, t, and b to change the left, right, top, and bottom edges of the sprite's bounding rectangle.

To move the sprite without resizing it, adjust only the x and y coordinates.

Positioning sprites with the Tweak window

You can use the Tweak window when you want to move sprites by a certain number of pixels.

To position sprites with the Tweak window:

1 Choose Modify > Tweak.

2 Select the sprite or sprites you want to move, as described in "Selecting sprites" on page 122.

3 In the Tweak window, drag the point on the left side of the window or enter the number of pixels in the fields for horizontal and vertical change; then click Tweak.

4 If you want to repeat the move, click Tweak again.

Positioning sprites using guides, the grid, or the Align window

On the Stage, you can align sprites using guides, the grid, or the Align window.

The grid consists of cell rows and columns of a specified height and width that you use to assist you in visually placing sprites on the Stage. The grid is always available.

Guides are horizontal or vertical lines you can either drag around the Stage or lock in place to assist you with sprite placement. You must create guides before they become available.

Moving a sprite with the Snap To Grid or Snap To Guides feature selected lets you snap the sprite's edges and registration point to the nearest grid or guide line. When you're not using the guides or the grid, you can hide them.

Guides and the grid are visible only during authoring.

You can create and modify the guides and the grid from the Property Inspector, or by using menu commands.

To add and configure guides:

1 With the Property Inspector open, click the Guides and Grid tab.

   The top half of the tab contains settings for Guides.

2 To change the guide color, click the Guide Color box and select a different color.

3 Select the desired options to make the guides visible, to lock them, and to make the sprites snap to the guides.

4 To add a guide, move the cursor over the new horizontal or vertical guide, then drag the guide to the Stage. Numbers in the guide tooltip indicate the distance, in pixels, the guide is from the top or left edge of the Stage.

5 To reposition a guide, move the pointer over the guide. When the sizing handle appears, drag the guide to its new position.

6 To remove a guide, drag it off the Stage.

7 To remove all guides, click Remove All on the Guides and Grid tab of the Property Inspector.

To display guides and align sprites:

1 If guides are not displayed on the Stage, choose View > Guides and Grid > Show Guides.

2 If Snap To Guides is not selected, choose View > Guides and Grid > Snap To Guides.

3 Move a sprite on the Stage near a guide line to make the sprite snap to that exact location.

To display a grid and align sprites:

1 If grid lines are not displayed on the Stage, choose View > Guides and Grid > Show Grid.

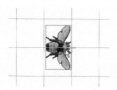

2 If Snap To Grid is not selected, choose View > Guides and Grid > Snap To Grid.

3 Move a sprite on the Stage near a grid line to make the sprite snap to that exact location.

Note: Press G while moving or resizing a sprite to temporarily turn Snap To Grid off or on.

To configure the grid:

1 With the Property Inspector open, click the Guides and Grid tab.

The bottom half of the tab contains Grid settings.

2 To change the grid color, click the Grid Color box and select a different color.

3 Select the desired options to make the grid visible and to make the sprites snap to the grid.

4 To change the size of the grid, enter numbers for Width and Height in the Spacing text box.

To align sprites using the Align window:

1 On the Stage or in the Score, select the sprites to align.

Select entire sprites, keyframes, or frames within sprites in as many different frames or channels as you need. All of the elements will align to the last sprite or frame selected.

2 Choose Modify > Align and do one of the following:

- Click an area in the preview window to view and select the way in which the sprites will align.

- Choose a vertical and/or horizontal alignment option from the pop-up menus.

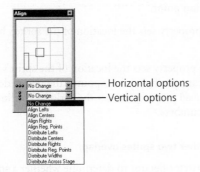

Horizontal options
Vertical options

3 Click Align.

4 Close the Align window when you finish aligning selections.

Positioning sprites with Lingo

Lingo lets you control a sprite's position by setting the sprite's coordinates on the Stage. You can also test a sprite's coordinates to determine a sprite's current position and whether two sprites overlap.

To check the location of a sprite's registration point or bounding rectangle on the Stage:

Test the bottom, left, loc, locH, locV, right, or top sprite property.

The bottom, left, right, and top sprite properties determine the location of the sprite's individual edges. See bottom, left, right, and top in the *Lingo Dictionary*.

To place a sprite at a specific location:

Set one of the following properties (see the *Lingo Dictionary* for entries on each property):

- The loc sprite property sets the horizontal and vertical distance from the upper left corner of the Stage to the sprite's registration point. The value is given as a point.

- The locV sprite property sets the number of pixels from the top of the Stage to a sprite's registration point.

- The locH sprite property sets the number of pixels from the left of the Stage to a sprite's registration point.

- The rect sprite property sets the location of the sprite's bounding rectangle on the Stage.

- The quad sprite property sets the location of the sprite's bounding rectangle on the Stage. You can specify any four points; the points do not have to form a rectangle. The quad property can set the sprite's coordinates as precise floating-point numbers.

To determine whether two sprites overlap:

Use the sprite...intersects operator to determine whether a sprite's bounding rectangle touches the bounding rectangle of a second sprite. Use the sprite...within operator to determine whether a sprite is entirely within a second sprite. See sprite...intersects and sprite...within in the *Lingo Dictionary*.

Changing when a sprite appears on the Stage

A sprite controls not only where media appears on the Stage, but also when. You change when a sprite appears on the Stage by moving the sprite to different frames in the Score and by changing the number of frames the sprite spans. You can either drag sprites to new frames or copy and paste them. Copying and pasting is easier when moving sprites more than one screen-width in the Score. You can also copy and paste to move sprites from one movie to another.

Moving a sprite in the Score

To change when a sprite appears on the Stage:

1 Choose Window > Score to display the Score.

2 Select a sprite or sprites, as described in "Selecting sprites" on page 122.

3 Drag the sprite to a different frame.

To move a sprite without spreading it over additional frames, hold down the Spacebar and drag. This technique is also useful for moving any sprite that consists mostly (or entirely) of keyframes.

To copy or move sprites between frames:

1 Select a sprite or sprites, as described in "Selecting sprites" on page 122.

2 Choose Edit > Cut Sprites or Edit > Copy Sprites.

3 Position the pointer where you want to paste the sprite and choose Edit > Paste Sprites.

If the pasting will overwrite existing sprites, choose a Paste option in the Paste Options dialog box:

• Overwrite Existing Sprites replaces the sprites with the content of the Clipboard.

• Truncate Sprites Being Pasted pastes the Clipboard contents in the space available without replacing existing sprites.

• Insert Blank Frames to Make Room adds new frames for the contents of the Clipboard.

Changing the duration of a sprite on the Stage

By default, Director assigns each new sprite a duration of 28 frames. You can change the duration of a sprite—that is, the amount of time the sprite appears in a movie—by adjusting its length, changing the number of frames in which it appears, or using the Extend command.

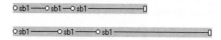

Director maintains the spacing proportions of keyframes when a sprite is lengthened. For a description of keyframes, see Chapter 8, "Animation."

To extend or shorten a sprite:

1 Choose Window > Score to display the Score.

2 Do one of the following:

• Drag the start or end frames. To extend a one-frame sprite, Alt-drag (Windows) or Option-drag (Macintosh).

• To extend a sprite and leave the last keyframe in place, Alt-drag (Windows) or Option-drag (Macintosh) a keyframe at the end of the sprite.

• To extend a sprite and leave all keyframes in place, Control-drag (Windows) or Command-drag (Macintosh) the end frame.

• Enter new values in the Start and End fields of the Sprite tab of the Property Inspector to change the start and end frames.

To extend a sprite to the current location of the playback head:

1 Select the sprite or sprites to extend.

2 Click the frame channel to move the playback head:

• To extend the sprite, move the playback head past the right edge of the sprite.

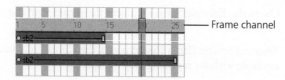
Frame channel

• To shorten the sprite, move the playback head to the left of the sprite's right edge, inside the sprite.

• To move the sprite's start frame, place the playback head to the left of the sprite.

3 Choose Modify > Extend Sprite.

Splitting and joining sprites

You may need to split an existing sprite into two separate sprites or join separate sprites. If, for example, you created a complex animation as separate sprites and now want to move the entire sequence in the Score, you would join the sprites. Splitting and joining also lets you update movies created with older versions of Director that may have several fragmented sprites.

To split an existing sprite:

1 In the Score, click the frame within a sprite where the split will occur.

The playback head moves to the frame you clicked.

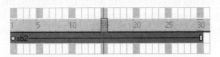

2 Choose Modify > Split Sprite.

Director splits the sprite into two new ones.

To join separate sprites into a single sprite:

1 Select the sprites you want to join, as described in "Selecting sprites" on page 122.

Director fills the gaps between the selected sprites. You can also select sprites in several channels. Director joins selected sprites in each individual channel.

2 Choose Modify > Join Sprite.

Changing the appearance of sprites

You can change the appearance of sprites on the Stage without affecting the cast member assigned to the sprite. You can resize, rotate, skew, flip, and apply new foreground and background colors to sprites. Applying these changes allows you to reuse the same cast member to create several different versions of an image. For example, you can create a flipped and rotated sprite with a new color. Since each cast member adds to downloading time, reusing cast members in this way reduces the number of cast members in your movie and makes it download faster.

Resizing and scaling sprites

You can resize sprites directly on the Stage by dragging their handles. To resize the sprite precisely, you can enter coordinates or scale sprites by a specified percentage in the Sprite tab of the Property Inspector. You can also set the sprite's size with Lingo.

Changing a sprite's size on the Stage doesn't change the size of the cast member assigned to the sprite, nor is the size of the sprite affected if you resize its cast member.

In some cases, resizing bitmap sprites can cause noticeable delays. If a bitmap sprite must be a particular size, make the cast members displayed in the sprite the proper size. You can do this with Modify > Transform Bitmap or in any image editing program. Scaling and resizing sprites works best with vector shapes.

Note: The procedure for resizing a rotated or skewed sprite is different from the procedures that follow. See "Rotating and skewing sprites" on page 144.

To resize a sprite by dragging its handles:

1 Select the sprite.

2 On the Stage, drag any of the sprite's resize handles. Hold down Shift while dragging to maintain the sprite's proportions.

To scale a sprite by pixels or by an exact percentage:

1   Select the sprite you want to scale and click the Sprite tab of the Property Inspector (Graphical view).

2   Click the Scale button.

The Scale Sprite dialog box appears.

3   Enter new values to scale the sprite by doing one of the following:

•   Specify a pixel size in the Width or Height field. If Maintain Proportions is selected, all of the updatable fields adjust to reflect the new scaled size. If Maintain Proportions in not selected, you can specify new proportions in the Width and Height fields.

•   Enter a percentage in the Scale field.

4   Click OK.

The sprite is scaled relative to its current size, not to the size of its parent cast member.

To restore a sprite to its original dimensions, do one of the following:

•   On the Sprite tab of the Property Inspector (Graphical view), click Restore All.

•   Choose Modify > Transform > Reset Width and Height or Reset All.

To resize a sprite's bounding rectangle with Lingo:

Set the sprite's quad or rect sprite property. See quad or rect (sprite) in the *Lingo Dictionary*.

The rect sprite property determines the coordinates of a sprite's bounding rectangle. The coordinates are given as a rect value, which is a list of the left, top, right, and bottom coordinates.

To change a sprite's height or width with Lingo:

Set the height or width sprite property. See height and width in the *Lingo Dictionary*.

Rotating and skewing sprites

You can rotate and skew sprites to turn and distort images and to create dramatic animated effects. You rotate and skew sprites on the Stage by dragging. To rotate and skew sprites more precisely, use Lingo or the Property Inspector to enter degrees of rotation or skew. The Property Inspector is also useful for rotating and skewing several sprites at once by the same angle.

Director can rotate and skew bitmaps, text, vector shapes, Flash movies, QuickTime videos, and animated GIFs.

Director rotates a sprite around its registration point, which is a marker that appears on a sprite when you select it with your mouse. By default, Director assigns a registration point in the center of all bitmaps. You can change the location of the registration point using the Paint window. See "Changing registration points" on page 315.

Rotation changes the angle of the sprite. Skewing changes the corner angles of the sprite's rectangle.

Rotated sprite

Skewed sprite

After a sprite is rotated or skewed, you can still resize it.

Director can automatically change rotation and skew from frame to frame to create animation. See "Tweening other sprite properties" on page 244.

To rotate or skew a sprite on the Stage:

1 Select a sprite on the Stage.

2 Choose Window > Tool Palette to display the Tool palette.

3 Click the Rotate tool in the Tool palette.

   You can also press Tab while the Stage window is active to choose the Rotate tool.

   The handles around the sprite change to indicate the new mode.

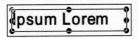

4 Do either of the following:

• To rotate the sprite, move the pointer inside the sprite and drag in the direction you want to rotate.

Pointer

• To skew the sprite, move the pointer to the edge of the sprite until it changes to the skew pointer and then drag in the direction you want to skew.

Pointer

To rotate or skew a sprite with the Property Inspector:

1 Select the sprite you want to rotate or skew and click the Sprite tab of the Property Inspector (List view).

2 To rotate the selected sprite, enter the number of degrees in the Rotation field.

3 To skew the selected sprite, enter the number of degrees in the Skew field.

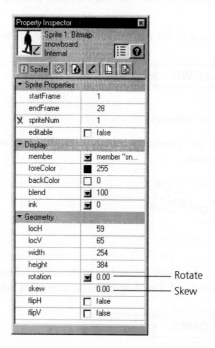

To resize a rotated or skewed sprite, do one of the following:

- Click the Rotate or Skew tool and drag any of the sprite's handles. Alt-drag (Windows) or Option-drag (Macintosh) to maintain the sprite's proportions as you resize.

- Enter new values in the Sprite tab of the Property Inspector.

  Director resizes the sprite at the current skew or rotation angle.

To restore a skewed or rotated sprite to its original orientation:

Choose Modify > Transform > Reset Rotation and Skew or Reset All.

To skew a sprite with Lingo:

Set the skew sprite property. See skew in the *Lingo Dictionary.*

Flipping sprites

Flipping a sprite creates a horizontally or vertically inverted image of the original sprite.

To flip a sprite:

1 Select a sprite.

2 Do any of the following:

- Click the Flip Vertical or Flip Horizontal button on the Sprite tab of the Property Inspector to flip the sprite without moving the registration point or changing the current skew or rotation angles.

- Choose Modify > Transform > Flip Horizontal in Place or Flip Vertical in Place to flip the sprite so that its bounding rectangle stays in place and the registration point is moved, if necessary.

- Choose Modify > Transform > Mirror Horizontal or Mirror Vertical to flip the sprite without moving the registration point, but inverting the skew and rotation angles.

Changing the color of a sprite

You can tint or color sprites by choosing new foreground and background colors from the Property Inspector or with Lingo. Choosing a new foreground color changes black pixels within the sprite to the selected color and blends dark colors with the new color. Choosing a new background color changes white pixels within the sprite to the selected color and blends light colors with the new color.

Director can animate foreground and background color changes in sprites, shifting gradually between the colors you specify in the start and end frames of a sprite. See "Tweening other sprite properties" on page 244.

To reverse the colors of an image, change the foreground color to white and the background color to black.

To change the color of a sprite:

1 Select a sprite.

2 Do one of the following:

• Choose colors from the Foreground and Background color boxes in the Sprite tab of the Property Inspector.

• Enter RGB values (hexadecimal) or palette index values (0-255) for the foreground and background colors in the Sprite tab of the Property Inspector.

To change the color of a sprite with Lingo, set the appropriate sprite property:

• The color sprite property sets the sprite's foreground color. The value is an RGB value. See color (sprite property) in the *Lingo Dictionary*.

• The bgColor sprite property sets the sprite's background color. The value is an RGB value. See bgColor in the *Lingo Dictionary*.

Setting blends

You can use blending to make sprites transparent. To change a sprite's blend setting, use the Sprite tab in the Property Inspector.

Blend setting
of 100%

Blend setting
of 30%

Director can gradually change blend settings to make sprites fade in or out. See "Tweening other sprite properties" on page 244.

The Blend percentage value affects only Copy, Background Transparent, Matte, Mask, and Blend inks.

To set blending for a sprite:

1 Select the sprite.

2 Choose a percentage from the Blend pop-up menu in the Property Inspector.

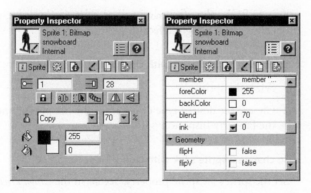

To set blending with Lingo:

Set the blend sprite property. See blend in the *Lingo Dictionary*.

Using sprite inks

You can change a sprite's appearance on the Stage by applying inks. Sprite inks change the display of a sprite's colors. Inks are most useful to hide white bounding rectangles around images, but they can also create many compelling and useful color effects. Inks can reverse and alter colors, make sprites change colors depending on the background, and create masks that obscure or reveal portions of a background.

You change the ink for a sprite in the Property Inspector or with Lingo.

Sprite with
Copy ink

Sprite with
Matte ink

For an animated demonstration and description of all the inks, see Director Help.

To achieve the fastest animation rendering on the screen, use Copy ink; other ink types may have a slight effect on performance.

To change a sprite's ink with the Property Inspector:

1   Select the sprite.

2   Choose the desired type of ink from the Ink pop-up menu in the Sprite tab of the Property Inspector.

To change a sprite's ink with Lingo:

Set the sprite's ink sprite property. See ink in the *Lingo Dictionary*.

Note: If Background Transparent and Matte inks don't seem to work, the background of the image may not be true white. Also, if the edges of the image have been blended or are fuzzy, applying these inks may create a halo effect. Use the Paint window or an image editing program to change the background to true white and harden the edges. You can also re-create the image with an alpha channel (transparency) and re-import the image.

Using Mask ink to create transparency effects

To reveal or tint certain parts of a sprite, you use Mask ink. Mask ink lets you define a mask cast member, which controls the degree of transparency for parts of a sprite.

The orignal cast member, its mask, and the sprite with mask ink applied.

Black areas of a mask cast member make the sprite completely opaque in those areas, and white areas make it completely transparent (invisible). Colors between black and white are more or less transparent; darker colors are more opaque.

When creating a bitmap mask for a sprite, use a grayscale palette if the mask cast member is an 8-bit (or less) image. An 8-bit mask affects only the transparency of the sprite and does not affect the color. Director ignores the palette of mask cast members that are less than 32-bit images; using a grayscale palette lets you view the mask in a meaningful way. If your mask cast member is a 32-bit image, the colors of the mask tint the sprite's colors.

If you do not need variable levels of opacity, use a 1-bit mask cast member to conserve memory and disk space.

There are many ways to use Mask ink, but the following procedure explains the most basic method.

To use Mask ink:

1 Decide which cast member you want to mask.

The cast member can be a bitmap of any depth.

2 In the next position in the same cast, create a duplicate of the cast member to serve as the mask.

The mask cast member can actually be any image, but a duplicate of the original is usually the most useful.

3 Edit the mask cast member in the Paint window or any image editor.

Black areas of the mask make the sprite completely opaque in those areas, and white areas make it completely transparent (invisible).

4 Drag the original cast member to the Stage or Score to create a sprite.

5 Make sure the new sprite is selected and choose Mask ink from the Ink pop-up menu in the Sprite tab of the Property Inspector.

Only the parts of the sprite revealed by the mask are visible on the Stage.

About Darken and Lighten inks

Darken and Lighten inks provide a great deal of control over the RGB properties of a sprite. You use them to create color effects in sprites varying from the subtle to the surreal.

Darken and Lighten both change how Director applies the foreground and background color properties of a sprite. Darken makes the background color equivalent to a color filter through which the sprite is viewed on the Stage. Lighten tints the colors in a sprite lighter as the background color gets darker. For both inks, the foreground color is added to the image to the degree allowed by the other color control. Neither ink has any effect on a sprite until you change the foreground or background color from the default settings of black and white.

Darken and Lighten are especially useful for animating unusual color effects. Because the Foreground and Background color properties of the sprite control the effects, you can animate color shifts to create dazzling effects without having to manually edit colors in a cast member. See "Tweening other sprite properties" on page 244.

Ink definitions

Following are definitions of all available ink types.

Copy displays all the original colors in a sprite. All colors, including white, are opaque unless the image contains alpha channel effects (transparency). Copy is the default ink and is useful for backgrounds or for sprites that do not appear in front of other artwork. If the cast member is not rectangular, a white box appears around the sprite when it passes in front of another sprite or is displayed on a nonwhite background. Sprites with the Copy ink animate faster than sprites with any other ink.

Matte removes the white bounding rectangle around a sprite. Artwork within the boundaries is opaque. Matte functions much like the Lasso tool in the Paint window in that the artwork is outlined rather than enclosed in a rectangle. Matte, like Mask, uses more RAM than the other inks, and sprites with this ink animate more slowly than other sprites.

Background Transparent makes all the pixels in the background color of the selected sprite appear transparent and permits the background to be seen.

Transparent makes all light colors transparent so you can see lighter objects beneath the sprite.

Reverse reverses overlapping colors. When applied to the foreground sprite, where colors overlap, the upper color changes to the chromatic opposite (based on the color palette currently in use) of the color beneath it. Pixels that were originally white become transparent and let the background show through unchanged. Reverse is good for creating custom masks.

Ghost, like Reverse, reverses overlapping colors, except nonoverlapping colors are transparent. The sprite is not visible unless it is overlapping another sprite.

Not Copy reverses all the colors in an image to create a chromatic negative of the original.

Not Transparent, Not Reverse, and **Not Ghost** are all variations of other effects. The foreground image is first reversed, then the Copy, Transparent, Reverse, or Ghost ink is applied. These inks are good for creating odd effects.

Mask determines the exact transparent or opaque parts of a sprite. For Mask ink to work, you must place a mask cast member in the Cast window position immediately following the cast member to be masked. The black areas of the mask make the sprite opaque, and white areas are transparent. Colors between black and white are more or less transparent; darker colors are more opaque. See "Using Mask ink to create transparency effects" on page 151.

Blend ensures that the sprite uses the color blend percentage specified in the Sprite tab of the Property Inspector. See "Setting blends" on page 149.

Darkest compares RGB pixel colors in the foreground and background and uses whichever pixel color is darkest.

Lightest compares RGB pixel colors in the foreground and background and uses whichever pixel color is lightest.

Add creates a new color that is the result of adding the RGB color value of the foreground sprite to the color value of the background sprite. If the value of the two colors exceeds the maximum RGB color value (255), Director subtracts 256 from the remaining value so that the result is between 0 and 255.

Add Pin is similar to Add. The foreground sprite's RGB color value is added to the background sprite's RGB color value, but the value of the new color cannot exceed the maximum color value (255).

Subtract subtracts the RGB color value of the foreground sprite's color from the RGB value of the background sprite's color to arrive at the new color. If the color value of the new color is less than 0, Director adds 256 so the remaining value is between 0 and 255.

Subtract Pin subtracts the RGB color value of pixels in the foreground sprite from the value of the background sprite. The value of the new color cannot be less than 0.

Darken changes the effect of the Foreground and Background color properties of a sprite to create dramatic color effects that generally darken and tint a sprite. Darken ink makes the background color equivalent to a color filter through which the sprite is viewed on the Stage. White provides no filtering; black darkens all color to pure black. The foreground color is then added to the filtered image, creating an effect similar to shining light of that color onto the image. Choosing Darken ink has no effect on a sprite until you select nondefault foreground and background colors. See "About Darken and Lighten inks" on page 152.

Lighten changes the effect of the Foreground and Background color properties of a sprite so that it is easy to create dramatic color effects that generally lighten an image. Lighten ink makes the colors in a sprite lighter as the background color gets darker. The foreground color tints the image to the degree allowed by the lightening. See "About Darken and Lighten inks" on page 152.

Note: Mask and Matte use more memory than other inks because Director must duplicate the mask of the artwork.

Assigning a cast member to a sprite with Lingo

Several Lingo properties specify the cast member assigned to a sprite. You can use these properties to determine a sprite's cast member and switch the sprite's cast members as the movie plays.

To specify the cast member, including its cast:

Set the member sprite property. See member (sprite property) in the *Lingo Dictionary*.

Setting this property is the most reliable way to specify a sprite's cast member. You can also set the memberNum sprite property, but this is reliable only when the new cast member is in the same cast as the current cast member.

To determine which cast contains the cast member assigned to a sprite:

Test the castLibNum sprite property. See castLibNum in the *Lingo Dictionary*.

This procedure can be useful for updating movies that serve as templates.

5

CHAPTER 5
Behaviors
· ·

A behavior is prewritten Lingo script that you use to provide interactivity and add interesting effects to your movie. You drag a behavior from the Library palette and drop it on a sprite or frame to attach it.

If the behavior includes parameters, a dialog box appears that lets you define those parameters. For example, most navigation behaviors let you specify a frame to jump to. You can attach the same behavior to as many sprites or frames as necessary and use different parameters for each instance of the behavior.

Most behaviors respond to simple events such as a click on a sprite or the entry of the playback head into a frame. When the event occurs, the behavior performs an action, such as jumping to a different frame or playing a sound.

Director comes packaged with customizable, reusable behaviors for many basic functions; you and other developers can also create your own behaviors by writing Lingo script. To modify behaviors, you use the Behavior Inspector or Property Inspector.

For more information about using included behaviors, see "Using Director 8 behaviors" in the Director Support Center.

Attaching behaviors

You use the Library palette to display behaviors included in Director.

Director allows you to attach the same behavior to several sprites or several frames at the same time. You can attach as many behaviors as you want to a sprite, but you can attach only one behavior to a frame. If you attach a behavior to a frame that already has a behavior, the new behavior replaces the old one. Behaviors attached to frames are best suited to actions that affect the entire movie. For example, you might attach Loop Until Media in Frame is Available to make the movie wait while the media for a particular frame downloads.

When you attach a behavior, and the Parameters dialog box appears, note that the parameters you specify apply to the behavior only as it is attached to the current sprite or frame. These settings do not affect the way the behavior works when attached elsewhere. Use the Behavior Inspector to change parameters for behaviors attached to sprites or frames.

Once you attach a behavior to a sprite or frame, Director copies the behavior from the Behavior Library to the currently selected cast in the movie. This means you don't have to include the Behavior Library when you distribute the movie.

To attach a behavior to a single sprite or frame using the Library palette:

1 Choose Window > Library Palette.

2 Choose a library from the Library pop-up menu in the upper left corner of the palette.

3 To view a brief description of included behaviors, move the pointer over a behavior icon.

If the behavior includes a longer description, you can view it in the Behavior Inspector. See "Getting information about behaviors" on page 161. The behaviors included with Director come with descriptions. Behaviors from other sources may not.

Choose Show Names from the Library pop-up menu to turn the display of behavior names off or on.

4 To attach a behavior to a single sprite, do one of the following:

- Drag a behavior from the Library palette to a sprite on the Stage or in the Score.

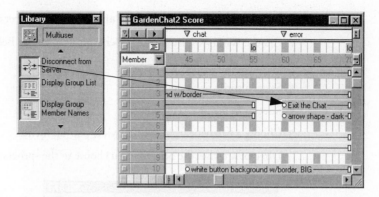

- Drag a behavior from the Library palette to a frame in the behavior channel.

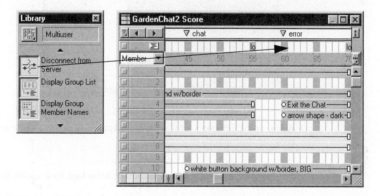

5 Enter parameters for the behavior in the Parameters dialog box.

Note: If you attach a behavior from a Director library of behaviors, the behavior is copied to an internal cast, to prevent you from accidentally changing the original behavior.

To attach the same behavior to several sprites at once using the Library palette:

Select the sprites on the Stage or in the Score and drag a behavior to any one of them.

To attach behaviors that are already attached to a sprite or frame:

1 Choose Window > Inspectors > Behavior to open the Behavior Inspector.

2 Do one of the following:

• Select a sprite or several sprites.

• Select a frame or several frames.

3 Choose a behavior from the Behaviors pop-up menu.

Director attaches the behavior you choose to the sprite(s) or frame(s).

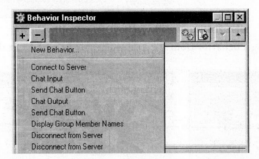

Note: Some behaviors work only when applied to either a sprite or a frame; read the behavior descriptions to learn more.

To change parameters for a behavior attached to a sprite or frame:

1 Select the sprite or frame to which the behavior is attached.

2 In the Behavior tab of the Property Inspector, use the pop-up menus or text fields to change any parameters.

The Behavior tab includes the same fields for the behavior as those included in the Parameters dialog box.

Changing the order of attached behaviors

Director executes behaviors in the order they were attached to a sprite, and they are listed in this order in the Property and Behavior Inspectors. It's sometimes necessary to change the sequence of behaviors so that actions occur in the proper order.

To change the order of the behaviors attached to a sprite:

1 Select the sprite in the Score or on the Stage.

2 Click the Behavior tab in the Behavior or Property Inspector.

3 Select a behavior from the list.

 4 Click the arrows in the toolbar to move the selected behavior up or down on the list.

Getting information about behaviors

Behaviors included with Director have pop-up descriptions that appear when you hold the pointer over a behavior in the Library palette. Some behaviors, however, have longer descriptions and instructions, which you can view in the Behavior Inspector. A scrolling pane in the Behavior Inspector displays the complete description provided by the behavior's author. The Behavior Inspector only displays information about a behavior attached to a sprite or frame.

To view a behavior description:

1 Open the Behavior Inspector.

2 Select a sprite or frame to which a behavior has been attached.

3 Click the arrow that expands the Behavior Inspector's description pane.

You can leave the description pane expanded and select different behaviors to see their descriptions.

Click to expand behavior descriptions

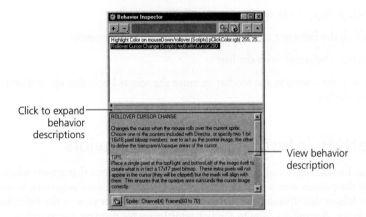

View behavior description

All of the behaviors included in the Director library have descriptions. Behaviors from other developers may not.

Creating and modifying behaviors

Without any scripting or programming experience, you can use the Behavior Inspector to create and modify behaviors to perform basic actions. To create behaviors with more complex structures, you need to understand Lingo.

 Using the Behavior Inspector is a good way to learn Lingo. You can examine the scripts created by the Behavior Inspector to see how basic functions are assembled. Select any behavior and click the Script button to view the associated Lingo script.

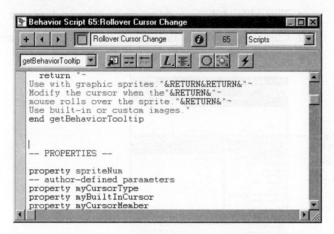

All behaviors detect an event and then perform one or more actions in response. The Behavior Inspector lists the most common events and actions used in behaviors.

For experienced Lingo programmers, the Behavior Inspector also provides a shortcut for writing simple scripts.

Note: To always edit behaviors in the Script window instead of the Behavior Inspector, choose File > Preferences > Editors. In the Editors Preferences dialog box, choose Behaviors from the list and then click Editor. In the Select Editor box, choose Script Window.

To create or modify a behavior:

1 Do one of the following:

 • To create a new behavior, click the Behaviors pop-up menu, choose New Behavior, and enter a name for the new behavior.

The behavior appears in the currently selected Cast window, in the first empty position. Select an empty cast position first if you want the behavior to appear in a different place.

• To modify a behavior, select it in the Behavior Inspector.

2 Click the arrow in the lower left of the Behavior Inspector to expand the editing pane.

Click here to
expand the
editing pane

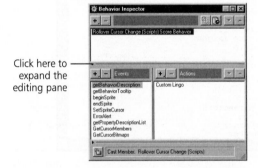

The editing pane shows the events and actions in the current behavior. If you're creating a new behavior, no events or actions appear.

• To add a new event or action group to the behavior, choose an event from the Events pop-up menu and then choose actions for the event from the Actions pop-up menu.

You can choose as many actions as you need for a single event.

• To change an existing event or action group, choose an event from the list and then add or remove actions in the Actions list.

• To delete an event or action group, choose the event and press Delete.

• To change the sequence of actions in an event or action group, choose an event from the Events list, choose an action from the Actions list, and then click the up and down arrows above the Actions list to change the order of actions.

• To lock the current selection so nothing changes in the Behavior Inspector when new sprites are selected, click the Lock Selection button in the lower left of the expanded Behavior Inspector.

If you are familiar with Lingo, you can also edit a behavior's script directly.

Events and actions in the Behavior Inspector

The actions and events included with Director are basic building blocks you can use to create simple or complex behaviors.

The Behavior Inspector makes the following events available:

Mouse Up indicates that the mouse button was released.

Mouse Down indicates that the mouse button was clicked.

Right Mouse Up indicates that the right mouse button was released. (On the Macintosh, Director treats a Control-click the same as a right mouse click on a Windows system.)

Right Mouse Down indicates that the right mouse button was clicked.

Mouse Enter indicates that the pointer entered a sprite's region.

Mouse Leave indicates that the pointer left a sprite's region.

Mouse Within indicates that the pointer is within the sprite's region.

Key Up indicates that a key was released.

Key Down indicates that a key was pressed.

Prepare Frame indicates that the playback head has left the previous frame but has not yet entered the next frame.

Enter Frame indicates that the playback head has entered the current frame.

Exit Frame indicates that the playback head has exited the current frame.

New Event indicates that a specified message was received from a script or behavior. You must specify a name for this event.

The Behavior Inspector makes the following actions available:

Go to Frame moves the playback head to the specified frame.

Go to Movie opens and plays the specified movie.

Go to Marker moves the playback head to the specified marker.

Go to Net Page goes to the specified URL.

Wait on Current Frame waits at the current frame until another behavior or script advances to the next frame.

Wait until Click waits at the current frame until the mouse button is clicked.

Wait until Key Press waits at the current frame until a key is pressed.

Wait for Time Duration waits at the current frame for the specified time.

Play Cast Member plays the specified sound cast member.

Play External File plays the specified external sound file.

Beep plays the current system beep.

Set Volume sets the system volume level to the specified setting.

Change Tempo changes the movie's tempo to the specified setting.

Perform Transition performs the specified transition.

Change Palette changes to the specified palette.

Change Location moves the current sprite to the specified coordinates.

Change Cast Member switches the sprite's cast member to the specified cast member.

Change Ink switches to the specified ink.

Change Cursor changes the pointer to a shape you choose from the pop-up menu.

Restore Cursor restores the current system pointer.

New Action executes any Lingo function or sends a message to a handler. You specify the new handler's name.

Writing behaviors with Lingo

If you are familiar with Lingo, you can author your own behaviors.

From the perspective of Lingo, a behavior is a script with these additional features:

- Each instance of the behavior has independent values for properties. Lingo uses a property statement to declare properties that can have independent values in each instance of the behavior. See property in the *Lingo Dictionary*.

- The same set of handlers can be shared by multiple sprites or frames.

  The handlers in a behavior are basically the same as other handlers. Include as many handlers as appropriate to implement the behavior.

  A behavior is usually attached to multiple sprites or frames. As a result, the sprites and frames share the same handlers. Director tracks which instance of the behavior is which by assigning each instance a reference number. The variable me contains the reference for the object that the instance of the behavior is attached to.

  In many cases it's most efficient to create behaviors dedicated to specific tasks and then attach a set of behaviors that perform the variety of actions you want.

- The behavior can have parameters that users edit from the Parameters dialog box. The optional on getPropertyDescriptionList handler sets up the Parameters dialog box. See on getPropertyDescriptionList in the *Lingo Dictionary*.

- A description of the behavior can be added to the Behavior Inspector. The optional on getBehaviorDescription handler displays a description of the behavior in the Behavior Inspector. See on getBehaviorDescription in the *Lingo Dictionary*.

- A brief description appears as a tooltip for the behavior in the Library palette if the optional on getBehaviorToolTip handler that creates the tooltip has been written. See on getBehaviorToolTip in the *Lingo Dictionary*.

Setting up a Parameters dialog box

It's impossible to predict exactly what a user will want behaviors to do. You can make behaviors more flexible by letting the user customize the behavior's parameters.

For example, this handler moves the sprite 5 pixels to the right each time the playback head enters a new frame:

```
on enterFrame me
    if the locH of sprite the spriteNum of me > the stageRight then
        set the locH of sprite the spriteNum of me = the stageLeft
    else
        set the locH of sprite the spriteNum of me to ¬
        (the locH of sprite the spriteNum of me + 5)
    end if
end
```

However, users could adjust the speed of each sprite if they could specify how far individual sprites move to the right in each frame.

To allow users to set different values for a property in different instances of the behavior, the behavior's script needs two types of Lingo:

- A property statement that allows each instance to maintain a separate value for the property

- An on getPropertyDescriptionList handler that sets up the property

Setting behavior properties with Lingo

Behaviors usually have properties for which each instance of the behavior maintains its own values. (An instance is each sprite or frame that the behavior is attached to.) These properties are shared among handlers in a behavior's script the same way that properties are shared among handlers in an object.

To declare which properties can have independent values in each instance of the behavior:

Put the property statement at the beginning of the behavior's script.

A property statement starts with the word property followed by the names of the individual properties. For example, the statement property movement declares that movement is a property of the behavior.

Customizing a behavior's property

If a behavior's script includes an on getPropertyDescriptionList handler, Director lets users set the property's initial values from the Parameters dialog box. The behavior's Parameters dialog box opens in three circumstances:

- After the user drags a behavior to a sprite or frame
- When the user double-clicks the behavior in the Behavior Inspector dialog box
- When the user clicks the Parameters button in the Behavior Inspector

The on getPropertyDescriptionList handler generates a property list that specifies these attributes of the property:

- The default initial value
- The type of data the property contains, such as Boolean, integer, string, cast member, or a specific type of cast member
- A comment in the Parameters dialog box to describe what the user is setting

The definition of a behavior's property must include the property's name, default value, and data type and the descriptive string that appears in the Parameters dialog box. The definition can also include an optional specification for the range of values allowed for the property.

The name of the property comes first in the definition. The remainder of the definition is a property list that assigns a value to each of the property's attributes.

For example, to define the property movement as an integer that can be set to a value from 1 to 10 and whose default value is 5, use a phrase similar to this:

```
#movement: [#default: 5, #format:#integer, ¬
#comment: "Set motion to the right:", #range: [#min:1, #max:10]]
```

- #movement is the property's name. A symbol (#) operator must precede the name in the property definition. A colon separates the name's definition and the list of parameters.

- #default specifies the property's default value. This example sets 5 as the default.

- #format specifies the property's type. This example sets the type as an integer. Some other possible types are Boolean, string, cast member, event, and sound. For a complete list of possible values for #format, see on getPropertyDescriptionList in Director Help or the *Lingo Dictionary.*

- #comment specifies a string that appears next to the parameter in the Parameters dialog box. This example makes "Set motion to the right" the comment that appears in the Parameters dialog box.

- #range specifies a range of possible values that the user can assign to the property. Specify the possible values as a list.

  To specify a range between a minimum and maximum number, use the form [#min:minimum, #max:maximum]. The example sets the range from 1 to 10. When the range is between a maximum or minimum number, the Parameters dialog box provides a slider that sets the value.

  To specify no range, omit the #range parameter. If the property's definition doesn't include #range, a text entry field appears for the user to enter a value in the Parameters dialog box.

  To specify a set of possible choices, use a linear list. For example, the list [#mouseUp, #mouseDown, #keyUp, #keyDown] makes these four events possible choices for a parameter. When you specify values in a linear list, the choices appear in a pop-up menu in the Parameters dialog box. (For this example list, you need to specify #format: #symbol for the list to display correctly.)

As another example, this statement defines the property whichSound:

```
addProp description, #whichSound, [#default: "", #format:#sound, #comment: ¬
"Which cast member"]
```

The value #sound assigned to #format provides a pop-up menu in the Parameters dialog box that includes every sound cast member available in the movie.

If the behavior includes a command that plays a sound, this property can be used to specify a sound cast member to play. For example, if the user chooses Growl from the pop-up menu in the Parameters dialog box, the statement puppetSound whichSound would play the sound cast member Growl.

Creating an on getPropertyDescriptionList handler

To build a list of properties for a behavior, add each property to the list that the on getPropertyDescriptionList handler returns. Then use the return command to return the list.

For example, this handler creates a property list named Description that contains the definitions for movement and whichSound:

```
on getPropertyDescriptionList

    set description = [:]

    addProp description, #Movement, [#default: 5, #format:#integer, #comment: ¬
    "Set motion to the right:", #range: [#min:1, #max:10]]

    addProp description, #noise, [#default:"", format: #sound, ¬
    #comment:"Sound cast member name"]

    return description

end
```

Alternatively, you can use this syntax to do the same as the previous handler:

```
on getPropertyDescriptionList

    return [¬

    #Movement: [#default: 5, #format:#integer, #comment: ¬
    "Set motion to the right:", #range: [#min:1, #max:10]],

    #noise: [#default:"", format: #sound, ¬
    #comment:"Sound cast member name"]
    ]

end
```

Including a description for the Behavior Inspector

An on getBehaviorDescription handler in a behavior's script provides a description that appears in the bottom pane of the Behavior Inspector when the behavior is selected. For example, this handler displays the phrase "This changes sprite color and position" in the Behavior Inspector:

```
on getBehaviorDescription
    return "This changes sprite color and position"
end
```

Example of a complete behavior

If the handlers described here were in one behavior, the script would look like this (the puppetSound command was added to the on mouseUp handler in this example):

```
property movement, noise

on getPropertyDescriptionList
    set description = [:]

    addProp description, #movement, [#default: 5, ¬
    #format:#integer, #comment: "Set motion to ¬
    the right:", #range: [#min:1, #max:10]]

    addProp description, #noise, [#default:"", ¬
    #format: #sound, #comment:"Sound cast ¬
    member name"]

    return description
end

on getBehaviorDescription
    return "This changes sprite color and position"
end

on mouseUp me
    set the foreColor of sprite the spriteNum of me ¬
    to random(255)
    puppetSound noise
end

on enterFrame me
    if the locH of sprite the spriteNum of me > ¬
    the stageRight then
        set the locH of sprite the spriteNum ¬
        of me = the stageLeft
    else
        set the locH of sprite the spriteNum of me to ¬
        (the locH of sprite the spriteNum of me + ¬
        movement)
    end if
end
```

When this behavior is attached to a sprite, each time the playback head enters a frame, the sprite moves to the right by the amount the user specifies. When the user clicks a sprite, its color changes and a specified sound plays.

Sending messages to behaviors attached to sprites

Lingo can run handlers in behaviors attached to specific sprites by sending messages to the behaviors attached to one sprite, all sprites, or several specific sprites.

Sending messages to a sprite

The sendSprite command sends a message to a specified sprite. If none of the sprite's behaviors has a handler that corresponds to the message, the message passes to the cast member script, the frame script, and then the movie script. See sendSprite in the *Lingo Dictionary*.

For example, this handler sends the custom message bumpCounter and the argument 2 to sprite 1 when the user clicks the mouse:

```
on mouseDown me
    sendSprite (1, #bumpCounter, 2)
end
```

Note: The symbol (#) operator must precede the message in the sendSprite command.

Sending messages to all sprites

The sendAllSprites command sends a message to every sprite in the frame. If no behavior of the specified sprite has a handler that corresponds to the message, the message passes to the cast member script, the frame script, and then the movie script. See sendAllSprites in the *Lingo Dictionary*.

For example, this handler sends the custom message bumpCounter and the argument 2 to all sprites in the frame when the user clicks the mouse:

```
on mouseDown me
    sendAllSprites (#bumpCounter, 2)
end
```

Note: The symbol (#) operator must precede the message in the sendAllSprites command.

Sending messages to specific behaviors only

The call command sends an event to specific behaviors. Unlike the sendSprite command, the call command doesn't pass the message to frame scripts, scripts of the cast member, or movie scripts.

Before sending a message to a specific behavior, check the scriptInstanceList sprite property to find a behavior script reference to use with the call command.

The scriptInstanceList property provides a list of references for the behaviors attached to a sprite while a movie is playing.

For example, this handler displays the list of references for all behaviors attached to the same sprite as this behavior's handler:

```
on showScriptRefs me
    put the scriptInstanceList of sprite the ¬
    spriteNum of me
end
```

This handler sends the message bumpCounter to the first script reference attached to sprite 1 (the getAt function identifies the first script reference in the scriptInstanceList):

```
on mouseDown me
    xref = getAt (the scriptInstanceList of sprite 1,1)
    call (#bumpCounter, xref, 2)
end
```

Note: The symbol (#) operator must precede the message in the call command.

To remove instances of a sprite while the movie is playing:

Set the sprite's scriptInstanceList property to an empty list([]). See scriptInstanceList in the *Lingo Dictionary*.

Using inheritance in behaviors

Behaviors can have ancestor scripts in the same way that parent scripts do. (Ancestor scripts are additional scripts whose handlers and properties a parent script can call on and use.)

- The ancestor's handlers and properties are available to the behavior.

- If a behavior has the same handler or property as an ancestor script, Lingo uses the property or handler in the behavior instead of the one in the ancestor.

For more information about the concept of ancestors and inheritance, see Chapter 11, "Parent Scripts."

To make a script an ancestor:

- Declare that ancestor is a property in the property statement at the beginning of the behavior's Score script.

  For example, the statement property ancestor declares that ancestor is a property.

- Include a statement that specifies which script is the ancestor. Put the statement in an on beginSprite handler in the behavior.

  For example, this handler makes the script Common Behavior an ancestor of the behavior when Director first enters the sprite:

```
on beginSprite
    set the ancestor of me to new (script "Common Behavior")
end
```

  This handler will let the behavior also use the handler in the script Common Behavior.

6

CHAPTER 6
Writing Scripts with Lingo
. . . .

Lingo, Director's scripting language, adds interactivity to a movie. You can use
Lingo to control a movie in response to specific conditions and events. For
example, Lingo can play a sound after a specified amount of the sound has
streamed from the Internet.

Scripting basics

The information in this section introduces and explains basic Lingo scripting
concepts that Director uses. If you are new to scripting, review this section before
you begin writing scripts in Lingo.

Types of scripts

Director uses four types of scripts: behaviors, movie scripts, parent scripts, and scripts attached to cast members. Behaviors, movie scripts, and parent scripts all appear as cast members in the Cast window.

Behaviors are scripts that are attached to sprites or frames in the Score, and are referred to as sprite behaviors or frame behaviors. The Cast window thumbnail for each behavior contains a behavior icon in the lower right corner.

When used in this chapter, the term "behavior" refers to any Lingo script that you attach to a sprite or a frame. This differs from the behaviors that come in Director's Library Palette. For more information about Director's built-in behaviors, see Chapter 5, "Behaviors."

All behaviors that have been added to the cast appear in the Behavior Inspector's Behavior pop-up menu. (Other types of scripts don't appear there.)

You can attach the same behavior to more than one location in the Score. When you edit a behavior, the edited version is applied everywhere the behavior is attached in the Score.

Movie scripts respond to events such as key presses and mouse clicks, and can control what happens when a movie starts, stops, or pauses. Handlers in a movie script can be called from other scripts in the movie as the movie plays.

A movie script icon appears in the lower right corner of the movie script's Cast window thumbnail.

Movie scripts are available to the entire movie, regardless of which frame the movie is in or which sprites the user is interacting with. When a movie plays in a window or as a linked movie, a movie script is available only to its own movie.

Parent scripts are special scripts that contain Lingo used to create child objects. You can use parent scripts to generate script objects that behave and respond similarly yet can still operate independently of each other. A parent script icon appears in the lower right corner of the Cast window thumbnail.

For information about parent scripts, see Chapter 11, "Parent Scripts."

Scripts attached to cast members are attached directly to a cast member, independent of the Score. Whenever the cast member is assigned to a sprite, the cast member's script is available.

Unlike behaviors, movie scripts, and parent scripts, cast member scripts don't appear in the Cast window. However, if Show Cast Member Script Icons is selected in the Cast Window Preferences dialog box, cast members that have a script attached display a small script icon in the lower left corner of their thumbnails in the Cast window.

 — Script icon

How scripts flow

Director always executes Lingo statements starting with the first statement and continuing in order until it reaches the final statement or a statement that instructs Lingo to go somewhere else.

To set up statements so that they run when specific conditions exist, you use if...then, case, and repeat loop structures. For example, you can create an if...then structure that tests whether text has finished downloading from the Internet and, if it has, then attempts to format the text. See "Controlling flow in scripts" on page 210.

The order in which statements are executed affects the order in which you should place statements. For example, if you write a statement that requires some calculated value, you need to put the statement that calculates the value first. For instance, in the following example, the first statement adds two numbers, and the second assigns a string representation of the sum to a field cast member to be displayed on the Stage:

```
x = 2 + 2
put string(x) into member "The Answer"
```

About planning and debugging scripts

When you write scripts for an entire movie, the quantity and variety of scripts can be very large. Deciding which Lingo commands to use, how to structure scripts effectively, and where scripts should be placed requires careful planning and testing, especially as the complexity of your movie grows.

Before you begin writing scripts, formulate your goal and understand what you want to achieve. This is as important—and typically as time consuming—as developing storyboards for your work.

When you have an overall plan for the movie, you are ready to start writing and testing scripts. Expect this to take time. Getting scripts to work the way you want often takes more than one cycle of writing, testing, and debugging.

The best approach is to start simple and test your work frequently. When you get one part of a script working, start writing the next part. This approach helps you identify bugs efficiently and ensures that your Lingo is solid as you write more complex scripts.

Performing common tasks

The following are ways to perform common tasks for creating, attaching, and opening scripts.

To create a frame behavior (script attached to a frame):

Double-click the behavior channel in the frame that you want to attach a behavior to.

Behavior channel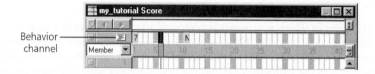

When you create a new behavior, the behavior receives the cast number of the first available location in the current Cast window.

When you create a new frame behavior, the Script window opens and already contains the line on exitFrame, followed by a line with a blinking insertion point, and then a line with the word end. This makes it easy for you to quickly attach a common behavior to the frame.

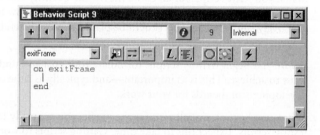

To create a sprite behavior (script attached to a sprite):

In the Score or on the Stage, select the sprite that you're attaching the behavior to. Then choose Window > Inspectors > Behavior and choose New Behavior from the Behavior pop-up menu.

When you create a new sprite behavior, the Script window opens and already contains the line on mouseUp, followed by a line with a blinking insertion point, and then a line with the word end. This makes it easy for you to quickly attach a common behavior to the sprite.

To open a behavior for editing:

1   Double-click the behavior in the Cast window.

The Behavior Inspector opens.

2   Click the Script Window icon in the Behavior Inspector.

The Script window displays the behavior.

Alternatively, you can open the Script window and cycle through the scripts until you reach the behavior.

To remove a behavior from a Score location:

Select the location and then delete the script from the list displayed in the Property Inspector (Behavior tab).

To attach existing behaviors to sprites or frames, do one of the following:

*   Drag a behavior from a cast to a sprite or frame in the Score or (for sprites) to a sprite on the Stage.

*   In the score, select the sprites or frames that you're attaching the behavior to. Then choose Window > Inspectors > Behavior and choose the existing behavior from the Behavior pop-up menu.

To create a movie script (script attached to a movie), do one of the following:

*   If the current script in the Script window is a movie script, click the New Script button in the Script window. (Clicking the New Script button always creates a script of the same type as the current script.)

*   If the current script in the Script window is not a movie script, click the New Script button and then change the new script's type with the Script Type pop-up menu in the Script tab of the Property Inspector.

*   If no sprites or scripts are selected in the cast, Score, or Stage, then open a new Script window; this will create a new movie script by default.

To open a movie script or parent script for editing:

Double-click the script in the Cast window.

To change a script's type:

1   Select the script in the Cast window or open it in the Script window.

2   Click the Script tab of the Property Inspector and choose a script type from the Type pop-up menu.

To cycle through the scripts in the Script window:

Use the Previous Cast Member and Next Cast Member arrows at the top of the Script window to advance or back up to a script.

To duplicate a script:

Select the script in the Cast window and choose Duplicate from the Edit menu.

To create and open scripts attached to cast members, do one of the following:

- Right-click (Windows) or Control-click (Macintosh) on a cast member in the Cast window and choose Cast Member Script from the context menu.

- Select a cast member in the Cast window and then click the Cast Member Script button.

- If the Script window is not open, choose Window > Script to open it. Then click the Previous Cast Member or Next Cast Member buttons until the script for the desired cast member appears in the window.

Note that the first two methods also let you create a new script if none is attached to the cast member.

Lingo terminology

Like any programming language, Lingo uses specific terminology and has rules of grammar and punctuation that you must follow. This information is summarized in this section.

Important Lingo terms are listed here in alphabetical order. References are included for terms that are discussed in more detail elsewhere in this chapter.

Arguments are placeholders that let you pass values to scripts (see "Using arguments to pass values to a handler" on page 191). For example, the following handler, called addThem, adds two values it receives in the arguments a and b.

```
on addThem a, b
    c = a + b
end
```

Commands are terms that instruct a movie to do something while the movie is playing. For example, go to sends the playback head to a specific frame, a marker, or another movie.

Constants are elements that don't change. For example, the constants TAB, EMPTY, and RETURN always have the same meaning.

Events are actions that occur while a movie is playing. For example, when a movie stops, a sprite starts, the playback head enters a frame, or the user types at the keyboard, these actions are events.

Expressions are any part of a statement that produces a value. For example, 2 + 2 is an expression.

Functions are terms that return a value. For example, the date() function returns the current date set in the computer. The key() function returns the key that was pressed last. Parentheses occur at the end of a function.

Handlers are sets of Lingo statements within a script that run when a specific event occurs in a movie (see "Using handlers" on page 191). For example, the following statements comprise a handler that plays a beep sound when the mouse is clicked:

```
on mouseDown
    beep
end
```

Keywords are reserved words that have a special meaning. For example, end indicates the end of a handler.

Lists are ordered sets of values used to track and update an array of data, such as a series of names or the values assigned to a set of variables (see "Using lists" on page 194). A simple example is a list of numbers such as [1, 4, 2].

Messages are notices that Director sends to scripts when specific events occur in a movie (see "Using messages to identify events" on page 188). For example, when the playback head enters a specific frame, the enterFrame event occurs and Directors sends an enterFrame message. If a script contains an on enterFrame handler, the statements within that handler will run, because the handler received the enterFrame message.

Operators are terms that calculate a new value from one or more values. For example, the addition (+) operator adds two or more values together to produce a new value.

Properties are attributes that define an object. For example, picture is a property of a bitmap cast member.

Statements are valid instructions that Director can execute (see "Writing Lingo statements" on page 186). For example, go to frame 23 is a statement.

Variables are elements used to store and update values (see "Storing and updating values in variables" on page 199). To assign values to variables or change the values of many properties, you use the equals (=) operator or the set command. For example, the statement set startValue = 0 places a value of 0 into a variable named startValue.

Lingo syntax

Lingo supports a variety of data types, including references to sprites and cast members, TRUE and FALSE (Boolean) values, strings, constants, integers, floating-point numbers, points, rects, colors, and dates.

The following are general syntax rules that apply to all Lingo. Most Lingo terms also have their own individual requirements about terms that they must be combined with. For the rules for a specific Lingo term, see the term's syntax in the *Lingo Dictionary*.

Parentheses

Functions that return values require parentheses. When you define functions in handlers, you need to include parentheses in the calling statement.

Use parentheses after the keyword sprite or member to refer to the object's identifier: for example, member("Patrice Lumumba") refers to the member named Patrice Lumumba.

You can also use parentheses to override Lingo's order of precedence in math operations or to make your Lingo statements easier to read.

For example, this math expression will yield a result of 13:

5 * 3 - 2

while this expression will yield a result of 5:

5 * (3 - 2)

Character spaces

Words within expressions and statements are separated by spaces. Lingo ignores extra spaces.

In strings of characters surrounded by quotation marks, spaces are treated as characters. If you want spaces in a string, you must insert them explicitly.

You can see Lingo that uses strings in "Writing strings" on page 202.

Uppercase and lowercase letters

Lingo is not case sensitive—you can use uppercase and lowercase letters however you want. For example, the following statements are equivalent:

Set the hiLite of member "cat" to True
set the hilite of member "Cat" to True
SET THE HILITE OF MEMBER "CAT" TO TRUE
Set The Hilite Of Member "Cat" To True

However, it's a good habit to follow script writing conventions, such as the ones that are used in this book, to make it is easier to identify names of handlers, variables, and cast members when reading Lingo code.

Also, note that literal strings are case sensitive. See "Writing strings" on page 202.

Comments

Comments in scripts are preceded by double hyphens (--). You can place a comment on its own line or after any statement. Lingo ignores any text following the double hyphen on the same line. For more information about comments in Lingo, see "Troubleshooting Lingo" in the Director Support Center.

Comments can consist of anything you want, such as notes about a particular script or handler or notes about a statement whose purpose might not be obvious. Comments make it easier for you or someone else to understand a procedure after you've been away from it for a while.

Double hyphens can also be used to make Lingo ignore sections of code you want to deactivate for testing or debugging purposes. By adding double hyphens rather than removing the code, you can temporarily turn it into comments. Select the code you want to turn on or off and then use the Comment or Uncomment buttons in the Script window to add or remove double hyphens easily.

Optional keywords and abbreviated commands

You can abbreviate some Lingo statements. Abbreviated versions of a command are easier to enter but may be less readable than the longer versions. The go command is a good example. All the following statements are equivalent, but the last one uses the fewest keystrokes.

```
go to frame "This Marker"
go to "This Marker"
go "This Marker"
```

It is good practice to use the same abbreviations throughout a movie so your Lingo is easier to read.

Describing conditions

A script often needs to determine whether a certain condition exists before carrying out a set of instructions. For example, a script may need to check whether a network operation is finished before doing something that requires the operation's result.

The term TRUE or the number 1 indicates that the condition you're testing for exists. The term FALSE or the number 0 indicates that a condition doesn't exist.

Writing Lingo statements

When you are writing statements in a Lingo script, you can choose between two types of syntax: verbose syntax and dot syntax.

Verbose syntax

Verbose syntax is similar to English. Because of this, verbose syntax is an excellent way to learn to program for the first time: as a new programmer, you can read verbose Lingo and get a fairly good idea of what it is doing. Most users will start out writing Lingo exclusively with verbose syntax because it is so easy to understand.

Here are three examples of verbose Lingo that is very English-like and has a literal meaning:

```
set the stageColor to 255
```

```
put the text of member "Instructions" after member "Introduction"
```

```
if x=5 then
    go to frame 22
end if
```

Almost all of Lingo's functionality is available through verbose syntax, but there are a few exceptions. Most of these exceptions are found in Lingo used for manipulating text.

The disadvantage of verbose Lingo is that it can quickly become very long when you write complex scripts. Longer scripts are harder to read and debug. Once your scripts reach a certain level of complexity, you may find it easier to use dot syntax.

The next section contains several examples that compare verbose and dot syntax.

Dot syntax

Dot syntax is a concise form of Lingo that makes longer scripts easier to read and comprehend for users who have at least a novice understanding of the language. By understanding and using dot syntax, you can make your scripts shorter and easier to read and debug.

If you are just beginning to learn Lingo, you will probably want to start with verbose syntax and then begin using dot syntax as your understanding of Lingo improves. You can use verbose syntax and dot syntax in combination. You may want to do this as you begin the process of learning dot syntax.

Because most users will want to use dot syntax after they achieve a basic understanding of Lingo, most of the Lingo examples in this book are written with dot syntax. However, this chapter will provide extensive examples of both syntaxes.

Almost any Lingo statement can be written with either verbose syntax or dot syntax. The following example demonstrates how the two types of syntax relate to each other.

This statement sets the forecolor of sprite 12 to 155 using verbose syntax:

```
set the forecolor of sprite 12 to 155
```

The following statement does the same thing by using dot syntax. It also omits the set command, which is optional:

```
sprite(12).forecolor = 155
```

You can use dot syntax to express the properties or functions related to an object or to specify a chunk of text within a text object. A dot syntax expression begins with the name of the object, followed by a period (dot), and then the property, function, or text chunk that you want to specify.

For example, the loc of sprite property indicates a sprite's horizontal and vertical position on the Stage. The expression sprite(15).loc refers to the loc of sprite property of sprite 15.

As another example, the number cast member property specifies a cast member's number. The expression member("Hot Button").number refers to the cast member number of the Hot Button cast member.

Expressing a function related to an object follows the same pattern. For example, the pointInHyperLink text sprite function reports whether a specific point is within a hyperlink in a text sprite. In addition to the syntax demonstrated in the *Lingo Dictionary*, you can use the dot syntax *textSpriteObject*.pointInHyperlink() to express this function.

The following put statement will evaluate the specified expression and return TRUE or FALSE depending on whether the pointer is located over a hyperlink in the text sprite in channel 3:

```
put sprite(2).pointInHyperlink(mouseLoc)
```

This is how the same statement is written with verbose syntax:

```
put pointInHyperlink(sprite 2, the mouseLoc)
```

To identify chunks of text, include terms after the dot to refer to more specific items within text. For example, the expression member("News Items").paragraph(1) refers to the first paragraph of the text cast member News Items. The expression member("News Items").paragraph(1).line(1) refers to the first line in the first paragraph. These text chunk expressions are available only with dot syntax.

Using messages to identify events

To run the appropriate set of Lingo statements at the right time, Director must determine what is occurring in the movie and which Lingo to run in response to certain events.

Director sends messages to indicate when specific events occur in a movie, such as when sprites are clicked, keyboard keys are pressed, a movie starts, the playback head enters or exits a frame, or a script returns a certain result. Handlers within scripts contain instructions that run when a specific message is received.

Although you can define your own message names (see "Defining custom messages" on page 189), most common events that occur in a movie have built-in message names. See the following categories in the "Lingo by Feature" section of the *Lingo Dictionary* for the built-in messages that describe events.

- Keyboard and mouse events.

- Frame events.

- Browser and Internet events.

- Sprite events.

- Movie in a window (MIAW) events.

- Movie events.

- Synchronizing media events.

- Idle events.

- Timeout events.

- Authoring behavior events.

Defining custom messages

In addition to using built-in message names, you can define your own messages and corresponding handler names. A custom message can call another script, another handler, or the statement's own handler. When the called handler stops executing, the handler that called it resumes.

Director can send a custom message from any location. The message is first available to handlers in the script from which the message was sent. If no handler is found, the message is available to movie scripts.

If more than one movie script contains a handler for the message, the handler in the movie script that has the lowest cast member number is executed.

A custom handler name must meet the following criteria:

- It must start with a letter.

- It must include alphanumeric characters only (no special characters or punctuation).

- It must consist of one word or of several words connected by an underscore—no spaces are allowed.

- It must be different from the name of any predefined Lingo element.

Using Lingo keywords for handler names can create confusion. Although it is possible to explicitly replace or extend the functionality of a Lingo element by using it as a handler name, this should be done only in certain advanced situations.

When you have multiple handlers with similar functions, it is useful to give them names that have similar beginnings so they appear together in an alphabetical listing, such as the listing that can be displayed by the Edit > Find > Handler command.

Understanding the order of messages in a movie

Director follows a definite order when sending messages about events that occur during the course of a movie.

When the movie first starts, events occur in the following order:

1 prepareMovie

2 beginSprite

This event occurs when the playback head enters a sprite span.

3 prepareFrame

Immediately after the prepareFrame event, Director plays sounds, draws sprites, and performs any transitions or palette effects. This event occurs before the enterFrame event. An on prepareFrame handler is a good location for Lingo that you want to run before the frame draws.

4 startMovie

This event occurs in the first frame that plays.

When Director plays a frame, events occur in this order:

1 beginSprite

This event occurs only if new sprites begin in the frame.

2 stepFrame

3 prepareFrame

Immediately after the prepareFrame event, Director plays sounds, draws sprites, and performs any transitions or palette effects. This event occurs before the enterFrame event.

4 enterFrame

After enterFrame and before exitFrame, Director handles any time delays required by the tempo setting, idle events, and keyboard and mouse events.

5 exitFrame

6 endSprite

This event occurs only if the playback head exits a sprite in the frame.

When a movie stops, events occur in this order:

1 endSprite

This event occurs only if sprites currently exist in the movie.

2 stopMovie

Using handlers

As described in "Using messages to identify events" on page 188, Director sends messages to handlers within scripts when specific events occur. You attach a set of handlers to an object by attaching the handlers' script to the object. See "Creating and attaching scripts with the Script window" on page 213.

Each handler begins with the word on followed by the message that the handler should respond to. The last line of the handler is the word end. You can repeat the handler's name after end, but this is optional.

When an object receives a message that corresponds to a handler attached to the object, Director runs the Lingo statements within the handler. For example, the mouseDown message indicates that the user clicked the mouse button. To indicate in your script that an action should be performed when the mouse is clicked, you include a line in your script that begins with onMouseDown. You follow this line with the Lingo statements that should execute when the script receives the mouseDown message.

Using arguments to pass values to a handler

By using arguments for values, you can give the handler exactly the values that it needs to use at a specific time, regardless of where or when you call the handler in the movie. Arguments can be optional or required, depending on the situation.

To create arguments for a handler:

Put the arguments after the handler name. Use commas to separate multiple arguments.

For example, the following handler, called addThem, adds two values it receives in the arguments a and b, stores the result in local variable c, and uses the Lingo term return to send the result back to the original handler:

```
on addThem a, b
    -- a and b are argument placeholders
    c = a + b
    return c
end
```

When you call a handler, you must provide specific values for the arguments that the handler uses. You can use any type of value, such as a number, a variable that has a value assigned, or a string of characters. Values in the calling statement must be in the order they follow in the handler's arguments, and they must be surrounded by parentheses.

The following statement is a calling statement for the on addThem handler:

```
set mySum = addThem(4, 8)
```

Because 4 is first in the list of arguments, Lingo substitutes it for a in the handler. Likewise, because 8 is second in the list of arguments, Lingo substitutes 8 for b everywhere in the handler.

After the calling statement sends these parameters to the handler, the handler returns the value 12, which corresponds to the variable c inside the on addThem handler. The variable mySum in the calling statement is then set to 12.

You can also use expressions as values. For example, the following statement substitutes 3+6 for a and 8>2 (or 1, representing TRUE) for b, and would return 10:

set mySum = addThem(3+6, 8>2)

Returning results from handlers

Often you want a handler to report some condition or the result of some action.

To return results from a handler:

Use the return function to have a handler report a condition or the result of an action. For example, the following handler returns the current color of sprite 1:

```
on findColor
      return sprite(1).foreColor
end
```

When you define a handler that returns a result, you must use parentheses after the handler when you call it from another handler. For example, the statement put findColor() calls the on findColor handler and then displays the result in the Message window.

Deciding where to place handlers

You can place handlers in any type of script, and a script can contain multiple handlers. It's a good idea to group related handlers in a single place, though, for easier maintenance.

The following are some useful guidelines for many common situations:

- To set up a handler that affects a specific sprite or runs in response to an action on a specific sprite, put the handler in a behavior attached to the sprite. To set up a handler that should be available any time the movie is in a specific frame, put the handler in a behavior attached to the frame.

  For example, to have a handler respond to a mouse click while the playback head is in a frame, regardless of where the click occurs, place an on mouseDown or on mouseUp handler in the frame behavior rather than in a sprite behavior.

- To set up a handler that runs in response to messages about events anywhere in the movie, put the handler in a movie script.

- To set up a handler that runs in response to an event that affects a cast member, regardless of which sprites use the cast member, put the handler in a cast member script.

Determining when handlers receive a message

A movie can contain more than one handler for the same message. Director manages this situation by sending the message to objects in a definite order.

The general order in which messages are sent to objects is as follows:

1 Messages are sent first to behaviors attached to a sprite involved in the event. If a sprite has more than one behavior attached to it, behaviors respond to the message in the order in which they are attached to the sprite.

2 Messages are sent next to a script attached to the cast member assigned to the sprite.

3 Messages are then sent to behaviors attached to the current frame.

4 Messages are sent last to movie scripts.

When a message reaches a script that contains a handler corresponding to the message, Director executes the handler's instructions.

After a handler intercepts a message, the message doesn't automatically pass on to the remaining locations. (You can use the pass command to override this default rule and pass the message to other objects.) If no matching handler is found after the message passes to all possible locations, Director ignores the message.

The exact order of objects to which Director sends a message depends on the message. For details about the sequence of objects to which Director sends specific messages, see the *Lingo Dictionary* entry for the message.

Using lists

Lists provide an efficient way to track and update an array of data, such as a series of names or the values assigned to a set of variables. For example, if you know you will need to keep track of many names or numbers in your Director project, you may want to store them in a list. The list operator ([ ]) designates that the items within the brackets comprise a list.

You can create two types of lists with Lingo: linear lists and property lists.

- In a linear list, each element is a single value. For example, this linear list is a simple set of numbers:

  [100, 150, 300, 350]

- In a property list, each element contains two values separated by a colon. One value is a property name, always preceded by a pound (#) sign; the other value is the value associated with that property. For example, the following statement sets the variable myList to a property list containing values for the properties #speed, #direction, and #weight. These could be the properties of an asteroid.

  myList = [#speed: 155, #direction: 237, #weight: 8746]

  Properties can appear more than once in a property list.

Both kinds of lists can be empty, containing no values at all. An empty linear list consists of two square brackets ([ ]). An empty property list consists of two square brackets surrounding a colon ([:]).

It's usually easier to manipulate a list by assigning it to a variable when you create the list. The value contained in the variable is actually a reference to the list, not the list itself.

For more information on lists, see list() in the *Lingo Dictionary*.

Creating linear lists

The most common way to create a linear list is to use the list operator ([ ]). You can also use the list() function to create a linear list.

To create a linear list, do one of the following:

- Place the list elements within the list operator ([ ]).

- Specify the list's elements as parameters of the list() function. (This function is useful when you use a keyboard that doesn't provide square brackets.)

In both cases, you use commas to separate items in the list.

For example, the following statements have the same effect; each statement creates a linear list of three names:

```
set workerList = ["Bruno", "Heather", "Carlos"]
set workerList = list("Bruno", "Heather", "Carlos")
```

To create an empty linear list:

Set the list to [ ].

Creating property lists

The only way to create a property list is to use the list operator ([ ]). You cannot use the list() function to create a property list.

To create a property list:

Place the list elements within the list operator, and use commas to separate the elements. Precede each property with the pound (#) sign, and separate each property from its value with a colon.

For example, the following statements create two different property lists. Each list specifies the Stage coordinates of a sprite.

```
sprite1Location = [#left:100, #top:150, #right:300, #bottom:350]
sprite2Location = [#left:400, #top:550, #right:500, #bottom:750]
```

To create an empty property list:

Set the list to [:].

Setting and retrieving items in a list

Lingo lets you set and retrieve individual items in a list. The syntax differs for linear and property lists.

To set a value in a linear list:

Use the equals (=) operator. (You can also use the setAt command introduced in earlier versions of Director.)

For example, the statement workerList[2] = "Tiffany" makes Tiffany the new value for the second item in the list workerList.

To retrieve a value in a linear list:

Use the list variable followed by the number that indicates the value's position in the list. Place square brackets around the number. (You can also use the getAt or getaProp commands, which were introduced in earlier versions of Director.)

For example, in the linear list set workerList = ["Bruno ", "Heather ", "Carlos "], the expression workerList[2] represents the second value in the list workerList. The value is Heather.

To set a value in a property list, do one of the following:

- Use the equals (=) operator. (You can also use the setAProp command, which was introduced in earlier versions of Director.)

  For example, the statement foodList[#Bruno] = "sushi" makes sushi the new value associated with the property Bruno.

- Use dot syntax.

  For example, the statement foodList.Bruno = "sushi" makes sushi the new value associated with the property Bruno in the list foodList.

To retrieve a value in a property list, do one of the following:

- Use the list variable followed by the name of the property associated with the value. Place square brackets around the property. (You can also use the getaProp or getAt commands, or the getPropAt() function, which were introduced in earlier versions of Director.)

  For example, in the property list foodList = [#breakfast:"Waffles", #lunch:"Tofu Burger", #dinner:"Hungarian Goulash"], the expression foodList[#breakfast] represents the value associated with the property #breakfast. The value is Waffles.

- Use dot syntax.

  For example, using the foodList property list above, foodList.breakfast represents the value Waffles.

Checking items in a list

You can determine the characteristics of a list and the number of items the list contains by using the following commands and functions. See entries for individual commands in the *Lingo Dictionary*.

- To display the contents of a list, use the put command followed by the variable that contains the list.

- To determine the number of items in a list, use the count() function.

- To determine a list's type, use the ilk() function.

- To determine the maximum value in a list, use the max() function.

- To determine the minimum value in a list, use the min() function.

- To determine the position of a specific property, use the findPos, findPosNear, or getOne command.

Adding and deleting items in a list

You can add or delete items in a list by using the following commands. See entries for individual commands in the *Lingo Dictionary*.

- To add an item at the end of a list, use the append command.

- To add an item at its proper position in a sorted list, use the add or addProp command.

- To add an item at a specific place in a linear list, use the addAt command.

- To add an item at a specific position in a property list, use the addProp command.

- To delete an item from a list, use the deleteAt, deleteOne, or deleteProp command.

- To replace an item in a list, use the setAt or setaProp command.

You do not have to explicitly remove lists. Lists are automatically removed when they are no longer referred to by any variable.

Copying lists

Assigning a list to a variable and then assigning that variable to a second variable does not make a separate copy of the list. For example, the statement landList = ["Asia", "Africa"] creates a list that contains the names of two continents. The statement continentList = landList assigns the same list to the variable continentList. However, adding Australia to landList using the statement add landList, "Australia" automatically adds Australia to continentList also. This happens because both variable names point to the same object in memory.

To create a copy of a list that is independent of the first list:

Use the duplicate() function. See duplicate() (list function) in the *Lingo Dictionary*.

For example, this statement creates a list and assigns it to the variable oldList:

oldList = ["a", "b", "c"]

This statement uses the duplicate() function to make an independent copy of the list and assign it to the variable newList:

newList = duplicate(oldList)

After newList is created, editing either oldList or newList has no effect on the other.

Sorting lists

Lists can be unsorted. However, Lingo can sort a list in alphanumeric order, with numbers before strings. Strings are sorted according to their initial letters, regardless of how many characters they contain.

Lingo sorts a linear list according to the values in the list. Lingo sorts a property list according to the properties in the list.

To sort a list:

Use the sort command followed by the list's name. See sort in the *Lingo Dictionary*.

About variables

Director uses variables to store and update values. As the name implies, a variable contains a value that can be changed or updated as the movie plays. By changing the value of a variable as the movie plays, you can do things such as store a URL, track the number of times a user takes part in an online chat session, or record whether a network operation is complete.

It's a good idea always to assign a variable a known value the first time you define the variable. This is known as initializing a variable. Initializing variables makes it easier to track and compare the variable's value as the movie plays.

Variables can be global or local. A global variable can exist and retain its value as long as Director is running, while a local variable exists only as long as the handler in which it is defined is running. See "Using global variables" on page 201 and "Using local variables" on page 202.

Storing and updating values in variables

Variables can hold any of the types of information found in Director: numbers, strings, TRUE or FALSE values, symbols, lists, or the result of a calculation. To store and retrieve the values of properties and variables, Lingo uses the equals (=) operator and the set and put commands.

Also, a variable in Lingo can contain different types of data at different times. (The ability to change a variable's type distinguishes Lingo from other languages such as Java, in which a variable's type cannot be changed.)

For example, the statement set x = 1 creates the variable x, which is an integer variable because you assigned the variable an integer. If you subsequently use the statement set x = "one", the variable x becomes a string variable, because the variable now contains a string.

Some properties cannot be set, but can only be tested. Often these are properties that describe some condition that exists outside Director's control. For example, you cannot assign a value to the numChannels cast member property, which indicates the number of channels within a Shockwave movie. However, you can retrieve the number of channels by referring to the numChannels property of a cast member.

To assign a value to a variable:

Use the equals (=) operator. For improved readability, you can use the optional set command at the beginning of the statement.

For example, any of these statements will change the cast member assigned to sprite 2 by setting the sprite's member property to a different cast member. The last two statements use dot syntax:

```
set the member of sprite 2 = member "Big Flash"
set sprite (2).member = member ("Big Flash")
sprite (2).member = member ("Big Flash")
```

As another example, each of these statements assigns a URL to the variable placesToGo:

```
placesToGo = "http://www.macromedia.com"
set placesToGo = "http://www.macromedia.com"
```

Variables can also hold the results of mathematical operations. Both of these statements add the result of an addition operation to the variable mySum:

```
mySum = 5 + 5
set mySum = 5 + 5
```

It's good practice to use variable names that indicate what the variable is used for. This will make your Lingo easier to read. For example, the variable mySum indicates that the variable contains the sum of numbers.

To test the values of properties or variables:

Use the put command in the Message window or check the values in the Watcher window.

For example, the statement put myNumber displays the value assigned to the variable myNumber in the Message window.

As another example, the following statement returns the cast member assigned to sprite 2 by retrieving the sprite's member property:

```
put the member of sprite 2
```

Using global variables

Global variables can be shared among handlers and movies. A global variable exists and retains its value as long as Director is running or until you issue the clearGlobals command.

In Shockwave, global variables persist among movies displayed by the Lingo goToNetMovie command, but not among those displayed by the goToNetPage command.

Every handler that declares a variable as global can use the variable's current value. If the handler changes the variable's value, the new value is available to every other handler that treats the variable as global.

It's good practice to start the names of all global variables with a lowercase *g*. This helps identify which variables are global when you examine Lingo code.

Because you usually want global variables to be available throughout a movie, it is good practice to declare global variables in an on prepareMovie handler. This ensures that the global variables are available from the very start of the movie.

To declare that a variable is global, do one of the following:

- Use the term global before the variable name at the top of the Script window, before any individual handlers. This makes the variable global for every handler in the script.

- Declare the variable as global by using the term global before the variable name on a separate line in every handler that uses the global variable.

When you use the term global to define global variables, the variables automatically have VOID as their initial value.

The following statements make gName a global variable and give it the value Mary:

```
global gName
gName = "Mary"
```

To display all current global variables and their current values:

Use the showGlobals command in the Message window.

To clear all current global variables:

Use the clearGlobals command in the Message window to set the value of all global variables to VOID.

See global, clearGlobals, and showGlobals in the *Lingo Dictionary*.

Using local variables

A local variable exists only as long as the handler in which it is defined is running. However, after a local variable is created, you can use the variable in other expressions or change its value while Lingo is still within the handler that defined the variable.

Treating variables as local is a good idea when you want to use a variable only temporarily in one handler. This helps you avoid unintentionally changing the value in another handler that uses the same variable name.

To create a local variable:

Assign the variable a value using the equals (=) operator or the set...= command.

Unless the handler uses the term global to declare that a variable is global, the variable is automatically a local variable.

To display all current local variables in the handler:

Use the showLocals command.

You can use this command in the Message window or in handlers to help with debugging. The result appears in the Message window. The Director debugger can also track the value of local variables. For more information about using the debugger, see "Troubleshooting Lingo," in the Director Support Center.

Expressing literal values

A literal value is any part of a statement or expression that is to be used exactly as it is, rather than as a variable or a Lingo element. Literal values that you encounter in Lingo are character strings, integers, decimal numbers, cast member names and numbers, frame and movie names and numbers, symbols, and constants.

Note: The value() function can convert a string into a numerical value. The string() function can convert a numerical value into a string.

Each type of literal value has its own rules.

Writing strings

Strings are characters that Lingo treats as characters instead of as variables. Strings must be enclosed in double quotation marks. For example, in the statement

member ("Greeting").text = "Hello"

"Hello" and "Greeting" are both strings. "Hello" is the literal text being put into a text cast member; "Greeting" is the name of the cast member.

Similarly, if you test a string, double quotation marks must surround each string, as in the following example:

```
if "Hello Mr. Jones" contains "Hello" then soundHandler
```

Lingo treats spaces at the beginning or end of a string as a literal part of the string. The following expression includes a space after the word *to*:

```
put "My thoughts amount to "
```

Although Lingo does not distinguish between uppercase and lowercase when referring to cast members, variables, and so on, literal strings are case sensitive. For example, the following two statements place different text into the specified cast member, because "Hello" and "HELLO" are literal strings.

```
member ("Greeting").text = "Hello"
member ("Greeting").text = "HELLO"
```

Using integers

An integer is a whole number, without any fractions or decimal places.

Director works with integers between -2,147,483,648 and +2,147,483,647. (For numbers outside this range, use decimal numbers, sometimes called floating-point numbers.) Enter integers without using commas. Use a minus (-) sign for negative numbers.

You can convert a decimal number to an integer by using the integer() function. For example, the statement set theNumber = integer(3.9) rounds off the decimal number 3.9 and converts it to the integer 4.

Some Lingo commands and functions require integers for their parameters. The requirements for specific Lingo elements can be found in Director Help or the *Lingo Dictionary*.

Using decimal numbers

A decimal number, sometimes called a floating-point number, is any number that includes a decimal point. The floatPrecision property controls the number of decimal places used to display these numbers. (However, Director always uses the complete number in calculations.) See the floatPrecision entry in Director Help or the *Lingo Dictionary* for information about setting the number of decimal places used for decimal numbers.

You can also use exponential notation with decimal numbers: for example, -1.1234e-100 or 123.4e+9.

You can convert an integer or string to a decimal number by using the float() function. For example, the statement set theNumber = float(3) stores the value 3.0 in the variable.

Identifying cast members and casts

Note: If you rearrange (and thus renumber) cast members while creating a movie, Director doesn't automatically update references to cast member numbers in Lingo scripts. Therefore, although some of the examples in this section illustrate how to reference cast members by number, the best practice is to always name cast members and refer to them by name in Lingo scripts.

Lingo refers to a cast member by using the term member followed by a cast member name or number in parentheses. (Cast member names are strings and follow the same syntax rules as other strings.) An alternative syntax is the term member, without parentheses, followed by the cast member name or number.

For example, the following all refer to cast member 50, which has the name Hammer:

```
member("Hammer")
member(50)
member "Hammer"
member 50
```

If more than one cast contains a cast member with the same name, you must use a second parameter to specify the cast member's cast. When your movie uses more than one cast and you identify a cast member by its number, you must also specify the cast. Otherwise, the second parameter is optional.

To specify a cast without parentheses when using member, include the term of castLib followed by the cast's name or number. When the cast member's name is unique in the movie, the cast's name or number isn't required, but you can include it for clarity.

For example, the following statements refer to cast member 50, which is named Hammer, in castLib 4, which is named Tools:

```
member(50, 4)
member 50 of castLib 4

member("Hammer", 4)
member "Hammer" of castLib 4

member(50, "Tools")
member 50 of castLib "Tools"

member("Hammer", "Tools")
member "Hammer" of castLib "Tools"
```

If more than one cast member has the same name and you use the name in a script without specifying the cast or cast member number, Lingo uses the first (lowest numbered) cast member in the lowest numbered cast that has the specified name.

Identifying frames and movies

Use these Lingo terms to refer to frames in a movie:

- The function the frame refers to the current frame.

- The keyword frame followed by the frame number or the frame marker label refers to a specific frame. For example, frame 60 indicates frame 60.

- The keyword loop refers to the marker at the beginning of the current segment. If the current frame has a marker, loop refers to the current frame; if not, loop refers to the first marker before the current frame. If there are no markers in the movie, loop refers to the first frame.

- The word next or previous refers to the next marker or the marker before the current scene, respectively.

- The term the frame followed by a minus or plus sign and the number of frames before or after the current frame refers to a frame that's a specific number of frames before or after the current frame. For example, the frame - 20 refers to the frame 20 frames before the current frame.

- The term the frameLabel identifies the label assigned to the current frame.

- The function marker(), with a positive or negative number of markers used as the parameter, refers to the marker that's a specific number of markers before or after the current frame. For example, marker(-1) returns the frame number of the previous marker and marker(2) returns the frame number of the second marker after the current frame. If the frame is marked, marker(0) returns the frame number of the current frame; if not, marker(0) gives the frame number of the previous marker.

- The term movie followed by the movie name refers to the beginning of another movie. For example, movie "Navigation" refers to the beginning of the movie called Navigation.

- The word frame plus a frame identifier, the word of, the word movie, and the movie name refers to a specific frame in another movie; for example, frame 15 of movie "Navigation" refers to frame 15 of the movie called Navigation.

Using symbols

A symbol is a string or other value that begins with the pound (#) sign.

Symbols are user-defined constants. Comparisons using symbols can usually be performed very quickly, providing more efficient code.

For example, the statement

```
userLevel = #novice
```

runs more quickly than the statement

```
userLevel = "novice"
```

Symbols can't contain spaces or punctuation.

Convert a string to a symbol by using the symbol() function. Convert a symbol back to a string by using the string() function.

See # (symbol) and string() in the *Lingo Dictionary*.

Expressing constants

A constant is a named value whose content never changes. For example, TRUE, FALSE, VOID, and EMPTY are constants because their values are always the same.

The constants BACKSPACE, ENTER, QUOTE, RETURN, SPACE, and TAB refer to keyboard characters. For example, to test whether the user is pressing the Enter key, use the following statement:

```
if the key = ENTER then beep
```

Using operators to manipulate values

Operators are elements that tell Lingo how to combine, compare, or modify the values of an expression. They include the following:

- Arithmetic operators (such as +, -, /, and *)

- Comparison operators (for example, <>, >, and >=), which compare two arguments

- Logical operators (not, and, or), which combine simple conditions into compound ones

- String operators (& and &&), which join strings of characters

Understanding operator precedence

When two or more operators are used in the same statement, some operators take precedence over others in a precise hierarchy that Lingo follows to determine which operators to execute first. This is called the operators' precedence order. For example, multiplication is always performed before addition. However, items in parentheses take precedence over multiplication. For example, without parentheses, Lingo performs the multiplication in this statement first:

total = 2 + 4 * 3

The result is 14.

When parentheses surround the addition operation, Lingo performs the addition first:

total = (2 + 4) * 3

The result is 18.

Descriptions of the operators and their precedence order follow. Operators with higher precedence are performed first. For example, an operator whose precedence order is 5 is performed before an operator whose precedence order is 4. Operations that have the same order of precedence are performed left to right.

Arithmetic operators

Arithmetic operators add, subtract, multiply, divide, and perform other arithmetic operations. Parentheses and the minus sign are arithmetic operators.

Operator	Effect	Precedence
( )	Groups operations to control precedence order.	5
-	When placed before a number, reverses the sign of a number.	5
*	Performs multiplication.	4
mod	Performs modulo operations.	4
/	Performs division.	4
+	Performs addition.	3
-	When placed between two numbers, performs subtraction.	3

Note: When only integers are used in an operation, the result is an integer. Using integers and floating-point numbers in the same calculation results in a floating-point number.

When dividing one integer by another doesn't result in a whole number, Lingo rounds the result down to the nearest integer. For example, the result of 4/3 is 1.

To force Lingo to calculate a value without rounding the result, use float() on one or more values in an expression. For example, the result of 4/float(3) is 1.333.

Comparison operators

Comparison operators compare two values and determine whether the comparison is true or false. These are the comparison operators available in Lingo:

Operator	Meaning	Precedence
<	Is less than	1
<=	Is less than or equal to	1
<>	Is not equal to	1
>	Is greater than	1
>=	Is greater than or equal to	1
=	Equals	1

Logical operators

Logical operators test whether two logical expressions are true or false. These are the logical operators available in Lingo:

Operator	Effect	Precedence
and	Determines whether both expressions are true.	4
or	Determines whether either or both expressions are true.	4
not	Negates an expression.	5

The not operator is useful for toggling a TRUE or FALSE value to its opposite. For example, the following statement turns on the sound if it's currently off and turns off the sound if it's currently on:

```
set the soundEnabled = not (the soundEnabled)
```

String operators

String operators combine and define strings. These are the string operators available in Lingo:

Operator	Effect	Precedence
&	Concatenates two strings.	2
&&	Concatenates two strings and inserts a space between the two.	2
"	Marks the beginning or end of a string.	1

Controlling flow in scripts

Lingo uses if...then...else, case, and repeat statements to perform an action depending on whether a condition exists.

Using if statements

Statements that check whether a condition is true or false begin with the Lingo term if. If the condition exists, Lingo executes the statement that follows then. If the condition doesn't exist, Lingo skips to the next statement in the handler.

To optimize your script's performance, test for the most likely conditions first.

The following statements test several conditions. The term else if specifies alternative tests to perform if previous conditions are false:

```
if the mouseMember = memberNum("map 1") then
    go to "Cairo"
else if the mouseMember = member ("map 2") then
    go to "Nairobi"
else
    alert "You're lost."
end if
```

When writing if...then structures, you can place the statement following then in the same line as then, or you can place it on its own line by inserting a carriage return after then. If you insert a carriage return, you must also include an end if statement at the end of the if...then structure.

For example, the following statements are equivalent:

```
if the mouseMember = member("map 1") then go to "Cairo"
```

```
if the mouseMember = member("map 1") then
    go to "Cairo"
end if
```

For more information, see if in the *Lingo Dictionary*.

Using case statements

The case statement is a shorthand alternative to repeating if...then statements when setting up a multiple branching structure. A case statement is often more efficient and easier to read than a large number of if...then...else statements.

The condition to test for follows the term case in the first line of the case structure. The comparison goes through each line in order until Lingo encounters an expression that matches the test condition. When a matching expression is found, Director executes the Lingo that follows the matching expression.

For example, the following case statement tests which key the user pressed most recently and responds accordingly:

```
case (the key) of
    "A": go to frame "Apple"
    "B", "C":
        puppetTransition 99
        go to frame "Oranges"
    otherwise beep
end case
```

- If the user pressed A, the movie goes to the frame labeled Apple.

- If the user pressed B or C, the movie performs the specified transition and then goes to the frame labeled Oranges.

- If the user pressed any other letter key, the computer beeps.

A case statement can use comparisons as the test condition.

For more information, see case in the *Lingo Dictionary*.

Repeating an action

Lingo can repeat an action a specified number of times or while a specific condition exists.

To repeat an action a specified number of times:

Use a repeat with structure. Specify the number of times to repeat as a range following repeat with.

This structure is useful for performing the same operation on a series of objects. For example, the following repeat loop makes Background Transparent the ink for sprites 2 through 10:

```
repeat with n = 2 to 10
    set the ink of sprite n = 36
end repeat
```

This example performs exactly the same action as above, but uses dot syntax:

```
repeat with n =2 to 10
    sprite(n).ink = 36
end repeat
```

To repeat a set of instructions as long as a specific condition exists:

Use a repeat...while statement.

For example, these statements instruct a movie to beep continuously whenever the mouse button is being pressed:

```
repeat while the mouseDown
    beep
end repeat
```

Lingo continues to loop through the statements inside the repeat loop until the condition is no longer true or until one of the instructions sends Lingo outside the loop. In the previous example, Lingo exits the repeat loop when the mouse button is released because the mouseDown condition is no longer true.

To exit a repeat loop:

Use the exit repeat command.

For example, the following statements make a movie beep while the mouse button is pressed, unless the mouse pointer is over sprite 1. If the pointer is over sprite 1, Lingo exits the repeat loop and stops beeping. (The term rollover followed by a sprite number indicates that the pointer is over the specified sprite.)

```
repeat while the stillDown
    beep
    if rollover (1) then exit repeat
end repeat
```

See repeat with, repeat while, and exit repeat in the *Lingo Dictionary*.

Creating and attaching scripts with the Script window

To create scripts and write the Lingo statements that make up handlers, you use the Script window.

To open the Script window, do one of the following:

- Choose Window > Script.

- Double-click a script in a Cast window.

For more ways to create and open scripts, see "Performing common tasks" on page 180.

You can change the font of text in the Script window and define different colors for various code components. See the next section.

Setting Script window preferences

To change the default font of text in the Script window and the color of various code elements, you use Script window preferences. Director automatically colors different types of code elements unless you turn off Auto Coloring.

To set Script window preferences:

1 Choose File > Preferences > Script.

2 To choose the default font, click the Font button and choose settings from the Font dialog box.

3 To choose the default color of text in the Script window, choose a color from the Color menu.

4 To choose the background color for the Script window, choose a color from the Background color menu.

5 To make the Script window automatically color certain code elements, select Enable for Auto Coloring. This option is on by default.

    With Auto Coloring off, all text appears in the default color.

6 If Auto Coloring is on, choose colors for the following code elements from the corresponding color menus:

- Keywords

- Comments

- Literals

- Custom (terms you define in your own code)

Inserting common Lingo terms

The Script window provides a pop-up menu of common Lingo terms that you can use to insert Lingo in a script.

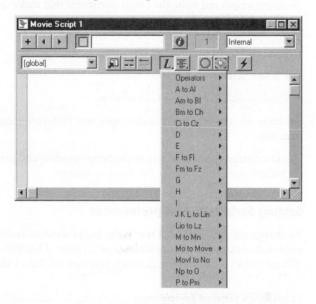

 • The Alphabetical menu lists every element in alphabetical order.

 • The Categories menu lists categories of elements according to the features they are often used for.

When you choose an element from the Lingo pop-up menu, Director inserts the element at the insertion point in the Script window.

When an element requires additional parameters, Lingo includes placeholder names that indicate the additional required information. When more than one argument or parameter is required, Lingo highlights the first one for you, so all you have to do is type to replace it. You must select and change the other parameters yourself.

Some cast member types and scripting Xtras provide Lingo terms that do not appear in the Lingo menus. These member types and Xtras often have their own documentation, and you can find some information from within Director.

To display a list of available Xtras:

Issue the command showXlib in the Message window.

To display a list of methods for an Xtra:

Issue the command put mmessageList("*XtraName*") in the Message window.

Entering and editing text

Entering and editing text in a Script window is similar to entering and editing text in any other field.

The following are common editing tasks you perform in the Script window:

- To select a word, double-click the word.
- To select an entire script, choose Select All from the Edit menu.
- To start a new line, enter a carriage return.
- To wrap a long line of code with a continuation symbol, press Alt+Enter (Windows) or Option+Return (Macintosh) where you want to insert a soft line break.

  The continuation symbol (¬) that appears indicates that the statement continues on the next line.

- To locate a handler in the current script, choose the handler's name from the Handler pop-up menu in the Script window.
- To compile the Lingo you have written, click the Script window's Recompile button or close the Script window.
- To reformat a script, press Tab in the Script window.

  Lingo automatically indents statements when the syntax is correct. If a line doesn't indent properly, there is a problem in the Lingo syntax on that line.

Finding handlers and text in scripts

The Find command in the Edit menu is useful for finding handlers and for finding and editing text and handlers.

To find handlers in scripts:

1 Choose Edit > Find > Handler.

   The Find Handler dialog box appears.

   The leftmost column in the Find Handler dialog box displays the name of each handler in the movie. The middle column displays the number of the cast member associated with the handler's script. The rightmost column lists the cast that the cast member is in.

2 Select the handler that you want to find.

3 Click Find.

   The handler appears in the Script window.

   The title bar at the top of the Script window indicates the script's type.

To find text in scripts:

1 Make the Script window active.

2 Choose Edit > Find > Text.

   The Find Text dialog box appears.

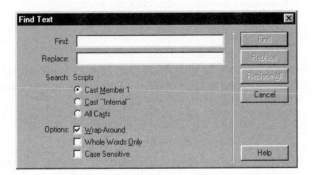

3 Enter text that you want to find in the Find field, and then click Find.

   Find is not case sensitive: ThisHandler, thisHandler, and THISHANDLER are all the same for search purposes.

To specify which cast members to search:

Select the appropriate option under Search: Scripts.

To start the search over from the beginning after the search reaches the end:

Select the Wrap-Around option.

To search only for whole words and not fragments of other words that match the word:

Select the Whole Words Only option.

To find the next occurrence of the text specified in the Find field:

Choose Edit > Find Again.

To find occurrences of selected text:

1 Select the text.

2 Choose Edit > Find > Selection.

Using linked scripts

In addition to scripts stored as internal cast members, you can choose to keep scripts in external text files and link them to your Director movie. These linked scripts are similar to linked image or digital video files you can import into Director movies.

Advantages of using linked scripts include the following:

- One person can work on the Director file while another works on the script.

- You can easily exchange scripts with others.

- You can control the scripts separately from the Director file in a source code control application such as Microsoft Visual SourceSafe. Applications such as this prevent multiple programmers working on the same Director project from overwriting each other's work.

Linked scripts are used by Director only during authoring. At run time, Director projectors and Shockwave use a special internal copy of the script data stored in the movie. This way, your linked scripts need not be distributed with your movies and cannot be copied by end users.

To import a script as a linked text file:

1 Choose File > Import.

2 Choose Script as the type of file to import.

3 Select the script file(s) you want to import.

   You can import files with the file extensions .txt or .ls; the .ls extension is Director's linked script extension.

   To create a list of files you want to import, you can use the Add and Add All buttons. This is especially useful if you want to import scripts from multiple locations.

4 Select Link to External File from the Media pop-up menu.

5 Click Import.

You can edit linked scripts normally in Director's script window. Changes you make are written to the external files each time you save your Director movie. (If you imported the linked script from a UNIX server, UNIX line endings are preserved.) If you import a script whose text file is locked, you will not be able to edit the script in Director.

You cannot apply custom text colors to linked scripts in the script window. Script auto coloring, however, is enabled for linked scripts.

To turn an internal script cast member into an external, linked script cast member:

1 Select the internal cast member and click the Script tab of the Property Inspector.

2 Click Link Script As.

3 Enter a name for the script file in the Save As dialog box.

4 Click Save.

To reload a linked script after it is edited:

Use the unloadMember command.

If a linked script is edited outside of Director, you can reload it by using the unloadMember command in the Message window. The following statement will cause the script myScript to be unloaded and then reloaded:

```
unloadMember member "myScript"
```

CHAPTER 7
Color, Tempo, and Transitions

A number of behind-the-scenes functions in Director are important to the appearance and performance of a movie.

To control the way Director manages colors, it's important to understand the difference between RGB and index color and how to assign colors to various elements in your movie. See "Controlling color" on page 220.

To control the speed at which your movie plays, you use settings in the tempo channel. See "About tempo" on page 232.

To make scenes in your movie flow together without creating the animation yourself, you can use predefined transitions. See "Using transitions" on page 236.

All of these features involve using the channels at the top of the Score.

Controlling color

Choosing colors for movie elements is as simple as making a selection from a menu. To make sure that the colors you choose are displayed correctly on as many systems as possible, it helps to understand how Director controls color.

Director provides a variety of color controls. The following list describes the most important:

- Use the Movie tab in the Property Inspector to change modes for selecting colors. The modes are RGB values or palette index.

- Also use the Movie tab to turn on the Remap Palettes If Needed option, which causes Director to either dither or remap colors in bitmap images to the best available colors. If the option is off, Director assumes that all bitmaps use the movie's color palette and does not perform remapping or dithering, regardless of the settings for individual cast members. See "Setting Stage and movie properties" on page 61.

- Use the pop-up Color menu to choose colors for movie elements. The Color menu is available throughout the Director application—for example, in the Tool palette.

- Use Transform Bitmap to remap bitmap images to new palettes and change their color depth. You can also make the same changes when you import a bitmap. See "Changing size, color depth, and color palette for bitmaps" on page 317, and "About importing bitmaps" on page 302.

- Use the Score's palette channel to change the movie's color palette as a movie plays.

- Use the Color Palettes window to change the colors in a color palette or to create a custom color palette cast member.

Specifying palette index and RGB color

Director can use either palette index values or RGB values to specify colors. RGB values are much more reliable and accurate for specifying colors than palette index values. RGB is the system that most Web pages use.

Director identifies a palette index color by the number of its position in a set of colors called a color palette. Color number 12, for example, might be blue. If a different palette is active, color number 12 might be red. When a computer is set to display 256 colors or fewer, it can display only the colors in the palette currently active in the system. This means that images created to display with the colors of one palette do not appear correctly when a different palette is active. If you use palette index color in a movie and then switch palettes during the movie, or never make sure that the correct palette is active, the images in your movie may appear with the wrong colors.

Director identifies an RGB color as a set of hexadecimal numbers that specify the amounts of red, green, and blue required to create the color. When a computer is set to display thousands or millions of colors, Director always displays RGB colors accurately. When a computer is set to 256 colors, Director finds the closest color in the current color palette to approximate the RGB color.

To choose the color mode for the current movie, you use the Color Selection options in the Movie tab of the Property Inspector. When you choose RGB, all the colors you choose from the Color menu in Director are specified in RGB values. When you choose Palette Index, the colors you choose are specified according to their position in the current palette. The Color menu indicates which method is being used.

To change the color mode of a movie:

1 Display the Movie tab of the Property Inspector.

2 For Color Selection, choose either RGB or Palette Index.

Changing the color depth of a movie

When you save a Director movie, it is set to the same color depth as the system on which you are authoring it. You can use Lingo to reset the system color depth to match the color depth of a movie. See switchColorDepth in the *Lingo Dictionary*.

If you want to set the color depth of a movie without using Lingo, you can use system utilities to change the color depth of your system before you save the movie file. On the Macintosh, you can also make the movie reset the system color depth by choosing File > Preferences > General and selecting Reset Monitor to Movie's Color Depth.

Choosing colors for movie elements

Use the Color menu to choose colors for movie elements such as the Stage, vector shapes, and the foreground and background of sprites. For some elements, such as Stage and sprite colors, you can also enter hexadecimal values for any RGB color. The Color menu displays the colors in the current palette; the 16 larger color chips at the top of the menu identify your favorite colors.

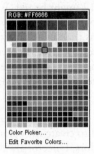

If the movie is set to specify colors as RGB values, choosing a color from the Color menu specifies the RGB value of the color, not its index value. (For an explanation of the difference between index and RGB color, see "Specifying palette index and RGB color" on page 221.) The bar at the top of the Color menu indicates whether the movie is set to RGB or index color.

If you want to choose a color that is not in the current palette (and therefore not available on the Color menu), you can use the system color picker to specify any color. You can also change the set of colors available on the Color menu by displaying a different color palette.

To open the Color menu:

1 Do one of the following:

- Select a sprite and display the Sprite tab of the Property Inspector.

- Choose Window > Tool Palette.

2 Click and hold the mouse button while pointing at the Foreground Color and Background Color buttons.

Note: To open the Color menu in the opposite mode (RGB or index), hold down the Alt key (Windows) or Option key (Macintosh) while clicking the color chip.

To choose colors not on the Color menu:

1 Open the Color menu.

2 Click Color Picker.

3 Use the color picker that is displayed to choose colors.

To edit the favorite colors on the Color menu:

1 Open the Color menu.

2 Choose Edit Favorite Colors.

3 Choose the color chip you want to change.

4 Choose a new color for the chip using one of the following options:

• Click the color box to open the Color menu and choose a color from the current palette.

• Enter an RGB value for a color in the box to the right of the color box.

• Click Color Picker and then use the system color picker to specify a new color.

5 Click OK.

To change the color palette displayed on the Color menu:

1 Choose Window > Color Palettes or double-click the mouse button on the Foreground Color and Background Color buttons in the Tool palette.

2 Choose a color palette from the Palettes pop-up menu.

Changing color palettes during a movie

The palette channel in the Score determines which palette is active for a particular frame in a movie. To define the palette that is active in a particular frame of a movie, use Modify > Frame > Palette. When the playback head reaches the frame with the palette change, Director switches to the new palette.

The settings in the palette channel have no effect on a movie playing in a Web browser. Do not use any of these settings for movies on the Web.

For a stand-alone disk-based movie that takes over the entire screen, changing palettes during a movie is a viable option for displaying 8-bit graphics with the best possible colors.

If you place a cast member that has its own custom palette on the Stage—and if it's the first cast member that has a different palette in the frame—Director automatically assigns the new palette to the palette channel. The new palette becomes the active palette unless you clear it from the palette channel or replace it with a different palette, and it remains in effect until you set a different palette in the palette channel.

Only one palette can be active at any time. If an 8-bit image appears with the wrong colors, it requires a different palette. See "Solving color palette problems" on page 231.

Director contains several color palettes. The Windows and Macintosh system palettes are the default selections. Web216 is nearly identical to the palettes used by Netscape Navigator and Microsoft Internet Explorer. Use it for any movie you plan to play in a browser. Any additional palettes you create or import appear as cast members.

While working on a movie, you can change the active palette in the authoring environment by choosing a new palette in the Color Palettes window. The palette that is active in the authoring environment while you work does not change the palette in the movie you're working on. Any settings in the palette channel reset the active palette as soon as the movie plays.

To specify a palette:

1 In the Score, do one of the following:

- Double-click the cell in the palette channel where you want the new palette setting to appear.

- Right-click (Windows) or Control-click (Macintosh) the cell in the effects channel where you want the new palette setting to appear, and then choose Palette from the Context menu.

- Select a frame in the palette channel and choose Modify > Frame > Palette.

    (If you don't see the palette channel, the effects channel is hidden. To display it, click the Hide/Show Effects Channel tool in the top right of the score window.)

Palette channel —————

2 Select the options you want to use in the Frame Properties: Palette dialog box.

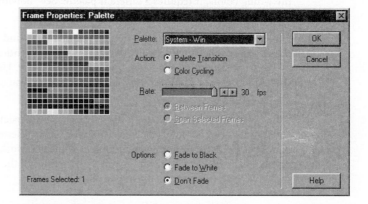

- Choose a new palette.

- Specify how you want Director to manage the palette change. For example, to hide a palette change within a fade, first choose a new palette from the pop-up menu. Select the Palette Transition option and then select Fade to Black or Fade to White. Use the Rate slider to set the speed of the fade.

    To stop the movie while the palette changes, first choose a new palette from the Palettes pop-up menu. Select the Palette Transition option and then select Between Frames. Use the Rate slider to set the speed of the transition.

3 Click Set.

The palette you chose now appears in the cell you selected in the Score's palette channel. The setting remains in effect in the movie until you set a different palette in the palette channel.

Using the Color Palettes window

Use the Color Palettes window to change and rearrange color palettes and to determine which colors in a palette are used in an image. This section explains basic features of the Color Palettes window. For a description of specialized features, see "Special Color Effects" in the Director Support Center.

Select a palette Reserve, select, and
to change   rearrange colors

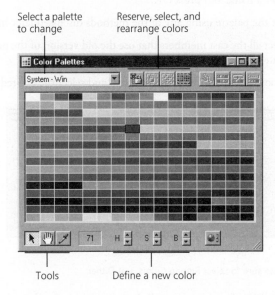

Tools   Define a new color

If you add new palettes to your movie from other graphics applications, those palettes appear in the palette list and in the Cast window.

The row of buttons on the right side of the Color Palettes window are for reserving, selecting, and rearranging colors in the current palette. If you attempt to change one of the nine built-in palettes, Director creates a copy of the palette for you to modify.

Note: Choosing a new palette in the Color Palettes window does not change the palette for the movie or any frame in the movie. Use the Movie tab in the Property Inspector to choose the movie color palette or choose Modify > Frame Palette to change the color palette at a particular frame.

When you modify a palette, all the cast members using the palette change as well, so make sure you always keep a copy of the original palette.

To open the Color Palettes window:

Choose Window > Color Palettes.

To edit a palette already used in a movie:

1   Choose Window > Color Palettes.

2   Select the palette you want to edit from the Palettes pop-up menu.

3   Double-click any color within the palette.

Director makes a copy of the palette and prompts you to enter a name.

4   Enter a name and press OK.

5   Edit the palette using any of the methods discussed later in this section.

6   Select all the cast members that use the old version of the palette, or use Find to locate all the cast members using a particular palette.

7   Choose Modify > Transform Bitmap and select the desired options.

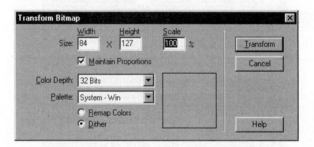

Note: Be sure to select Remap Colors, not Dither.

8   Click Transform to remap all the cast members to the new palette.

To select one or more colors:

 1   Click a color in the Color Palettes window. If the selection arrow is not active, click the Arrow tool at the bottom of the window.

2   To select a range, drag across colors—or click the first color in the range, and then Shift-click the last.

3   Control-click (Windows) or Command-click (Macintosh) to select multiple discontiguous colors.

To match the color of any pixel on the Stage with the same color in the palette:

 1 Click the Eyedropper tool.

2 Drag any color in the Color Palettes window to any point on the Stage.

The selection in the Color Palettes window and the foreground color in the Tool palette changes to the color at the pointer location.

To select colors in the palette used by the current cast member:

1 Select the cast member or open the cast member in the Paint window.

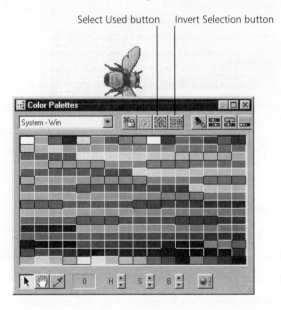

Select Used button   Invert Selection button

 2 Click the Select Used button in the Color Palettes window.

To select all colors not currently selected:

Click the Invert Selection button in the Color Palettes window.

Changing colors in a color palette

You can define a new color for a color palette by selecting a color you want to change and then using either the controls at the bottom of the Color Palettes window or the system color.

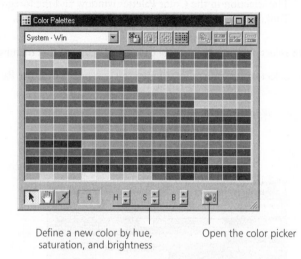

Define a new color by hue, saturation, and brightness

Open the color picker

To edit selected colors in the Color Palettes window:

1 Choose Window > Color Palettes.

2 Select the palette you want to change from the Palettes pop-up menu.

3 Select a color within the palette to change.

   If you attempt to change one of the default palettes, Director makes a copy of the palette and prompts you to enter a name.

4 To change the color using the H, S, and B (hue, saturation, and brightness) controls, click the arrows next to the controls.

• Hue is the color created by mixing primary colors.

• Saturation is a measure of how much white is mixed in with the color. A fully saturated color is vivid; a less saturated color is a washed-out pastel or, in the case of black, a shade of gray.

• Brightness controls how much black is mixed in with a color. Colors that are very bright have little or no black. As more black is added, the brightness is reduced, and the color gets darker. If brightness is reduced to 0, then no matter what the values are for Hue or Saturation, the color is black.

5 To change the color using the system color picker, click the Color Picker button.

   For instruction on using the Windows or Macintosh color picker, see your system documentation.

Controlling color palettes with Lingo

By using the puppetPalette command, you can change the current palette and specify how quickly a new palette fades in. This command is useful when you want to change the palette to suit changing conditions in the movie without entering a new frame. For example, you can change the palette when you switch a cast member assigned to a sprite.

The new palette remains in effect until a new puppetPalette command is issued, a new palette is set in the palette channel, or a new movie starts.

See puppetPalette in the *Lingo Dictionary*.

Solving color palette problems

When images in your movie appear with the wrong colors, you probably have the wrong color palette active. Color palette problems occur only if you are using 8-bit bitmaps and you want your movie to be displayed correctly on 256-color systems (8-bit bitmaps always appear correctly on computers set to display thousands or millions of colors).

Eight-bit bitmaps don't store information about actual colors; they identify colors by referring to positions in the current color palette. When saving an 8-bit bitmap, a graphics program creates a palette with the colors required for that particular image. This palette is saved with the file and must be active when the bitmap appears in a Director movie for the bitmap to appear with the proper colors. Only one palette can be active at once. Whenever it's necessary to display more than one 8-bit bitmap on the screen at one time, as is often the case in Director movies, all the images must refer to the same palette.

To solve color palette problems, follow these guidelines:

- To avoid color problems in movies for the Web, map all 8-bit bitmaps in your movie to Director's built-in Web216 color palette. This is essentially the same palette used by Netscape Navigator and Microsoft Internet Explorer.

- Do not attempt to change palettes while a movie is playing in the browser. The browser, not the Director movie, controls the palette. Browsers ignore all palette channel settings.

- Make sure all 8-bit images that are on the Stage at the same time refer to the same palette.

- If bitmaps are not dithering or remapping to the current palette, make sure the Remap Palettes If Needed option in the Movie tab of the Property Inspector is selected. See "Setting Stage and movie properties" on page 61.

- Make sure there are no palette changes in the palette channel that you are unaware of. For example, when a cast member you are placing on the Stage has a palette different from the currently active palette, Director adds the new palette to the palette channel. If you don't realize that this has happened, you may find the palette changing unexpectedly when the movie plays.

- For disk-based movies, simplify your work and avoid frequent palette changes by mapping all the images in your movie to as few palettes as possible.

- Remap existing cast members to a new color palette using the Modify > Transform Bitmap command.

- If the Import option for Palette is not available while you are importing an image, the image's palette may not meet standard system requirements. Use an image editor to make sure the image's palette meets the following requirements: The palette must contain exactly 16 or 256 colors. The first and last colors in the palette must be black or white, and there must be only one black and one white in the entire palette.

- Don't change colors that are used by your system software for interface elements. In Windows, these colors always appear as the first ten and the last ten colors in the palette.

About tempo

Tempo is the number of frames per second that Director tries to play. You can control tempo using the Score tempo channel or Lingo's puppetTempo command.

Director tempo settings control the maximum speed at which the playback head moves from frame to frame. The tempo doesn't affect the duration of any transitions set in the transition channel, nor does it control the speed at which a sound or digital video plays. Note that tempo settings don't always control animated GIFs; see "Using animated GIFs" on page 303.

Settings in the tempo channel can also make a movie pause and wait for a mouse click or key press. For information on making a movie wait for a cue point in a sound or video, see "Synchronizing media" on page 384.

For simple movies, using the tempo channel is often the best way to define tempos. For more sophisticated control of the speed of a movie, use Lingo's puppetTempo command to control tempo.

You can't make a movie go faster than the computer allows. Many factors can make movies play more slowly than the specified tempo, such as the following:

- Playing the movie on a slower computer

- Making the movie wait for cast members to download from a slow Internet connection

- Animating several large sprites at the same time

- Animating stretched sprites

- Color depth differences between the movie and monitor

- Animating sprites that have blend values

Specifying tempo properties

It's best to begin a movie with a tempo setting in the first cell of the tempo channel. If you don't set a tempo until later in the movie, the beginning tempo is determined by the setting in the Control Panel. Director plays a movie at the tempo you've set until it encounters a new tempo setting in the tempo channel or a puppetTempo command is issued.

Enter tempo changes in the tempo channel at the top of the Score. (If you don't see the tempo channel, the effects channel is hidden. To display it, click the Hide/Show Effects Channel tool in the top right of the score window.)

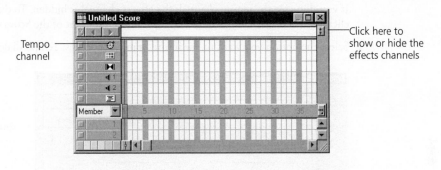

Tempo channel

Click here to show or hide the effects channels

To specify a tempo setting:

1 In the score, do one of the following:

- Double-click the cell in the tempo channel where you want the new tempo setting to appear.

- Right-click (Windows) or Control-click (Macintosh) the cell in the effects channel where you want the new tempo setting to appear, and then choose Tempo from the Context menu.

- Select a frame in the tempo channel and choose Modify > Frame > Tempo.

  If you don't see the tempo channel, the effects channel is hidden. To display it, click the Hide/Show Effects Channel tool in the top right of the Score window.

2 Select the option you want to use in the Frame Properties: Tempo dialog box.

- To set a new tempo for the movie, use the Tempo arrows or drag the slider.

- To pause the movie at the current frame for a certain amount of time, use the Wait arrows or drag the slider.

- To pause the movie until the user clicks the mouse or presses a key, select Wait for Mouse Click or Key Press.

- To pause the movie until a sound or digital video cue point passes, select Wait for Cue Point and choose a channel and cue point. See "Synchronizing media" on page 384.

3 Click OK.

  A number that matches the setting you've chosen appears in the tempo channel. If you can't read the number, you may need to zoom the score. To do so, click the Zoom Menu button at the right edge of the sprite channel or choose View > Zoom. Then choose a percentage from the pop-up menu.

Comparing actual speed with tempos you've set

It's good practice to test the performance of your movie on a system similar to what your users have. Make sure the movie plays well on the slowest systems likely to be used.

The tempo you've set and the actual speed of a movie both appear in the Control Panel.

Step forward button

Tempo setting

Actual tempo

To compare the actual speed of a movie with the tempos you've set:

1 Play the movie from start to finish, then rewind it to the beginning.

2 Use the Step Forward button to step through the movie frame by frame,

3 In each frame, compare the tempo setting shown in the Control Panel with the actual speed shown there.

If you haven't recorded the actual speed of a movie in a particular frame, the Control Panel displays two dashes (--).

Locking frame durations

To make Director play a movie at the same tempo on all types of computers, use the Lock Frame Durations option in the Movie Playback Properties dialog box ("Setting movie playback options" on page 414). For frames without tempo settings, Director uses the current tempo. Lock Frame Duration prevents a movie from playing too fast on a fast system, but it cannot prevent a movie from playing slowly on a slow system.

To turn on Lock Frame Durations:

1 Choose Modify > Movie > Playback.

2 Select Lock Frame Durations.

Controlling tempo with Lingo

To override the tempo set in the movie's tempo channel, you use the puppetTempo command. This approach is useful when you want to change the movie's tempo in response to conditions that you can't control, such as the type of computer the movie is playing on or a user's action.

The puppetTempo command doesn't retain control of the tempo channel. If the movie encounters any tempo settings in the tempo channel, the puppetTempo settings will be overridden.

See puppetTempo in the *Lingo Dictionary*.

Using transitions

Transitions create brief animations that play between frames to create a smooth flow as sprites move, appear, or disappear or as the entire Stage changes. Director provides dozens of transitions built into the application, and many third-party Xtras include transitions as well. For example, you can dissolve from one scene to the next, display a new scene strip by strip, or switch to a scene as though revealing it through venetian blinds. You can also use many of the transitions to make individual elements appear or disappear from the screen.

Once they are defined, transitions appear in the Cast window as cast members. You can place them in the transition channel by dragging them from the cast to the Score.

Creating transitions

Transitions, like tempos, palettes, sounds, and behaviors, have a channel set aside for them in the Score.

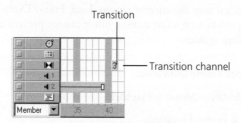

A transition always takes place between the end of the current frame and the beginning of the frame where the transition is set. If you want to create a dissolve between two scenes, set the transition in the first frame of the second scene, not in the last frame of the first scene.

To add a transition:

1 In the transition channel, select the frame in which you want the transition to occur.

2 Choose Modify > Frame > Transition or double-click the frame in the transition channel.

3 In the Frame Properties Transition dialog box, choose a category if desired, then select the transition you want. You can quickly scroll through transitions by typing the first letter of the transition's name.

Many transitions have default settings for Duration and Smoothness. You can adjust the sliders to change the settings.

For many transitions, you can also select whether the transition affects the entire Stage or just the area that's changing.

Xtra transitions may offer additional options provided by the developer. If the Options button is available when you choose an Xtra transition, click it to view and change the transition options.

4 Click OK.

Director displays the cast member number that corresponds to the transition in the transition channel. The transition also appears in the cast.

Tips for using transitions

Here are some points to keep in mind when working with transitions:

- To play a sound while a transition occurs, place the sound in the frame immediately before the transition.

- The Dissolve Pixels, Dissolve Pixels Fast, or Dissolve Patterns transitions may look different on Windows and Macintosh systems. Test to ensure satisfactory results.

- If you export a movie that contains transitions as a digital video or PICS file, the transitions may not be preserved.

- A transition that occurs while a sound or digital video is decompressing may require more system resources than are available on less powerful systems. This may cause the sound to stop playing. If you notice this behavior while testing on low-end systems, try making the transition shorter, and avoid complex transitions such as Dissolve.

- Avoid looping on a frame that contains a transition. Playing a transition continuously may cause performance issues.

- Options will become available only when transition Xtras are available.

Using transition Xtras

You can add custom transitions that are available as transition Xtras. Transition Xtras appear in the Frame Properties: Transitions dialog box. Transition Xtras are often more complex than the transitions provided with Director and may include an additional dialog box for specialized settings.

To install a transition Xtra:

Place the transition Xtra in the Xtras folder in the Director application folder. The transition Xtra must be present when the movie runs.

Controlling transitions with Lingo

To set a transition with Lingo, you use the puppetTransition command. This command gives you the flexibility to select a transition appropriate for current movie conditions or to apply a transition to sprites before the playback head exits the current frame.

For example, use the puppetTransition command to specify one of several transitions, depending on which sprites are on the Stage when the playback head enters a new frame, or apply a transition to a new sprite when it appears but the playback head doesn't exit the frame.

The puppetTransition command applies only to the frame in which you issue the command. You do not need to explicitly return control of the transition channel to the Score after the transition occurs.

The puppetTransition command's parameters perform the same functions as the options in the Frame Properties: Transition dialog box.

See puppetTransition in the *Lingo Dictionary*.

CHAPTER 8
Animation

Animation is the appearance of an image changing over time. The most common types of animation involve moving a sprite on the Stage (tweening animation) and using a series of cast members in the same sprite (frame-by-frame animation).

- Tweening is a traditional animation term that describes the process in which a lead animator draws the animation frames where major changes take place, called keyframes. Assistants draw the frames in between.

- Frame-by-frame animation involves manually creating every frame in an animation, whether that involves switching cast members for a sprite or manually changing settings for sprites on the Stage.

Other forms of animation include making a sprite change size, rotate, change colors, or fade in and out.

To specify tweening properties for a sprite, you use the Sprite Tweening dialog box.

To open the Sprite Tweening dialog box:

1 Select a sprite.

2 Choose Modify > Sprite > Tweening.

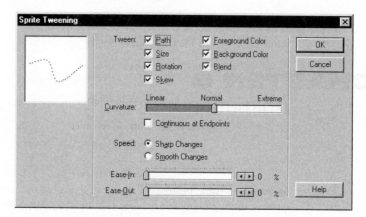

About tweening in Director

To use tweening in Director, you define properties for a sprite in frames called keyframes and let Director change the properties in the frames in between. Tweening is very efficient for adding animation to movies for Web sites, since no additional data needs to download when a single cast member changes.

A keyframe usually indicates a change in sprite properties. Properties that can be tweened are position, size, rotation, skew, blend, and foreground and background color. Each keyframe defines a value for all of these properties, even if you only explicitly define one.

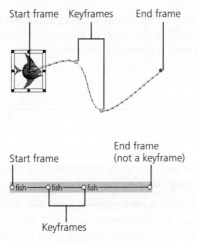

Tweening the path of a sprite

Sprite paths are the lines Director displays on the Stage to show the movement of a sprite. Sprite paths are controlled by the Sprite Overlay Settings dialog box. You can change settings to make the paths appear for all sprites, for selected sprites, or only when the pointer rolls over a sprite. See "Using the Sprite Overlay" on page 128.

You can tween a sprite directly on the Stage by editing the sprite's path. Director displays the path of the selected sprite directly on the Stage. You can adjust the path by dragging keyframe indicators.

To tween the path of a sprite:

1 Place a sprite on the Stage where you want the path to start. If the sprite is already on the Stage, select it.

This places the start frame of the sprite in the proper location. The start frame is also the first keyframe of the sprite.

2 If necessary, choose View > Sprite Overlay > Show Paths.

The Show Paths option is on by default. With this option turned on, Director displays the paths of moving sprites on the Stage. Keyframes appear as hollow circles. Small tick marks show the sprite's position in tweened frames.

3 Insert keyframes in any additional frames where you want the sprite's animation path to change.

4 Drag the red handle within the sprite to the place on the Stage where you want the sprite's path to end.

The red handle represents the sprite's location in the end frame. For bitmaps, the red handle is usually in the center of the image. For vector shapes and other media types, the handle is often in the upper left corner.

5 Director displays the path the sprite will follow. The tick marks along the path show the sprite location in each frame in between.

6 To make the sprite's path curve between more points, hold down the Alt key (Windows) or Option key (Macintosh) and move the pointer on the Stage over a tick mark. When the pointer changes color, drag the tick mark to a new location.

This creates a new keyframe and records the new location. Repeat this step to create additional keyframes.

7 To make the property changes defined by a keyframe occur at a different time, drag the keyframe in the Score to a new frame within the sprite.

8 To change the degree of curvature between keyframes, choose Modify > Sprite > Tweening and adjust the Curvature slider. To make the sprite move in the same direction at the beginning and end, select Continuous at Endpoints in the Sprite Tweening dialog box. This creates a circular motion. See "Changing tweening settings" on page 246.

Accelerating and decelerating sprites

To create more natural motion in tweened sprites, use the following settings in the Sprite Tweening dialog box:

- Ease-In and Ease-Out control how a sprite moves from its start frame to its end frame, no matter how many keyframes are in between. Ease-In makes a sprite move more slowly in the beginning frames; Ease-Out makes the sprite slow down in the ending frames. This setting makes the sprite move more like an object in the real world.

- The Speed settings control how Director moves a sprite between each keyframe. The Sharp Changes option is the default setting. Using this option, Director calculates how to move the sprite between each pair of keyframes separately. If a sprite's keyframes are separated by unequal numbers of frames in the Score, or by different amounts of space on the Stage, abrupt changes in speed may occur as the sprite moves between keyframe locations. Smooth out these speed changes by choosing the Smooth Changes option.

Sprite with modified ease-in and ease-out settings

To change the acceleration or deceleration of a sprite:

1 Use one of the tweening methods to create a moving sprite.

2 Turn on View > Sprite Overlay > Show Paths to see how far the sprite moves between each frame.

3 Select the sprite and choose Modify > Sprite > Tweening.

4 Use the Ease-In and Ease-Out sliders to specify the percentage of the sprite's path through which the sprite should accelerate or decelerate.

5 Choose one of the following speed settings:

- Sharp Changes moves the sprite between keyframe locations without adjusting the speed.

- Smooth Changes adjusts the sprite's speed gradually as it moves between keyframes.

Tweening other sprite properties

In addition to tweening a sprite's path, Director can tween the size, rotation, skew, blend, and foreground and background color of a sprite. Tweening size works best for vector-based cast members created in the Vector Shape window or Flash (bitmaps can become distorted when resized). Director can tween all of these properties at once.

To make a sprite fade in or out, you can tween blend settings. To make sprites spin or tilt, use rotation. To create gradual shifts in color, you can tween color settings.

Note: To prevent Director from tweening a certain sprite property, choose Modify > Sprite > Tweening and turn off any of the tweening options.

To tween sprite properties:

1 If the Score isn't open, choose Window > Score.

2 Position a sprite on the Stage and make sure it spans all the frames in which you want the sprite to change.

3 Select the start frame of the sprite in the Score.

4 To tween size, scale the sprite or resize the sprite on the Stage. See "Resizing and scaling sprites" on page 142.

5 To define the beginning property settings, click the Sprite tab of the Property Inspector and do any of the following:

• To make the sprite fade in or out, enter a blend setting in the Property Inspector (in List view). Enter 0 to make the sprite fade in or 100 to make it fade out. For more information, see "Setting blends" on page 149.

• To tween rotation or skew, manually rotate or skew the sprite to the beginning position on the Stage or enter an angle in the Property Inspector. See "Rotating and skewing sprites" on page 144.

• To tween color, use the color boxes in the Property Inspector to open the color menu for foreground and background color, or enter the RGB values for a new color in the boxes at the right.

6 In the Score, select the end frame of the sprite.

7 Choose Insert > Keyframe.

Note that the end frame is not a keyframe unless you create one there.

8 Make sure only the keyframe is selected (not the entire sprite), and then enter the ending values of the sprite properties you are tweening.

For example, if you entered a blend setting of 0 in the first frame, you could enter a blend setting of 100 in this frame.

9 If necessary, create additional keyframes in the sprite and enter new values for the tweened properties.

10 To make the property changes defined by a keyframe occur at a different time, drag a keyframe in the Score to a new frame within the sprite.

To view the tweening, rewind and play the movie. Director gradually changes the value of the tweened property in the frames between the keyframes.

Suggestions and shortcuts for tweening

Follow the suggestions listed here to improve results and productivity while tweening sprites.

- For smoother movements, tween across more frames, increasing the tempo if necessary.

- To achieve some types of motion, you may need to split the sprite and tween the sprites separately. See "Accelerating and decelerating sprites" on page 243.

- To quickly make duplicates, Alt-drag (Windows) or Option-drag (Macintosh) keyframes. This technique is useful when you want the start and end frames to have the same settings. This shortcut also provides a quick way to create a complex path. Insert a single keyframe, drag several duplicates to the proper frames, and then select the various keyframes and set positions on the Stage.

- To extend the sprite and leave the last keyframe in place, Alt-drag (Windows) or Option-drag (Macintosh) a keyframe at the end of a sprite.

- To move many keyframe positions at once, Control-click (Windows) or Command-click (Macintosh) multiple keyframes to select them and then move the sprite on the Stage.

- To make the animation look smoother, use an image editor to blur the edges of bitmaps.

- When tweening sprites that have a series of cast members, consider using a film loop instead. For more information, see "Using film loops" on page 255.

- Turn off all tweening options to make a sprite jump instantly between settings in different keyframes.

Changing tweening settings

To change tweening properties for sprites, you use the Sprite Tweening dialog box. You can turn tweening on and off for certain properties and control the curve of a tweening path and the way the speed changes as a sprite moves. For information on creating tweened animation, see "Tweening the path of a sprite" on page 241.

To change tweening settings:

1 Select a tweened sprite on the Stage or in the Score.

2 Choose Modify > Sprite > Tweening to open the Sprite Tweening dialog box.

   The diagram in the upper left corner shows the sprite's path as specified by the Curvature, Speed, Ease-In, and Ease-Out settings. This does not show the actual path of the sprite, just the type of curve it will follow.

   If the start and end points of the sprite are the same, the diagram is circular, indicating that the sprite travels in a circle when tweened. If the start and end points are not the same, the diagram describes a curved path, indicating that the sprite ends at a point different from the starting point.

3 To change which properties of the sprite are tweened, change the values for Tween.

   A check mark indicates that the property will be tweened. The available properties are Path, Size, Rotation, Skew, Foreground Color, Background Color, and Blend.

4 To change how the sprite curves between positions defined by keyframes, adjust the Curvature slider.

   • Linear makes the sprite move in a straight line between the keyframe positions.

   • Normal makes the sprite follow a curved path inside the keyframe positions.

   • Extreme makes the sprite follow a curved path outside the keyframe positions.

5 To make the sprite move smoothly through start and end frames when it moves in a closed path, select Continuous at Endpoints.

6 To define how the tweened sprite positions change between keyframes, choose an option for Speed. See "Accelerating and decelerating sprites" on page 243.

   • Sharp Changes makes the changes in position occur abruptly.

   • Smooth Changes makes the changes in position occur gradually.

7 To define how tweened sprite positions change over the whole length of the sprite, use the sliders to change the values for Ease-In and Ease-Out.

   • Ease-In defines the percentage of the sprite span through which the sprite accelerates.

   • Ease-Out defines the percentage of the sprite span through which the sprite decelerates.

Switching a sprite's cast members

To show different content while maintaining all other sprite properties, you exchange the cast member assigned to a sprite. This technique is useful when you've tweened a sprite and you decide to use a different cast member. When you exchange the cast member, the tweening path stays the same.

To exchange cast members in the Score:

1 To change a cast member in every frame, select an entire sprite. To change a cast member only in certain frames, select part of a sprite.

   To select part of a sprite, press Alt and click the first frame that you want to select. Then press Control-Alt (Windows) or Option-Alt (Macintosh) and click each additional frame that you want to select.

2 Open the Cast window and select the cast member you want to use next in the animation.

3 Choose Edit > Exchange Cast Members.

If you selected an entire sprite, Director replaces the cast member for the entire sprite.

Before cast members are exchanged, the sprite moves like this.

After cast members are exchanged, the sprite still moves in the same way, but it displays a different cast member.

You can also use Lingo to switch the cast member assigned to a sprite. See "Assigning a cast member to a sprite with Lingo" on page 155.

Editing sprite frames

To change how a sprite is selected and how keyframes are created, you use the Edit Sprite Frames option. Use this option with sprites that have animation you need to adjust frequently; it's especially useful for cell animation in which each frame contains a different cast member in a different position.

Ordinarily, clicking a sprite on the Stage or in the Score selects the entire sprite.

When Edit Sprite Frames is turned on for a certain sprite, clicking the sprite selects a single frame. Any change you make to a tweenable property, such as moving a sprite on the Stage, defines a new keyframe.

To use Edit Sprite Frames:

Select sprites and choose Edit > Edit Sprite Frames. You can also Alt-double-click (Windows) or Option-double-click (Macintosh) a frame within the sprite.

To return sprites to their normal state:

Select sprites and choose Edit > Edit Entire Sprite. You can also Alt-double-click (Windows) or Option-double-click (Macintosh) a frame within the sprite.

Frame-by-frame animation

To create animation that is more complex than is possible with simple tweening, you can use a series of cast members in frame-by-frame animation. Sprites usually refer to only one cast member, but they can refer to different cast members at different times during the life of the sprite.

For example, an animation of a man walking may display several cast members showing the man in different positions. By placing all the images in a sequence within a single sprite, you can work with the animation as if it were a single object.

Single sprite in the Score

Cast members in the sprite

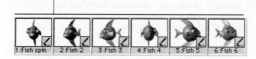

A single sprite can display several cast members.

Sprite animating

Use this approach sparingly for movies that will be downloaded from the Internet, because all cast members must be downloaded before the animation can run. As an alternative to this type of animation, consider using vector shapes, rotation and skewing on bitmap cast members, or a Flash movie.

You can create multiple-cast-member animations in a variety of ways in Director. The following procedure explains a basic approach. The Cast to Time command provides an effective shortcut; see "Shortcuts for animating with multiple cast members" on page 252.

Note: The best way to prepare cast members for use in multiple-cast-member animation is with onion skinning in the Paint window. For more information, see "Using onion skinning" on page 327.

To animate a sprite with multiple cast members:

1 Create a sprite by placing the first cast member in the animation on the Stage in the appropriate frame.

2 Change the length of the sprite as needed.

   Drag the start or end frame in the Score, or enter a new start or end frame number in the Sprite Inspector.

3 Choose View > Display > Cast Member.

   This setting displays the name of the cast member on each sprite. For more information, see "Displaying sprite labels in the Score" on page 130.

4 Choose View > Sprite Labels > Changes Only.

   This setting changes the view of the Score to show the name of each sprite's cast member when it changes. This makes it easy to identify frames where the cast member changes. You may also want to zoom the score to 800% so the frames are wide enough to display the cast member information.

5 Choose Edit > Edit Sprite Frames.

   Edit Sprite Frames makes it easier to select frames within a sprite. See "Editing sprite frames" on page 248.

6 Select the frames in the sprite where you want a different cast member to appear.

7 Open the Cast window and select the cast member you want to use next in the animation.

8 Choose Edit > Exchange Cast Members.

Director replaces the cast member in the selected frame with the cast member selected in the Cast window.

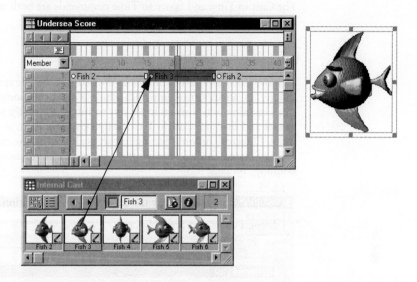

9 Repeat these steps to complete the animation. Choose Edit Entire Sprite when you're done.

Sometimes a series of cast members placed in the Score jumps unexpectedly when you play the movie. This occurs because the cast members' registration points aren't aligned properly. When you exchange cast members, Director places the new cast member's registration point precisely where the previous cast member's registration point was. By default, Director places registration points in the center of a bitmap cast member's bounding rectangle.

For information about aligning registration points, see "Changing registration points" on page 315. You can also align sprites relative to their bounding rectangles. See "Positioning sprites using guides, the grid, or the Align window" on page 135.

Shortcuts for animating with multiple cast members

The Cast to Time and Space to Time commands are both useful shortcuts for animating with multiple cast members.

Using the Cast to Time command

To move a series of cast members to the Score as a single sprite, you use the Modify > Cast to Time command, which is one of the most useful methods for creating animation with multiple cast members. Typically, you create a series of images and then use Cast to Time to quickly place them in the Score as a single sprite. Director's onion skinning feature is also useful for creating and aligning a series of images for use in animation. For more information, see "Using onion skinning" on page 327.

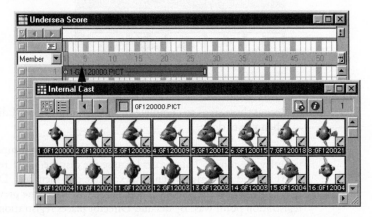

Cast to Time places selected cast members in the Score as a single sprite.

To create a sprite from a sequence of cast members:

1 Select the frame in the Score where you want to place the new sprite.

2 Make the Cast window active.

3 Select the series of cast members to be placed in the new sprite.

4 Choose Modify > Cast to Time, or hold down Alt (Windows) or Option (Macintosh) and drag the cast members to the Stage.

The selected series of cast members becomes a single sprite.

Using the Space to Time command

To move sprites from adjacent channels to a single sprite, you use the Modify > Space to Time command. This method is convenient when you want to arrange several images on the Stage in one frame and then convert them to a single sprite.

Arrange sprites on the Stage in a single frame.

Space to Time converts sprites from adjacent channels to a single sprite.

Onion skinning provides a benefit in the Paint window similar to that provided by Space to Time on the Stage. For more information, see "Using onion skinning" on page 327.

To use the Space to Time command:

1 Choose File > Preferences > Sprite and set Span Duration to 1 frame.

Set the span duration to any setting you like, but Space to Time works best with shorter sprites.

2 Select an empty frame in the Score.

This is usually at the end of the Score.

3 Drag cast members onto the Stage to create sprites where you want them to appear in the animation.

As you position the sprites on the Stage, Director places each sprite in a separate channel. Make sure all the sprites are in consecutive channels.

4 Select all the sprites that are part of the sequence in the Score or on the Stage.

5 Choose Modify > Space to Time.

The Space to Time dialog box appears. Set the number of frames you want between each cast member.

6 Enter an interval.

Director rearranges the sprites so that instead of being arranged from top to bottom in a single frame, they're arranged in sequence from left to right in a single sprite.

Note: Space to Time is a fast way to set up keyframes for a sprite to move along a curve. Arrange the cast members in one frame, choose Modify > Space to Time, and add 10 to 20 cells between each cast member to produce a smooth curve.

Using film loops

A film loop is an animated sequence that you can use like a single cast member. For example, to create an animation of a bird flying across the Stage, you can create a film loop of the sequence of cast members that shows the bird flapping its wings. Instead of using the frame-by-frame technique, you create a sprite containing only the film loop and then animate it across as many frames as you need. When you run the animation, the bird flaps its wings and at the same time moves across the Stage.

You can also use film loops to consolidate Score data. Film loops are especially helpful when you want to reduce the number of sprite channels you're using. You can combine several Score channels into a film loop in a single channel.

To determine if a film loop is cropped or scaled within a sprite's bounding rectangle and to make the film loop repeat or mute its sounds, you use the Film Loop Cast Member properties. See "Setting film loop properties" in Director Help.

Film loops are useful for animating repetitive motions and combining sprites to use fewer channels.

To create a film loop:

1   In the Score, select the sprites you want to turn into a film loop.

    Use sprites in as many channels as you need in film loops—even in the sound channel. Select sequences in all the channels you want to be part of the film loop. You can select sprite fragments if you first select a sprite and choose Edit > Edit Sprite Frames. Control-click (Windows) or Command-click (Macintosh) to select sequences that aren't in adjacent channels.

2   Choose Insert > Film Loop.

    A dialog box appears asking you to name the film loop.

3   Enter a name for the film loop.

    Director stores all the Score data and cast member references as a new film loop cast member.

Note: Drag a selection from the Score to the Cast window to quickly create a film loop cast member in that position.

A film loop behaves just like any other cast member, with a few exceptions:

- When you step through an animation that contains a film loop (either by using Step Forward or Step Backward or by dragging the playback head in the Score), the film loop doesn't animate. Animation occurs only when the movie is running.

- You can't apply ink effects to a film loop. If you want to use ink effects with a film loop, you need to apply them to the sprites that make up the animation before you turn the animation into a film loop.

- Lengthening or shortening a sprite that contains a film loop doesn't affect how fast the film loop plays. It changes the number of times the film loop cycles.

Director provides three other ways of incorporating a completed animation into a movie as a discrete element: you can export it as a digital video (QuickTime or AVI), save and import it as a linked Director movie, or play it in a window in another Director movie.

Note: If you need to edit a film loop and you've deleted the original Score data it was based on, it's possible to restore the Score data for editing. Copy the film loop cast member to the Clipboard, select a cell in the Score, and then paste. Director pastes the original Score data instead of the film loop.

Animating sprites with Lingo

Lingo can create animation regardless of the settings in the Score. This lets you create or modify animation depending on movie conditions.

To move a sprite on the Stage, you use Lingo that controls the sprite's location. See bottom, left, right, and top in the *Lingo Dictionary*.

To animate a sprite by switching the sprite's cast members, change the sprite's member property. See member (sprite property) in the *Lingo Dictionary*.

CHAPTER 9
Navigation and User Interaction

Adding interactivity lets you involve your audience in your movies. Using the keyboard, the mouse, or both, your audience can download content from the Internet, jump to different parts of movies, enter information, move objects, click buttons, and perform many other interactive operations.

Unless made to do otherwise, a movie plays through every frame in the Score from start to finish. Behaviors and Lingo can make the movie jump to a different frame, movie, or URL when a specified event occurs. With Lingo, you can include simple navigation instructions as part of more complex handlers; you can also place navigation Lingo in movie scripts and scripts attached to cast members such as buttons.

There are several other interactive features that you can add to your movie:

- Draggable sprites give your audience the ability to move sprites anywhere on the Stage. You can also create boundaries beyond which sprites cannot move.

- Editable fields are fields in which your audience can enter or edit information.

- Rollovers make certain sprites change in appearance when the mouse pointer passes over them, even if the user has not clicked the mouse. Using rollovers is an excellent way to give your audience feedback based on their actions.

- The cursor (that is, the mouse pointer) can be changed based on criteria you choose. Using Lingo, you can provide animated cursors or specify one of the standard cursors or a bitmap cast member as a cursor image. See cursor (command) and cursor (sprite property) in the *Lingo Dictionary*.

Creating basic navigation controls with behaviors

Director provides behaviors that allows you to create basic navigation controls without knowing Lingo. You can use behaviors to move the playback head to a frame number or marker. You can also stop the playback head at any frame and wait for the user to act.

The following examples explain the basic use of the Hold on Current Frame and Go Next Button behaviors. You can also create your own navigation behaviors or get them from third-party developers.

To use basic navigation behaviors:

1 Create a movie that contains a sprite in frame 1, and at least one marker in a later frame.

2 Choose Window > Library Palette and select the Navigation library.

3 Drag Hold on Current Frame to frame 1 in the script channel.

Typically, you use this behavior in a frame that requires user interaction such as selecting a menu command.

4 Play the movie.

The playback head remains in frame 1 where you attached the behavior. Notice that the movie is still playing, but the playback head remains on the single frame. Use Go Next Button to send the playback head to a new frame and continue playing, as described in the following steps.

5 Stop the movie.

6 Drag the Go Next Button behavior from the Library palette to the sprite in frame 1.

7 Rewind and play the movie again.

The playback head is again stopped in the first frame by the Hold on Current Frame behavior.

8 Click the sprite to which you attached the Go Next Button behavior.

The playback head jumps to the frame containing the next marker and continues playing.

Jumping to locations with Lingo

Lingo's navigation features can make a movie jump to other frames, to other movies, or to Internet movies and Web pages. You can also use Lingo to make a movie appear to pause by looping in one frame or a group of frames.

For details about specifying the locations of frames, markers, and movies, see "Identifying frames with Lingo" on page 74.

Jumping to a different frame

Lingo lets you jump to a different frame in the current movie or in another movie. See individual commands in the *Lingo Dictionary*.

- To jump to a specific frame in the current movie, use the go to command, followed by an identifier for the frame.

  For example, the statement go to "Begin Over" jumps to the frame labeled Begin Over.

- To jump to the beginning of a different movie, use the go to command followed by an identifier for the movie.

  For example, the statement go to movie "Citizen_Kane" goes to the beginning of the movie Citizen_Kane.dir.

- To jump to a frame in a different movie, use the go to command followed by an identifier for the frame and the movie; use frame followed by the frame identifier and movie followed by the name of the movie.

  For example, the statement go to frame "Rosebud" of movie "Citizen_Kane" goes to the frame labeled Rosebud in the movie Citizen_Kane.dir.

  See go in the *Lingo Dictionary*.

Jumping to a URL

Lingo lets you jump to a URL that represents an Internet movie or a Web page.

- To jump to an Internet movie, use the gotoNetMovie command.

  For example, the statement gotoNetMovie "http://www.yourserver.com/movies/movie1.dcr" retrieves and plays the movie named movie1.dcr. See gotoNetMovie in the *Lingo Dictionary*.

- To jump to a Web page, use the gotoNetPage command.

  For example, the statement gotoNetPage "http://www.yourserver.com/movies/intro.html" displays the Web page named intro.html in a browser window. See gotoNetPage in the *Lingo Dictionary*.

Looping in a group of frames

Looping within frames lets you create animation that recycles or makes a movie appear to pause. Such looping is useful for allowing a network operation to complete before the movie proceeds. Looping a movie by jumping from the current frame back to the first frame in the sequence can create a recycling animation effect.

- To loop within one segment of the Score, use the statement go loop to return to the first marker to the left of the frame containing the go loop statement. If there is no previous marker, the playback head jumps to frame 1.

- To pause a movie in one frame but keep it playing so the movie can react to events, use the statement go to the frame to loop in the current frame.

- To resume playing a movie that is looping in one frame, use the statement go to the frame + 1.

Jumping away and returning to the original location

You may want a movie to jump to a different frame or a separate movie and then return to the original frame. For example, at a Web site that describes the weather, you could jump to a movie segment that explains a weather term, and then return to the original location.

To jump away and return to the original location:

Use the play and play done commands.

The play command branches a movie to another frame, another movie, or a specified frame in another movie. The play done command remembers the original frame and returns to it without requiring that you specify where to return.

Use the play and play done commands in these situations:

- When the movie you want to play does not have instructions about where to return.

- When you want to play several movies sequentially from a single script. When one movie finishes, Lingo returns to the script that issued the play command.

- When you want to put one sequence inside another sequence and easily return to where you were in the outer sequence.

- When you want to jump to one loop from several different locations.

See play and play done in the *Lingo Dictionary*.

Detecting mouse clicks with Lingo

Users can click the mouse button in several ways, each of which Lingo can detect. The following are ways that you can use Lingo to detect what the user does with the mouse. See individual properties and functions in the *Lingo Dictionary*.

- To determine the last place the mouse was clicked, use the clickLoc() function.
- To determine the last active sprite (a sprite with a script attached) that the user clicked, use the clickOn function.
- To determine whether the last two clicks were a double-click, use the doubleClick function.
- To determine the time since the mouse was last clicked, use the lastClick() function.
- To determine whether the mouse button is pressed, check the mouseDown property.
- To determine whether the mouse button is released, check the mouseUp property.
- To determine whether the user presses the right mouse button (Windows) or Control+click (Macintosh), check the rightMouseDown property.
- To determine whether the user releases the right mouse button (Windows) or Control+click (Macintosh), check the rightMouseUp property.

For example, this handler checks whether the user double-clicked the mouse button and, if so, runs the handler openWindow:

```
on mouseDown
    if the doubleClick = TRUE then openWindow
end
```

Making sprites editable and draggable

Using the Property Inspector, you can make a sprite editable, draggable, or both while your movie is running. See "Displaying sprite properties in the Property Inspector" on page 94.

To make a sprite draggable on the Stage:

Click the Moveable button in the Property Inspector.

To make a text sprite editable:

Click the Editable button in the Property Inspector.

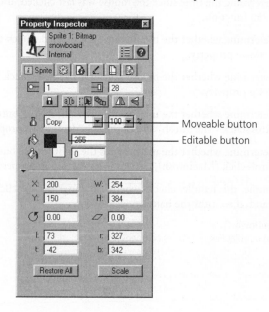

Making sprites editable or moveable with Lingo

Lingo can make sprites editable or moveable regardless of the settings in the Score. You can also use Lingo to constrain a moveable sprite to a certain region. For example, you can create a draggable slider with an indicator that moves across a gauge. For more information, see individual properties and functions in the *Lingo Dictionary*.

- To make a text sprite editable with Lingo, set the text sprite's editable property to TRUE. For best results, set this property in a script attached to the sprite or the frame where the sprite is located.

- To make a sprite moveable with Lingo, set the moveableSprite sprite property to TRUE. For best results, set this property in a script attached to the sprite or the frame where the sprite is located.

- To restrict the registration point of a moveable sprite so it stays within the bounding rectangle of a second sprite, use the constraint sprite property.

- To constrain a sprite along a horizontal or vertical path, use the constrainH() or constrainV() function.

Checking which text is under the pointer with Lingo

Lingo can detect which text component in a text or field cast member is currently under the mouse pointer. See individual properties and functions in the *Lingo Dictionary*.

Use Lingo that applies to text and field cast members as follows:

- To detect which character in a text or field cast member is under the pointer, use the pointToChar() function.

- To detect which item in a text or field cast member is under the pointer, use the pointToItem() function.

- To detect which word in a text or field cast member is under the pointer, use the pointToWord() function.

- To detect which paragraph in a text or field cast member is under the pointer, use the pointToParagraph() function.

Use Lingo that applies only to text cast members as follows: To detect whether a specific point is in a hyperlink within a text cast member and is under the pointer, use the pointInHyperlink() function.

Use Lingo that applies only to field cast members as follows:

- To detect which line in a field is under the pointer, use the mouseLine function.

- To detect which word in a field is under the pointer, use the mouseWord function.

Responding to rollovers with Lingo

You often want some action to occur when the user rolls the mouse pointer over a sprite or a particular place on the Stage. You can use Lingo to specify how the movie responds to such rollovers.

Director provides several event handlers that run when the pointer rolls over a sprite. Messages for each of these events are sent to the sprite script, the script of the cast member, the frame script, and then the movie script. See individual event handlers and functions in the *Lingo Dictionary*.

- To set up Lingo that runs when the mouse pointer enters a sprite's bounding rectangle, place the Lingo in an on mouseEnter event handler.

- To set up Lingo that runs when the mouse pointer leaves a sprite's bounding rectangle, place the Lingo in an on mouseLeave event handler.

- To set up Lingo that runs when the user clicks a sprite, rolls the pointer off the sprite, and then releases the mouse button, place the Lingo in an on mouseUpOutside event handler.

- To set up Lingo that runs when the mouse pointer is within a sprite's bounding rectangle when the playback head enters the frame that contains the sprite, place the Lingo in an on mouseWithin event handler.

  The mouseWithin event can occur repeatedly as long as the mouse pointer remains inside the sprite.

- To determine whether the cursor is over a specific sprite, use the rollOver() function.

Finding mouse pointer locations with Lingo

Determining where the mouse pointer is on the Stage is a common need in Director.

To determine the mouse pointer's horizontal and vertical positions, use the mouseH() and mouseV() functions. See mouseH and mouseV in the *Lingo Dictionary*.

The mouseV() function returns the distance, in pixels, between the mouse pointer and the upper left corner of the Stage. The mouseH() function returns the distance, in pixels, between the mouse pointer and the upper left corner of the Stage.

The statements put the mouseH and put the mouseV display the mouse pointer's location in the Message window.

For example, this handler directs the Message window to display the distance (in pixels) between the pointer and the upper left corner of the Stage:

```
on exitFrame
    put the mouseH
    put the mouseV
    go to the frame
end
```

Checking keys with Lingo

Lingo can detect the last key the user pressed. See individual properties and functions in the *Lingo Dictionary*.

- To obtain the ANSI value of the last key that was pressed, use the key() function.

- To obtain the keyboard's numerical (or ASCII) value for the last key pressed, use the keyCode() function.

A common place for using key and keyCode is in an on keyDown handler. This instructs Lingo to check the value of key only when a key is actually pressed. For example, the following handler in a frame script sends the playback head to the next marker whenever the user presses Enter (Windows) or Return (Macintosh):

```
on keyDown
    if the key = RETURN then go to marker (1)
end
```

Equivalent cross-platform keys

Because of inherent differences between Windows and Macintosh keyboards, keys on Windows and Macintosh computers don't always correspond directly.

This can create confusion, because Lingo often uses the same term to refer to corresponding keys on Windows and Macintosh computers, even though the key's name differs on the two platforms.

The following table lists Lingo elements that refer to specific keys and the keys they represent on each platform.

Lingo term	Windows key	Macintosh key
RETURN	Enter	Return
commandDown	Control	Command
optionDown	Alt	Option
controlDown	Control	Control
ENTER	Enter key on the numeric keypad (during authoring, pressing Enter starts playing the movie)	Enter key on the numeric keypad (during authoring, pressing Enter starts playing the movie)
BACKSPACE	Backspace	Delete

Identifying keys on different keyboards

Characters can vary on different keyboards. Avoid possible confusion by identifying a character by its ASCII value. See individual properties and functions in the *Lingo Dictionary*.

- To obtain a character's ASCII value, use the charToNum() function.

  For example, this statement finds the ASCII value for the letter *A* and displays it in the Message window:

  ```
  put charToNum("A")
  -- 65
  ```

- To find out which character corresponds to an ASCII value, use the numToChar() function.

  For example, this statement finds the character that corresponds to the ASCII value 65. The result is the letter *A*:

  ```
  put numToChar(65)
  -- A
  ```

About animated color cursors

Director supports animated cursors. You can use any 8-bit bitmap source in your Director cast as an image in the cursor animation, automatically scale images, and generate masks for 16 x16 pixel and 32 x 32 pixel cursors. (Macintosh computers don't support 32 x 32 pixel cursors.)

An animated cursor consists of a series of bitmap cast members. Each bitmap cast member is a frame of the cursor. You can control the rate at which Director plays the frames of an animated cursor. Using the Cursor Properties Editor, you designate one or more bitmap cast members as frames of a single cursor cast member.

Xtras that support animated cursors

The Director installation program places two animated color cursor files in the Media Support folder within the Director application's Xtras folder. The specific files depend on the platform you are using.

Windows	PowerPC	Purpose
Cursor Options.x32	Cursor Options	This file supports the creation of cursors while you author movies in Director. Do not distribute this file with projectors; it is not licensed for redistribution.
Cursor Asset.x32	Cursor Asset	Distribute this file with any movies or projectors that you create using the animated color cursors.

Requirements for animated color cursors

All cast members used for an animated color cursor must meet certain criteria:

- They must be bitmap cast members.
- They must have a color depth of 8 bits (256 colors).
- They must use only the first eight or the last eight colors that are in the standard System - Win palette. These provide the most predictable results when playing back across platforms. Other colors may not appear correctly.

The cast members need not be in sequence in the cast, and they need not be in the same cast.

A cursor's maximum size depends on the computer:

- In Windows 95 and 98, you can create cursors of either 16 x 16 pixels or 32 x 32 pixels (almost always 32 x 32 pixels, but some video cards may support only 16 x 16 pixels).
- In Windows NT, you can create cursors of 16 x 16 pixels or 32 x 32 pixels.
- On the Macintosh, you can create cursors of 16 x 16 pixels.

When you are creating cursors in the Cursor Properties Editor, Director dims any size option that is not available on your computer.

The 16 x16 pixel and 32 x 32 pixel sizes are the maximum sizes at which Director can display a cursor on the screen. The actual cast members you specify for the cursor can be larger than the maximum, and Director will scale the cast members to the appropriate size, maintaining the aspect ratio as it scales them. If you specify a cast member smaller than the maximum size, Director displays the cast member at its original size, without scaling. For example, if you select a maximum size of 16 x 16 pixels and then specify a cursor that is 12 x 14 pixels, Director displays the cursor at 12 x 14 pixels.

Creating an animated color cursor cast member

Before creating an animated color cursor cast member, make sure that the cast members you want to use in the cursor are stored in a cast linked to the movie. See "Managing external casts" on page 114.

To create an animated color cursor cast member:

1 Choose Insert > Media Element > Cursor.

Director opens the Cursor Properties Editor, which you use to set up the cursor.

2 From the Cast pop-up menu, choose the cast that contains the cast member you want to add as a frame in your cursor.

The cast members used for a single cursor can be stored in different casts.

3 Use the < and > buttons to find the cast member you want.

As you click the buttons, the preview shows a thumbnail of the selected cast member. If you do not see the cast member you want, the cast member probably isn't a bitmap or has a color depth greater than 8 bits (256 colors). The Cursor Properties Editor shows only bitmaps that can be used in an animated color cursor.

You can also type a cast member number in the Member box and press Tab; Director will select the cast member that has that number or the cast member with the number closest to it.

4 Select the cast member you want and click Add.

You see the cast member in the Cursor Frames preview area. The Frame X of Y field shows where the cast member falls within an animated series of cursor frames.

5 Repeat steps 2 through 4 until you have added all the cast members for the cursor.

In the Cursor Frames area, you can use the < and > buttons to review the order of the cursor frames. Click the Remove button to delete the currently selected frame from the cursor (this deletes the cast member only from the cursor animation, not from the cast).

6 In the Interval field, specify the number of milliseconds that elapse between each frame of the cursor animation.

This interval affects all frames of the cursor and cannot vary for different frames. The cursor frame rate is independent of the frame rate set for the movie using the tempo channel or the puppetTempo Lingo command.

Note: By inserting the same bitmap in multiple frames of the cursor, you can create the illusion of variable-rate cursor animation.

7 In the Hotspot Position fields, specify the location of the mouse pointer's active point.

Director uses this point to track the mouse pointer's position on the screen. For example, Director uses this point's location when it returns values for the mouseH() and mouseV() functions. The hotspot also determines the point where a rollover occurs.

The first field specifies the horizontal (*x*) location, and the second field specifies the vertical (*y*) location. The upper left pixel is location 0,0. In a 16 x 16 pixel cursor, the lower right pixel is location 15,15. You can't enter a point that is beyond the bounds of the cursor.

8 Click one of the Size options to specify the maximum size of the cursor.

If a Size option is dimmed, your computer does not allow you to create cursors of that size.

9 Select the Automask option if you want the white pixels of the cursor frames to be transparent.

Note: The Automask option makes all white pixels transparent. If you want some white pixels to be opaque, you can't use white for those pixels, but you can achieve the same effect by instead using the lightest shade of gray available in the system palette.

10 Click OK to close the Cursor Properties Editor.

After you create a cursor cast member, use Lingo to switch to the cursor in a movie, as shown in the next section.

Using an animated color cursor in a movie

Once you have added an animated color cursor to the cast, use Lingo to switch to the animated cursor just as you would any other cursor. You can set up an animated cursor as the movie's cursor or a sprite's cursor.

To switch to an animated color cursor, use this command:

cursor (member *whichCursorCastMember*)

For *whichCursorCastMember*, substitute a cast member name (surrounded by quotation marks) or a cast member number. For example, this sprite script changes the cursor to the cast member named myCursor when the cursor is over the sprite:

```
on mouseEnter
    cursor (member "myCursor")
end
```

To reset the cursor to the regular arrow cursor, specify a cursor type of -1 (and do not use parentheses). This sample sprite script resets the cursor:

```
on mouseLeave
    cursor -1
end
```

Note: Do not place an animated color cursor cast member on the Stage.

For more information, see cursor (command) in the *Lingo Dictionary*.

10

CHAPTER 10
Movies in a Window

Director can play several movies simultaneously by creating windows that additional movies can play in. A movie in a window (MIAW) is a distinct Director movie that retains all its interactivity.

You can use a MIAW simply to play another movie in a separate window while the main movie plays on the Stage. In addition, movies in windows and the main movie can communicate and interact with each other. This lets you create a variety of interactive features, such as an interactive portfolio, a control panel for a second movie or digital video, or a status display window.

Here's the typical workflow for using a movie in a window:

- Create and set up the window.
- Assign a movie to the window.
- Open the window and play the movie.
- Delete the window when the reason for playing the movie no longer applies.

When creating a MIAW, first decide how you want it to behave and work. For example, decide how you want to display it, how users should be able to move the window around the screen and dismiss it, and how the window should appear. You can specify the window's size and whether the window is visible, has a frame and title, or is in front of or behind other windows on the screen.

You can create and control movies in windows using behaviors from the Behavior Library or by writing your own Lingo scripts.

Shockwave doesn't support MIAWs. Use MIAWs only with movies that you intend to distribute as projectors (see "About distribution formats" on page 438 and "About projectors" on page 449). However, you can use Lingo to have a Shockwave movie target a URL in a browser window. See "Jumping to a URL" on page 259.

Creating a MIAW using Lingo

In Lingo, you create a MIAW by specifying a window's rectangle on the Stage and then specifying the file name for the movie assigned to the window. You can also make the window visible, change its type, set its title, and set the window's size and location.

The simplest way to create a MIAW is to simply open a window for an existing movie.

To create a new MIAW by opening a window for an existing movie:

Follow this example:

```
open window("movieName")
```

This statement creates a window, assigns it the movie movieName, and opens it on the Stage at the location where movieName was originally authored. At this point, you can use the commands discussed in the rest of this chapter to set various attributes of the MIAW.

You can also use a movie's file name as the argument for the open window command. This approach assigns that movie to a window and instructs Director to use the file name as the window title.

To create a MIAW using a file name and the Open Window command:

Follow this example:

```
on beginNewMovie theMovie
    global newWindow
    set newWindow to window theMovie
    set newWindow.titleVisible to FALSE
    open newWindow
end beginNewMovie
```

This version of the handler uses the movie's rectangle to determine the size of the window's rectangle.

You can also assign a MIAW to a variable, which makes it easier to write the handler and reuse it.

To assign a MIAW to a variable:

Follow this example:

```
on beginNewMovie theMovie
    global newWindow
    set newWindow to window "The Big Picture"
    set newWindow.rect to rect(0, 0, 250, 200)
    set newWindow.filename to theMovie
    set newWindow.titleVisible to FALSE
    open newWindow
end beginNewMovie
```

The variable newWindow contains a new window named The Big Picture. The handler specifies the coordinates of a rectangle, instructs Director to use that rectangle as the window named The Big Picture, and then assigns a movie file to the window. The handler makes the title bar at the top of the window invisible and then opens the window.

Opening and closing a MIAW

Use the commands in this section to open and close movies in windows. For more information, see the *Lingo Dictionary*.

Opening a MIAW

To open a MIAW, use the open window command.

Unless Lingo explicitly preloads the movie, Director doesn't load the movie into memory until the window is first opened, which can cause a noticeable pause. To load the first frame of the movie, use preLoadMovie.

You can specify other window characteristics before or after you open the window.

Closing a MIAW

You can close the window for a MIAW but leave the movie in memory, or you can close the MIAW and remove the movie from memory when it's no longer in use.

- If you leave a MIAW in memory, you'll get better performance if the window is reopened; however, the movie still takes up space in memory. You may want to use this option if you expect a MIAW to be reopened after it initially runs, or if other windows or global variables refer to the MIAW.

- If you remove a MIAW from memory, performance will slow down if the window is reopened, because the movie has to reload; however, memory is freed up until the movie is reloaded. You may want to use this option if you don't expect a MIAW to be reopened after it initially runs, or if you want to optimize memory on the computer running the MIAW.

To close a MIAW but keep it in memory:

Use the close window command. After the window is closed, the window becomes invisible, but the movie continues playing. See close window in the *Lingo Dictionary*.

To close a MIAW and remove it from memory:

Use the forget window command. The window is closed and the movie is removed from memory. Use this command only if no other window or global variables still refer to the MIAW. See forget window in the *Lingo Dictionary*.

Setting the window type for a MIAW

You can choose from seven styles of windows:

- Four document window styles: the standard document window, a document window with a zoom box and variable resize box, a document window with the variable resize box disabled, and a document window without a resize box

- An alert box style

- A plain box style

- A curved-border style

To specify the window type for a MIAW:

Assign a value for the windowType property.

Different numerical values for the windowType property specify different types of window styles. When you don't specify a window type, Director uses a moveable, sizable window without a zoom box and with a title bar, which is type -1. You can set the title property only for windows of type -1.

In most cases, it's best to specify window settings before you actually open the window, to avoid delays as the window redraws.

See windowType in the *Lingo Dictionary*.

Setting the window size and location for a MIAW

Setting the screen coordinates for a MIAW lets you control how large the window is and where it appears. Setting the coordinates before the movie appears controls the initial position of the window; setting them after the window appears moves the window.

To specify the screen coordinates for a MIAW:

Set the rect property to the coordinates of the location where you want the window to appear, choosing from the following options:

- Define the coordinates as a rectangle in the order left, top, right, and bottom, as in this statement:

  ```
  set window.rect "Sample" = [0, 0, 200, 300]
  ```

- Use the rect() function to define the window rectangle's four coordinates, as in these statements:

  ```
  set aRect = rect(0, 0, 200, 300)
  set window.rect "Sample" = aRect
  ```

  For convenience, assign the coordinates to a variable and then use the variable in the statements you write.

See rect(window) and rect() in the *Lingo Dictionary*.

Cropping and scaling a MIAW

You can use Lingo to crop or scale a MIAW.

To crop a MIAW:

Set the rect window property to an area smaller than the MIAW. See rect(window) in the *Lingo Dictionary*.

To scale a MIAW:

Set the drawRect property to coordinates smaller than the MIAW's original size and apply the position to the window, as shown in the following example:

```
set aRect = [0, 0, 200, 300]
set window("Sample").drawRect = aRect -- sets window size to 200 x 300
set window("Sample").drawRect = aRect/2 -- scales the window to half its original size
```

When the drawRect property specifies a window rectangle that is smaller than the movie, the window appears in the upper left corner, and the movie is compressed to fit within the window. See drawRect in the *Lingo Dictionary*.

Controlling the appearance of a MIAW

You can use Lingo commands and properties to control whether a window is visible, is in front of or behind other windows, and has a title. For more information, see the *Lingo Dictionary*.

To specify whether the window is visible:

Set the window's visible window property. To avoid a potential time lag when the window opens, use preLoadMovie to preload the movie before it's needed and then open the window when it needs to be visible. See visible (window property) in the *Lingo Dictionary*.

To control whether a movie appears in front of or behind other windows:

Use the moveToFront and moveToBack commands. See moveToFront and moveToBack in the *Lingo Dictionary*.

To assign a title to a window:

Set the title window property. See title in the *Lingo Dictionary*.

Listing the current movies in windows

The windowList property displays a list of all known MIAWs in the main movie.

For example, the following statement displays a list of current MIAW names in the Message window.

put the windowList

See windowList in the *Lingo Dictionary*.

Controlling interaction between MIAWs

Movies can interact with each other by sending Lingo messages back and forth. This lets movies share current values for variables, share information about current conditions, and send each other Lingo instructions.

Global variables can be declared in the main movie (the Stage) or in a MIAW. No matter where they are declared, they are available to the main movie and to all movies playing in windows. For more information about global variables, see "Using global variables" on page 201.

At times, you may want only one movie to respond when the user clicks the mouse or types on the keyboard. To control when Director can respond to any events that occur outside a window, set the modal window property. When a window's modal property is set to TRUE, no other window, including the Stage, can respond to events such as mouse clicks and keystrokes.

To have a MIAW send a Lingo statement:

Use the tell command. See tell in the *Lingo Dictionary*.

When using the tell command, be sure to specify the MIAW to which the instructions are directed. When you want a MIAW to send a Lingo message to the main movie, use the stage to refer to the main movie. For example, the statement tell the stage to go to "Help" instructs the main movie to go to the frame marked Help in the main movie.

To have a MIAW open another MIAW:

In Lingo, only the main movie (the Stage) can open a MIAW. Therefore, to have one MIAW open another MIAW, you must use the tell command in the running MIAW to tell the Stage to open another MIAW.

For example, this statement in a MIAW tells the Stage movie to open the movie menuMovie in its own window:

```
tell the stage to open window "menuMovie"
```

Controlling events involving MIAWs

Lingo provides event handlers for typical events that can occur while a MIAW is playing, such as the movement of a window by the user. Such a handler is a good place for instructions that you want to run in response to an event that involves a window.

For example, to cause a sound to play whenever the user closes a MIAW, use the queue() and play() functions in an on closeWindow handler in a movie script within the movie that plays in the window. The on closeWindow handler will run whenever the MIAW that contains the handler closes.

See "Movie in a Window" in the "Lingo by Feature" section in the *Lingo Dictionary*.

CHAPTER 11
Parent Scripts
. . . .

Parent scripts provide the advantages of object-oriented programming within Director. These advantages include the ability to write less code and use simpler logic to accomplish tasks in Lingo. You can use parent scripts to generate script objects that behave and respond similarly yet can still operate independently of each other.

Lingo can create multiple copies (or instances) of a parent script. Each instance of a parent script is called a child object. You can create child objects on demand as the movie plays. Director doesn't limit the number of child objects that can be created from the same parent script. You can create as many child objects as the computer's memory can support.

Director can create multiple child objects from the same parent script, just as Director can create multiple instances of a behavior for different sprites. You can think of a parent script as a template and of child scripts as implementations of the parent template.

This chapter describes the basics of how to write parent scripts, and create and use child objects, and it provides script examples. It doesn't teach fundamental object-oriented programming concepts; however, to use parent scripts and child objects successfully, you must understand object-oriented programming principles. For an introduction to the basics of object-oriented programming, see one of the many third-party books on that subject.

Similarity with other object-oriented languages

If you are familiar with an object-oriented programming language such as Java or C++, you may already understand the concepts that underlie parent scripting but know them by different names.

Terms that Director uses to describe parent scripts and child objects correspond to the following common object-oriented programming terms:

Parent scripts correspond to classes.

Child objects correspond to instances.

Property variables correspond to instance variables or member variables.

Handlers correspond to methods.

Ancestor scripts correspond to the Super class or base class.

Parent script and child object basics

A parent script is a set of handlers and properties that will define a child object; it is not a child object itself. A child object is a self-contained, independent instance of a parent script. Children of the same parent have identical handlers and properties, so child objects in the same group can have similar responses to events and messages.

Typically, parent scripts are used to build child objects that make it easier to organize movie logic. These child objects are especially useful when a movie requires the same logic to be run several times concurrently with different parameters. You can also add a child object to a sprite's scriptInstanceList or the actorList as a way to control animation.

Because all the child objects of the same parent script have identical handlers, those child objects respond to events in similar ways. However, because each child object maintains independent values for the properties defined in the parent script, each child object can behave differently than its sibling objects—even though they are instances of the same parent script.

For example, you can create a parent script that defines child objects that are editable text fields, each with its own property settings, text, and color, regardless of the other text fields' settings. By changing the values of properties in specific child objects, you can change any of these characteristics as the movie plays without affecting the other child objects based on the same parent script.

Similarly, a child object can have a property set to either TRUE or FALSE regardless of that property's setting in sibling child objects.

Differences between child objects and behaviors

While child objects and behaviors are similar in that they both can have multiple instances, they have some important differences as well. The main difference between child objects and behaviors is that behaviors are associated with locations in the Score because they are attached to sprites. Behavior objects are automatically created from initializers stored in the Score as the playback head moves from frame to frame and encounters sprites with attached behaviors. In contrast, child objects from parent scripts must be created explicitly by a handler.

Behaviors and child objects differ in how they become associated with sprites. Director automatically associates a behavior with the sprite that the behavior is attached to, but you must explicitly associate a child object with a sprite.

Ancestor basics

Parent scripts can declare ancestors, which are additional scripts whose handlers and properties a child object can call on and use.

Ancestor scripting lets you create a set of handlers and properties that you can use and reuse for multiple parent scripts.

A parent script makes another parent script its ancestor by assigning the script to its ancestor property. For example, the following statement makes the script What_Everyone_Does an ancestor to the parent script in which the statement occurs:

```
set ancestor to new(script "What_Everyone_Does")
```

When handlers and properties are not defined in a child object, Director searches for the handler or property in the child's ancestors, starting with the child's parent script. If a handler is called or a property is tested and the parent script contains no definition for it, Director searches for a definition in the ancestor script. If a definition exists in the ancestor script, that definition is used.

A child object can have only one ancestor at a time, but that ancestor script can have its own ancestor, which can also have an ancestor, and so on. This lets you create a series of parent scripts whose handlers are available to a child object.

See ancestor in the *Lingo Dictionary*.

Writing a parent script

A parent script contains the Lingo needed to create child objects and define their possible actions and properties. First you need to decide how you want the child objects to behave. Then you can write a parent script that does the following:

- Optionally declares any appropriate property variables; these variables represent properties for which each child object can contain a value independent of other child objects. See "Parent script and child object basics" on page 280.

- Sets up the initial values of the child objects' properties and variables in the on new handler.

- Contains additional handlers that control the child objects' actions.

Declaring property variables

Each child object created from the same parent script initially contains the same values for its property variables. A property variable's value belongs only to the child object it's associated with. Each property variable and its value persists as long as the child object exists. The initial value for the property variable is typically set in the on new handler; if it's not set, the initial value is VOID.

To declare a property variable:

Use the property keyword at the beginning of the parent script. See property in the *Lingo Dictionary*.

To set and test property variables from outside the child object:

Set and test property variables in the same way you would any other property in Lingo, by using the syntax the *propertyName* of *whichObject* or *whichObject.propertyName*.

This statement sets the speed property of the object car1:

car1.speed = 55

Creating the on new handler

Each parent script typically uses an on new handler. This handler creates the new child object when another script issues a new(script *parentScriptName*) command, which tells the specified parent script to create a child object from itself. The on new handler in the parent script can also set the child object's initial property values, if you want. The on new handler always starts with the phrase on new, followed by the me variable and any arguments being passed to the new child object. See new() in the *Lingo Dictionary*.

The following is a sample on new handler:

```
property spriteNum

on new me, aSpriteNum
    spriteNum = aSpriteNum
    return me
end
```

Adding other handlers

You determine a child object's behavior by including in the parent script the handlers that produce the desired behavior. For example, you could add a handler to the code above to make the sprite change color.

The following parent script defines a value for the property spriteNum and contains a second handler that will change the forecolor property of the sprite.

```
property spriteNum

on new me, aSpriteNum
    spriteNum = aSpriteNum
    return me
end

on changeColor me
    spriteNum.forecolor = random(255)
end
```

Using the me variable

Typically, one parent script creates many child objects, and each child object contains more than one handler. The term me is a special parameter variable. It must always be the first parameter variable stated in every handler definition in a parent script.

The me variable tells the handlers in the child object that they are to operate on the properties of that object and not on the properties of any other child object. This way, when a handler within a child object refers to properties, the handler will use its own child object's values for those properties.

This is why it is always important to define me as the first parameter for parent scripts and to pass the same parameter if you need to call other handlers in the same parent script, since these will be the handlers in each of the script's child objects.

When referring to properties defined in ancestor scripts, you must use the me parameter as the source of the reference. This is because the property, while defined in the ancestor script, is nevertheless a property of the child object. For example, these statements both use me to refer to an object and access properties defined in an ancestor of the object:

```
--access ancestor property
x = me.y
```

or

```
x = the y of me
```

Because the me variable is present in each handler of the child object, it indicates that all the handlers control that same child object.

See me in the *Lingo Dictionary*.

Creating a child object

Child objects exist entirely in RAM; they are not saved with a movie. Only parent and ancestor scripts exist on disk.

To create a new child object, you use the new function and assign the child object a variable name or position in a list so you can identify and work with it later.

To create a child object and assign it to a variable, use the syntax:

set *variableName* = new(script "*scriptName*", *argument1*, *argument2*, *argument3*...)

where *scriptName* is the name of the parent script and *argument1*, *argument2*, *argument3*... are any arguments you are passing to the child object's on new handler.

The new() function creates a child object whose ancestor is *scriptName*. It then calls the on new handler in the child object with the specified arguments.

You can issue a new statement from anywhere in a movie. You can customize the child object's initial settings by changing the values of the arguments passed with the new statement.

Each child object requires only enough memory to record the current values of its properties and variables and a reference to the parent script. Because of this, in most cases you can create and maintain as many child objects as you require.

You can produce additional child objects from the same parent script by issuing additional new statements.

To create child objects without immediately initializing their property variables, use the rawNew() function. The rawNew() function does this by creating the child object without calling the parent script's on new handler. In situations where large numbers of child objects are needed, rawNew() allows you to create the objects ahead of time and defer the assignment of property values until each object is needed.

This statement creates a child object from the parent script Car without initializing its property variables and assigns it to the variable car1:

car1 = script("Car").rawNew()

To initialize the properties of one of these child objects, call its on new handler:

car1.new

Checking child object properties

You can check the values of specific property variables in individual child objects by using a simple *objectName.PropertyName* syntax. For example, this statement assigns the variable x the value of the carSpeed property of the child object in the variable car1:

x = car1.carSpeed

Querying object properties from outside the objects themselves can be useful for getting information about groups of objects, such as the average speed of all the car objects in a racing game. You might also use the properties of one object to help determine the behavior of other objects that are dependent on it.

In addition to checking the properties you assign, you can check whether a child object contains a specific handler or find out which parent script an object came from. This is useful when you have objects that come from parent scripts that are similar but that have subtle differences.

For example, you may want to create a scenario in which one of several parent scripts might be used to create a child object. You can then determine which parent script a particular child object came from by using the script() function, which returns the name of an object's parent script.

These statements check whether the object car1 was created from the parent script named Car:

```
if car1.script = script("Car") then
    beep
end if
```

You can also get a list of the handlers in a child object by using the handlers() function, or check whether a particular handler exists in a child object by using the handler() function.

This statement places a list of the handlers in the child object car1 into the variable myHandlerList:

myHandlerList = car1.handlers()

The list would look something like this:

[#start, #accelerate, #stop]

These statements use the handler() function to check whether the handler on accelerate exists in the child object car1:

```
if car1.handler(#accelerate) then
    put "The child object car1 contains the handler named on accelerate."
end if
```

Removing a child object

You can remove a child object from a movie by setting all variables that contain a reference to the child object to another value. If the child object has been assigned to a list, such as actorList, you must also remove the child object from the list. (The actorList property is useful for tracking and manipulating the child objects in a movie. For details, see "Using actorList" on page 288.)

To remove a child object and the variables that refer to it:

Set each variable to VOID.

Director deletes the child object when there are no more references to it. For example, if ball1 contains the only reference to a specific child object, then the statement set ball1 = VOID deletes the object from memory.

To remove an object from actorList:

Use the delete command to delete the item from the list. See delete in the *Lingo Dictionary*.

Using scriptInstanceList

You can use the scriptInstanceList property to dynamically add new behaviors to a sprite. Normally, scriptInstanceList is the list of behavior instances created from the behavior initializers defined in the Score. If you add child objects created from parent scripts to this list, the child objects receive the messages sent to other behaviors.

For example, this statement adds a child object to the scriptInstanceList property of sprite 10:

```
add sprite(10).scriptInstanceList, new(script "rotation", 10)
```

This is a possible parent script that the statement refers to:

```
-- parent script "rotation"
property spriteNum

on new me, aSpriteNum
  spriteNum = aSpriteNum
  return me
end

on prepareFrame me
    sprite(spriteNum).rotation = sprite(spriteNum).rotation + 1
end
```

When a child object is added to scriptInstanceList, you must initialize the child object's spriteNum property. Typically you do this from a parameter passed in to the on new handler.

Note: The beginSprite message is not sent to dynamically added child objects.

Using actorList

Lingo can set up a special list of child objects (or any other objects) that receives its own message each time the playback head enters a frame or the updateStage command updates the Stage.

The special list is actorList, which contains only objects that have been explicitly added to the list. See actorList in the *Lingo Dictionary*.

The message is the stepFrame message that is sent only when the playback head enters a frame or the updateStage command is used. See on stepFrame in the *Lingo Dictionary*.

Objects in actorList receive a stepFrame message instead of an enterFrame message at each frame. If the objects have an on stepFrame handler available, the Lingo in the on stepFrame handler runs each time the playback head enters a new frame or the updateStage command updates the Stage.

Some possible uses of the actorList and stepFrame are to animate child objects that are used as sprites or to update a counter that tracks the number of times the playback head enters a frame.

An on enterFrame handler could achieve the same results, but the actorList property and on stepFrame handler are optimized for performance in Director. Objects in the actorList respond to stepFrame messages more efficiently than to an enterFrame message or to a custom message sent after an updateStage command.

To add an object to actorList, **use the following statement:**

add the actorList, theObject

The object's on stepFrame handler in its parent or ancestor script will then run automatically each time the playback head advances. The object will be passed as the first argument (that is, the me argument) to the on stepFrame handler.

Director doesn't clear the contents of actorList when branching to another movie, which can cause unpredictable behavior in the new movie. If you don't want child objects in the current movie to be carried over into the new movie, insert a statement that clears actorList in the on prepareMovie handler of the new movie.

To clear child objects from actorList:

Set actorList to [ ], which is an empty list.

For more information, see actorList and stepFrame in the *Lingo Dictionary*

Creating timeout objects

You can create a timeout object—a script object that acts like a timer and sends a message when the timer expires. This is useful for scenarios that require specific things to happen at regular time intervals or after a particular amount of time has elapsed.

Timeout objects can send messages that call handlers inside child objects or in movie scripts. You create a timeout object by using the new() function. You must specify a name for the object, a handler to be called, and the frequency with which you want the handler to be called. Once a timeout object is created, Director keeps a list of currently active timeout objects, called timeOutList.

To create timeout objects, use the following syntax:

variableName = timeOut(*"theName"*).new(*integerMilliseconds*, *#handlerName*, *targetObject*)

This statement uses the following elements:

- *variableName* is the variable you are placing the timeout object into.

- timeOut indicates which type of Lingo object you are creating.

- *theName* is the name you give to the timeout object. This name will appear in the timeOutList. It is the #name property of the object.

- new is the Lingo function that creates a new object.

- *integerMilliseconds* indicates the frequency with which the timeout object should call the handler you specify. This is the #period property of the object. A value of 2000 will call the specified handler every 2 seconds.

- *#handlerName* is the name of the handler you want the object to call. This is the #timeOutHandler property of the object. You represent it as a symbol by preceding the name with the # sign. For example, a handler called on accelerate would be specified as #accelerate.

- *targetObject* indicates which child object's handler should be called. This is the #target property of the object. It allows specificity when many child objects contain the same handlers. If you omit this parameter, Director will look for the specified handler in the movie script.

This statement creates a timeout object named timer1 that will call the on accelerate handler in the child object car1 every 2 seconds:

myTimer = timeOut("timer1").new(2000, #accelerate, car1)

To determine when the next timeout message will be sent from a particular timeout object, check its #time property. The value returned is the point in time, in milliseconds, when the next timeout message will be sent.

This statement determines the time when the next timeout message will be sent from the timeout object timer1 and displays it in the Message window:

```
put timeout("timer1").time
```

Using timeOutList

When you begin creating timeout objects, you can use timeOutList to check the number of timeout objects that are active at a particular moment.

The following statement sets the variable x to the number of objects in timeOutList. See count() in the *Lingo Dictionary*.

```
x = (the timeOutList).count
```

You can also refer to an individual timeout object by its number in the list.

The following statement deletes the second timeout object in timeOutList. See forget() in the *Lingo Dictionary*.

```
timeOut(2).forget
```

Relaying system events with timeout objects

When you create timeout objects that target specific child objects, you enable those child objects to receive system events. Timeout objects relay these events to their target child objects. The system events that can be received by child objects include prepareMovie, startMovie, stopMovie, prepareFrame, and exitFrame. By including handlers for these events in child objects, you can make the child objects respond to them for whatever purposes you see fit. System events received by child objects are also received by movie scripts, frame scripts, and other scripts designed to respond to them.

This parent script contains a handler for the system event exitFrame as well as a custom handler:

```
property velocity

on new me
    velocity = random(55)
end

on exitFrame
    velocity = velocity + 5
end

on slowDown mph
    velocity = velocity - mph
end
```

For information on specific timeout properties, see timeout() in the *Lingo Dictionary*.

CHAPTER 12
Vector Shapes and Bitmaps
· ·

Vector shapes and bitmaps are the two main types of graphics used with Director. A vector shape is a mathematical description of a geometric form that includes the thickness of the line, the fill color, and additional features of the line that can be expressed mathematically. A bitmap defines an image as a grid of colored pixels, and it stores the color for each pixel in the image. A bitmap typically requires more RAM and disk space than a comparable vector shape. If not compressed, bitmaps take longer than vector shapes to download from the Internet. Fortunately, Director offers compression control to reduce the size of bitmaps in movies that you package to play on the Web. For more information about bitmap compression, see "Compressing bitmaps" on page 332.

Vector shape

Bitmap

A vector shape is most appropriate for a simple, smooth, clean-looking image. It typically includes less detail than a bitmap, but you can resize it without distortion. You can use Lingo to dynamically control a vector shape. You can create a vector shape entirely with Lingo or modify an existing one as the movie plays. Because vector shapes are stored as mathematical descriptions, they require less RAM and disk space than an equivalent bitmap image and they download faster from the Internet.

You can create vector shapes in the Director Vector Shape window by defining points through which a line passes. The shape can be a line, a curve, or an open or closed irregular shape that can be filled with a color or gradient.

Bitmaps are suited for continuous tone images, like photographs. You can easily make minute changes to a bitmap by editing single pixels, but resizing the image can cause distortion as pixels are redistributed. Anti-aliasing is a Director feature that blends the bitmap's colors with background colors around the edges to make the edge appear smooth instead of jagged.

You can create bitmaps in the Paint window or import them from any of the popular image editors in most of the popular formats, including GIF and JPEG. Director can also import bitmaps with alpha channel (transparency) data and animated GIFs. The Paint window includes a variety of tools for editing and applying effects to bitmaps.

Drawing vector shapes

You create vector shapes with drawing tools in the Vector Shape window. You can use the Pen tool to create irregular shapes, or use shape tools to create rectangles and ellipses. A vector shape can include multiple curves, and you can split and join the curves. Shape properties such as fill color, stroke color, and stroke width are set at the cast-member level and not for individual curves.

When you create vector shapes, you create vertices, which are fixed points. You can also create handles, which are points that determine the degree of curvature between vertices. These curves are known as Bézier curves. A vertex without a handle creates a corner.

As you draw vector shapes, control handles appear on the vertices: round curve points for vertices with handles and square corner points for vertices without handles.

- The first vertex in a curve is green.
- The last vertex in a curve is red.
- All other vertices are blue.
- Unselected vertices are solid.
- Selected vertices are unfilled.

To open the Vector Shape window:

Choose Window > Vector Shape.

Zooming in and out in the Vector Shape window

You can use the Magnify tool or the Zoom commands on the View menu to zoom in or out at four levels of magnification.

To zoom in or out, do one of the following:

- Choose View > Zoom and then choose the level of magnification.
- Right-click (Windows) or Control-click (Macintosh) and choose Zoom In or Zoom Out from the context menu.
- Press Control + the plus (+) key (Windows) or Command + the plus (+) key (Macintosh) to zoom in, or Control + the minus (-) key (Windows) or Command + the minus (-) key (Macintosh) to zoom out.

To return to normal view:

Choose View > Zoom > 100%.

Using vector shape drawing tools

You use the tools in the Vector Shape window to draw free-form shapes or geometric figures. You can define a shape with the Pen tool by creating curve or corner points through which a line passes.

To draw regular shapes, you use the Rectangle, Rounded Rectangle, and Ellipse tools.

To create a vector shape using the Pen tool:

1 In the Vector Shape window, click the New Cast Member button.

2 Click the Pen tool and begin to draw:

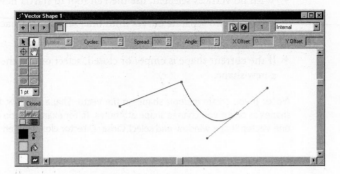

- To create a corner point, click once.

- To create a curve point, click and drag. Dragging creates control handles that define how the line curves through the point you define.

- To constrain a new point to vertical, horizontal, or a 45° angle, hold down Shift while clicking.

To draw using a basic shape tool:

1 In the Vector Shape window, click the New Cast Member button.

2 Select the Filled or Unfilled Rectangle, Rounded Rectangle, or Ellipse tool.

3 Hold down the mouse button to start a shape, drag to draw, and release the mouse button to end the shape.

To constrain a rectangle to a square, or to constrain an ellipse to a circle, hold down Shift while dragging.

To select a vertex or vertices:

- To select one vertex, select the Arrow tool and click the vertex.

- To select multiple vertices, either select the Arrow tool and hold Shift while clicking the vertices, or click and drag a selection rectangle over the vertices (marquee-select).

- To select all the vertices in a curve, select the Arrow tool and double-click one of the vertices in the curve.

To create multiple curves, do one of the following:

- If using the Pen tool, double-click the last vertex drawn. The next vertex will start a new curve.

- With no vertices selected, use the Pen tool to start a new curve.

- To create two separate curves from one, select two adjacent vertices in a curve and choose Modify > Split Curve.

- If the current shape is empty or closed, select one of the shape tools and draw a new shape.

Note: If you create multiple shapes in the Vector Shape window, Director treats all of the shapes as one if you change shape attributes. If, for example, you create ten open shapes in one Vector Shape window and select Close, Director closes all ten shapes.

Choosing fill and line settings for vector shapes

You can use either controls in the Vector Shape window or Lingo to choose a vector shape's fill color, line width and color, and background color. The background is the area outside of a vector shape but within the cast member's bounding rectangle.

Because a vector shape is a single object, you don't need to select any part of the vector shape to make the following changes.

To choose the fill and line settings:

1 Open a vector shape in the Vector Shape window.

2 Choose fill and line settings using the appropriate controls at the left of the window.

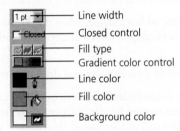

- Line width
- Closed control
- Fill type
- Gradient color control
- Line color
- Fill color
- Background color

- To choose the fill color, choose a color from the Fill Color menu.

- To choose the line color, choose a color from the Line Color menu.

- To set the line width, choose a point size option from the Line Width menu.

- To set the background color, choose a color from the Background Color menu. Choosing a background color that matches the color of the background results in better performance than using Background Transparent ink.

Specifying vector shape fills and strokes with Lingo

You can use Lingo to specify a vector shape's fills and strokes.

To specify the strokes that form a vector shape with Lingo:

Set the strokeColor and strokeWidth cast member properties. See strokeColor and strokeWidth in the *Lingo Dictionary*.

To specify a vector shape's fill with Lingo:

Set the fillColor, fillMode, fillOffset, and fillScale cast member properties. See fillColor, fillMode, fillOffest, and fillScale in the *Lingo Dictionary*.

Editing vector shapes

To edit vector shapes, you use the Vector Shape window. You change vector shapes by moving, adding, or deleting control points and changing the way they control curves. You can also change the way a vector shape is placed on the Stage by moving its registration point using either the Vector Shape window or Lingo.

To adjust the outline of a vector shape:

1 Open a vector shape in the Vector Shape window.

2 Click the Arrow tool and make any of the following changes:

- To move a curve or corner point, drag it to any location.

- To move multiple points, Shift-click or drag a selection rectangle around all the points you want to move and then drag any one of the selected points.

- To drag a single curve within a shape, select the Arrow tool and drag the curve. If the curve is filled, you can click anywhere within the filled area and drag the curve.

- To adjust a curve, select a curve point and drag a control handle.

  By default, the two control handles remain at a 180° angle from each other. If you want to drag one control handle independently from the other one, hold down Control (Windows) or Command (Macintosh) when you drag it. To constrain the control handles to vertical, horizontal, or a 45° angle, hold down Shift as you move them.

- To change a corner point to a curve point, Alt-click (Windows) or Option-click (Macintosh) and drag away from the handle to extend a control handle.

- To change a curve point to a corner point, drag the control handles directly over the curve point.

- To delete a point, select the point and press Backspace or Delete.

- To move the window view without using the scroll bars, click the Hand tool and drag anywhere inside the shape.

To add a point in the middle of a shape:

1 Open a vector shape in the Vector Shape window.

2 Click the Pen tool.

3 If the shape is closed, move the pointer over a line until it changes and then click the mouse button. If the shape is open, hold down Alt (Windows) or Option (Macintosh) and move the pointer over a line until it changes; then click the mouse button.

To add a new point that is connected to a certain end point:

1 Click the Arrow tool and select an end point.

2 Click the Pen tool and then click the location where you want to add the next point.

To join two curves:

1 Select a vertex in each curve.

If you select two endpoint vertices, you will join them. If you select points in the middle of the curve, you will join the start of the second curve to the end of the first curve.

2 Choose Modify > Join Curves.

To split two curves:

Select two adjacent vertices and choose Modify > Split Curves.

To change the registration point:

 1 Click the Registration Point tool.

The dotted lines in the window intersect at the registration point. The default registration point is the center of the cast member.

The pointer changes to a cross hair when you move it to the window.

2 Click to set the new registration point.

You can also drag the dotted lines around the window to reposition the registration point.

3 To reset the default registration point at the center of the cast member, double-click the Registration Point tool.

To change a vector shape cast member's registration point with Lingo:

Set the regPoint or regPointVertex cast member property. You can test the centerRegPoint property to determine whether Director automatically recenters the registration point when the cast member is edited. (If you specify a value for regPointVertex, any values in the regPoint and centerRegPoint properties are ignored.) See centerRegPoint, regPoint, and regPointVertex in the *Lingo Dictionary*.

To close or open vector shapes:

Select or deselect the Close box at the left side of the window.

If the shape is closed, Director draws a line between the last and first points defined; if it is open, Director removes the line between the last and first points.

To close a shape with Lingo:

Set the closed cast member property to TRUE. See closed in the *Lingo Dictionary*.

To scale a vector shape:

Control-Alt-drag (Windows) or Command-Option-drag (Macintosh) to proportionally resize a vector shape.

You can also enter a scaling percentage for a vector shape using the Cast Member Properties dialog box.

Defining gradients for vector shapes

You can use controls in the Vector Shape window or Lingo to specify the type of gradient, how it is placed within a shape, and how many times it cycles within the shape. A gradient for a vector shape shifts between the fill color and the end color you define. You can create linear or radial gradients. Changes you make to vector shape gradients have no effect on gradients for bitmaps in the Paint window. You can fill only closed vector shapes with gradients.

To define a gradient for a vector shape:

1 Create a closed vector shape in the Vector Shape window.

2 Click the Gradient button.

3 To choose colors for the gradient, click the color box on the left side of the Gradient Colors control and choose a starting color from the Color menu. To choose the ending color, repeat this step using the color box on the right side of the Gradient Colors control.

4 Choose Linear or Radial from the Gradient Type pop-up menu at the top of the window.

5 To define the number of times the gradient should change colors within the shape, use the Cycles control.

6 To specify the rate at which the gradient shifts between colors, use the Scale control to enter a percentage.

A setting of 100% uses the entire width or height of the shape to gradually shift colors. Lower settings make the shift more abrupt. For settings over 100%, the end color is reached at a theoretical location beyond the edges of the shape.

7 To rotate the gradient within the shape, use the Angle control to enter the number of degrees.

This setting affects only linear gradients.

8 To offset the gradient within the shape, enter X Offset (horizontal) and Y Offset (vertical) values.

To specify a gradient with Lingo:

Set the fillColor, fillDirection, fillMode, fillOffset, fillScale, gradientType, and endColor cast member properties. See fillColor, fillDirection, fillMode, fillOffset, fillScale, gradientType, and endColor in the *Lingo Dictionary*.

Controlling vector shapes with Lingo

You can use Lingo to modify a vector shape by setting properties and using commands and functions related to the shape's vertices. For more information, see the *Lingo Dictionary*.

- To display a list that contains the location of each vertex and control handle in a vector shape, test the vertexList property.

- To access a vertex directly, use the vertex chunk expression.

- To add or delete a vertex, use the addVertex() or deleteVertex() command.

- To move a vertex or a vertex handle, use the moveVertex() or moveVertexHandle() command.

- To display the vertex list for a vector shape, test the curve property.

- To add a new shape to the vector shape, use the newCurve() command.

- To display or specify the registration point for the vector shape's cast member, test or set the regPointVertex property.

- To display or specify the point around which a vector shape scales and rotates, test or set the originMode property.

About importing bitmaps

Importing bitmaps is similar to importing other types of media. If you import a bitmap with a color palette or depth different from that of the current movie, the Image Options dialog box appears. You must choose to import the bitmap at its original color depth or at the current system color depth. If you are importing an 8-bit image, you have the choice of importing the image's color palette or remapping the image to a palette already in Director. See"Choosing import image options" on page 111.

Director can import images with alpha channel (transparency) effects, which are 32 bits. If you reduce the image to a lower color depth, Director removes all the alpha channel data.

When importing bitmaps, you should always consider that they will be displayed on the screen at your monitor's resolution (generally 72 to 96 dots per inch). Higher-resolution images that you place on the Stage in Director may appear much larger than you expect. Other applications, particularly those focused on creating images for print, allow you to work on the screen with high-resolution images at reduced sizes. Within Director, you can scale high-resolution images to the right size, but this may reduce the quality of the image. Also, high-resolution images use extra memory and storage space, even after they've been scaled.

If you are working with a high-resolution image, convert it to between 72 and 96 dots per inch with your image editing program before you import it into Director.

Director supports JPEG compression at run time for internal cast members imported through the Standard or Include Original Data for Editing import options. A JPEG file imported with either of these options contains both the original compressed bits and decompressed bits. Once imported, the JPEG file decompresses in the authoring environment. The cast member size displays the member's size in RAM after it has been decompressed. The amount of RAM required to display a JPEG file is larger than its size on disk, so do not be surprised that your cast member size is larger than its original size on disk in the Cast Properties window.

Director takes advantage of compressed JPEG data at run time. The original compressed data bits are saved in a Shockwave movie or a projector (if the Shockwave compression option is on). If you edit the member within Director in the Paint window, the compressed data will be lost. An alert appears before the data is overwritten.

If the Shockwave compression option is on, Director also compresses bitmaps into the JPEG format. For more information about bitmap compression, see "Compressing bitmaps" on page 332.

Using animated GIFs

You can import an animated GIF into Director with File > Import, similar to the way in which you import any other bitmap cast member. The only difference is that when the Select Format dialog box appears, you select Animated GIF.

Director supports both the GIF89a and GIF87 formats. GIFs must have a global color table to be imported. You can import an animated GIF within a movie file or link to an external file. You also have the choice of importing the first frame of an animated GIF as a still image. Just as with an ordinary bitmap, you place an animated GIF in the Score in a sprite channel and extend it through all the frames in which you want it to appear. An animated GIF can play at the same frame rate as the Director movie, at a different rate that you specify, or at its original rate.

Director does not support the following inks for animated GIFs: Background Transparent, Reverse, Not Reverse, Darkest, Lightest, Add, Add Pin, Subtract, and Subtract Pin.

You can make an animated GIF play direct-to-Stage, meaning that it is immediately displayed on the Stage instead of being first composed in an offscreen buffer with other sprites. A direct-to-Stage GIF takes less time to load, but you cannot place other sprites in front of it or use any ink effect.

To set properties for an animated GIF:

1 To specify how Director removes the cast member from memory if memory is low, choose an option from the Unload pop-up menu on the Cast Member tab of the Property Inspector (Graphical view). See "Controlling cast member unloading" on page 114.

2 To achieve the fastest playback rate, click the Animated GIF tab and select Direct to Stage.

When Direct to Stage is on, you can use only Copy ink and you cannot place any sprites on top of the animated GIF sprite.

3 Choose an option from the Rate pop-up menu.

• Normal plays at the GIF's original rate, independent of the Director movie. The GIF cannot exceed Director's frame rate.

• Fixed plays at the frame rate you enter on the right.

• Locked-Step plays at the same rate as the Director movie.

4 To set additional animated GIF settings, click More Options.

• To change the file of a linked external cast member, enter a new pathname in the Import field or click Browse to choose a new file.

• To import a file from the Internet, click Internet and enter a new URL.

Using the Paint window

The Paint window has a complete set of paint tools and inks for creating and changing bitmap cast members for movies. Anything you draw in the Paint window becomes a cast member. When you make a change to a cast member in the Paint window, the image in the Cast window is instantly updated—as is the cast member wherever it appears on the Stage.

To open the Paint window, do any of the following:

- Choose Window > Paint.

- Click the Paint window icon on the toolbar.

- Press Control-5 (Windows) or Command-5 (Macintosh).

- Double-click a bitmap sprite on the Stage or in the Score or double-click the sprite's cast member in the Cast window.

Using Paint window tools and controls

If you see an arrow in the lower right corner of a tool, click it and hold down the mouse button to display a pop-up menu of options for that tool.

To select an irregular area:

- Click the Lasso tool in the Paint window and drag to enclose the pixels you want to select.

  The Lasso selects only those pixels of a color different from the color the Lasso was on when you first started dragging it.

- Press Alt (Windows) or Option (Macintosh) while dragging to create a polygon selection. Every time you click, you create a new angle in the selection polygon.

- Click the Lasso tool and hold down the mouse button to choose new settings from the pop-up menu.

  See "Using the Lasso" in Director Help.

To select a rectangular area:

- Click and drag the Marquee tool in the Paint window.

- Double-click the Marquee tool to select the entire bitmap.

- Click the Marquee tool and hold down the mouse button to choose new settings from the pop-up menu.

See "Using the Marquee tool" in Director Help.

To change the location of the registration point:

- Click the Registration Point tool and click the spot where you wish to set the registration point.

- Double-click the Registration Point tool to set the registration point in the center of the image.

See "Changing registration points" on page 315.

To erase:

- Click and drag the Eraser tool to erase pixels.

- Double-click the Eraser tool to erase the cast member.

To move the view of the Paint window:

- Click and drag the Hand tool to move the visible portion of the image within the Paint window.

- Shift-drag to move straight horizontally or vertically.

Press the Spacebar to temporarily activate this tool while using other paint tools.

To zoom in or out on an area:

Click the Magnifying Glass tool and click in the Paint window to zoom in. Shift-click to zoom out.

See "Zooming in and out in the Paint window" on page 310.

To select a color in a cast member:

 Click the Eyedropper tool and do one of the following:

- Click a color to select it as the foreground color.

- Shift-click a color to select it as the background color.

- Alt-click (Windows) or Option-click (Macintosh) to select the destination color for a gradient.

Press D to temporarily activate the Eyedropper while using other paint tools.

To fill all adjacent pixels of the same color with the foreground color:

- Click the Bucket tool and click the area you want to fill.

- To open the Gradient Settings dialog box, double-click the Bucket tool.

To enter bitmap text:

- Click the Text tool and then click in the Paint window and begin typing.

- Choose character formatting with the Modify > Font command.

Bitmap text is an image. Before you click outside the text box, you can edit text you've typed by using the Backspace key (Windows) or Delete key (Macintosh). Once you have clicked outside the text box, you cannot edit or reformat bitmap text.

To draw a 1-pixel line in the current foreground:

 Click the Pencil tool and drag in the Paint window. To constrain the line to horizontal or vertical, Shift-Click and drag.

If the foreground color is the same as the color underneath the pointer, the Pencil tool draws with the background color.

To spray variable dots of the foreground color:

- Click the Airbrush tool and drag in the Paint window.

- Click the Airbrush tool and hold down the mouse button to choose a new brush type from the pop-up menu. Choose Settings to change the selected brush.

See "Using the Airbrush tool" in Director Help.

To brush strokes of the foreground color:

- Click the Brush tool and drag in the Paint window. To constrain the stroke to horizontal or vertical, Shift-click and drag.

To choose a new brush type:

Click the Brush tool and hold down the mouse button to choose a new brush type from the pop-up menu. Choose Settings to change the selected brush.

See "Using the Brush tool" in Director Help.

To paint shapes or lines:

Click and drag the shape tools. To constrain lines to horizontal or vertical, ovals to circles, and rectangles to squares, Shift-click and drag.

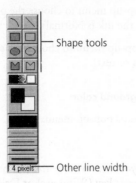 — Shape tools

— Other line width

The filled tools create shapes filled with the foreground color and the current pattern. The thickness of lines is determined by the line width selector.

To choose a foreground and destination color for color-shifting inks:

 Click the color box on the left to choose a foreground color; click the color box on the right to choose a destination color.

These colors affect Gradient, Cycle, and Switch inks. Each of these uses a range of colors that shifts between the foreground color and the destination color.

See "Using gradients" and "Using Paint window inks" in Director Help.

To choose the foreground and background colors:

Foreground
color

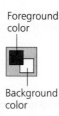

Background
color

- Use the Foreground Color pop-up menu to choose the primary fill color (used when the pattern is solid and the ink is Normal).

- Use the Background Color pop-up menu to choose the secondary color (the background color in a pattern or text).

To choose a pattern for the foreground color:

Choose an option from the Patterns pop-up menu:

 —— Patterns

- To change the pattern palette, choose Pattern Settings at the bottom of the menu.

- To define a tile—a pattern based on a rectangular section of an existing cast member—choose Tile Settings.

See "Editing patterns" in Director Help, and "Creating a custom tile" on page 323.

To choose a line thickness:

 —— Other line width

- Choose the None, One-, Two-, or Three-Pixel Line button to set the line width.

- Double-click the Other Line Width button to open Paint Window Preferences and assign a width to the line.

To change the color depth of the current cast member:

— Color Depth

Double-click the Color Depth button to open the Transform Bitmap dialog box.

The button displays the color depth of the current cast member.

See "Changing size, color depth, and color palette for bitmaps" on page 317.

To choose a Paint window ink:

Choose the type of ink from the Ink pop-up menu at the bottom left of the window.

See "Using Paint window inks" in Director Help.

Using rulers in the Paint window

The Paint window has vertical and horizontal rulers to help you align and size your artwork.

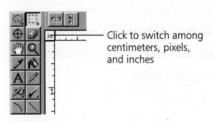

— Click to switch among centimeters, pixels, and inches

To hide or show the rulers in the Paint window:

Choose View > Rulers.

To change the location of the zero point, do one of the following:

- Drag along the ruler at the top or side of the window.
- Drag into the window to align the zero point with a specific point in the cast member.

Zooming in and out in the Paint window

You can use the Magnify tool or the Zoom commands on the View menu to zoom in or out at four levels of magnification.

To zoom in or out, do one of the following:

- Click the Magnify tool and then click the image. Click again to increase the magnification. Shift-click to zoom out.

- Choose View > Zoom and then choose the level of magnification.

- Press Control + the plus (+) key (Windows) or Command + the plus (+) key (Macintosh) to zoom in, or Control + the minus (-) key (Windows) or Command + the minus (-) key (Macintosh) to zoom out.

- Control-click (Windows) or Command-click (Macintosh) the image to zoom in on a particular place.

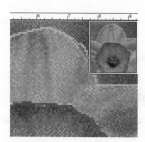

To return to normal view, do one of the following:

- Click the normal-sized image in the upper right corner.

- Choose View > Zoom > 100%.

Changing selected areas of a bitmap

Once you have selected part of an image in the Paint window with the Lasso or Marquee tool, you can change the selected area.

To reposition the selected area:

Move the cross hair inside the selected area (the cross hair becomes an arrow pointer). Drag the selected area.

To affect how the selected area behaves when you drag it, use the following key combinations:

- To make a copy of the selected area as you drag, Alt-drag (Windows) or Option-drag (Macintosh) the selection.

- To stretch the selection (Marquee tool only), Control-drag (Windows) or Command-drag (Macintosh) the selection.

- To stretch the selection proportionally (Marquee tool only), Control-Shift-drag (Windows) or Command-Shift-drag (Macintosh) the selection.

- To copy and stretch the selection (Marquee tool only), Control-Alt-drag (Windows) or Command-Option-drag (Macintosh) the selection.

- To constrain the movement of the selection to horizontal or vertical, Shift-drag the selection.

- To move the selection one pixel at a time, use the arrow keys.

Flipping, rotating, and applying effects to bitmaps

The toolbar at the top of the Paint window contains buttons to apply effects to bitmaps. Before using any of these options, you must select part of the bitmap with the Lasso or Marquee tool. Effects that change the shape of the selection work only when the selection is made with the Marquee tool. Effects that change colors within the selection work with both the Marquee and the Lasso tools.

Lingo flips and rotates bitmaps by flipping and rotating bitmap sprites. See "Rotating and skewing sprites" on page 144 and "Flipping sprites" on page 147.

Note: To repeat any of these effects after using them, press Control+Y (Windows) or Command+Y (Macintosh).

To flip, rotate, skew, or apply effects to part of a bitmap:

1 Select part of a bitmap in the Paint window with the Marquee tool.

2 Use any of the following effects:

 • To flip the selection, click the Flip Horizontal button to flip right to left, or click the Flip Vertical button to flip top to bottom.

 • To rotate the selection 90° counterclockwise or 90° clockwise, click the Rotate Left or Rotate Right buttons.

 • To rotate the selection by any amount in either direction, click the Free Rotate button and then drag the rotate handles in any direction. (You can rotate a sprite containing a bitmap instead of the bitmap itself. See "Rotating and skewing sprites" on page 144.)

 • To skew the selection, click the Skew button and drag any of the skew handles.

• To warp the shape of the selected area, click the Warp button and drag any handle in any direction.

 • To create a perspective effect, click the Perspective button and drag one or more handles to create the effect you want.

 • To create an outline around the edges of the selected artwork, click the Trace Edges button.

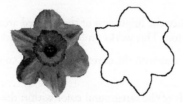

To apply color effects to a selected area:

1 Select an area within a bitmap cast member using either the Marquee or the Lasso tool.

2 Use any of the following effects:

 • To soften the edges of the selected artwork, click the Smooth button. This works only with 8-bit cast members.

• To reverse the colors of the selected area, click the Invert Color button.

• To increase or reduce the brightness of the selected area, click the Lighten or Darken Color button. This works on 8-bit (256 color) images only.

• To fill the selected area with the current foreground color and pattern, click the Fill Color button.

• To change all pixels of the foreground color within the selection to the currently selected destination color, click the Switch Colors button.

Changing registration points

A registration point is a marker that appears on a sprite when you select it with your mouse. (Registration points do not appear on unselected sprites or when a movie is playing.) Registration points provide a fixed reference point within an image, thereby helping you align sprites and control them from Lingo. Registration points are crucial to precisely placing vector shapes, bitmaps, and all cast members that appear on the Stage.

By default, Director assigns a registration point in the center of all bitmaps, but for many types of animation, you may want to move the registration point. To do this, you can use the Registration Point tool.

You can edit a bitmap's registration point in the Paint window or using Lingo.

Moving the registration point is useful for preparing a series of images for animation. When you use Cast to Time or exchange cast members, Director places a new cast member's registration point precisely where the previous one was. By placing the registration point in the different locations, you can make a series of images move around a fixed position without having to manually place the sprites on the Stage. Use onion skinning to set registration points when images are placed in relation to each other. See "Using onion skinning" on page 327.

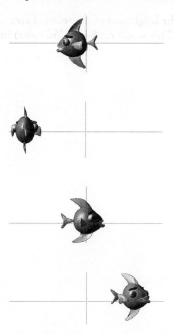

With the registration points set as shown, the series of fish swim in a circle without any tweening or manual placement of sprites.

To set a registration point:

1 Display the cast member you want to change in the Paint window.

 2 Click the Registration Point tool.

The dotted lines in the Paint window intersect at the registration point. The default registration point is the center of the cast member.

The pointer changes to a cross hair when you move it to the Paint window.

3 Click a location in the Paint window to set the registration point.

You can also drag the dotted lines around the window to reposition the registration point.

Note: To reset the default registration point at the center of the cast member, double-click the Registration Point tool.

To set a bitmap's registration point with Lingo:

Set the regPoint cast member property. Set the centerRegPoint property to specify whether Director automatically centers the registration point if the bitmap is edited. See centerRegPoint and regPoint in the *Lingo Dictionary*.

Changing size, color depth, and color palette for bitmaps

You can use Transform Bitmap to change the size, color depth, and palette of selected cast members. Any change you make to a cast member's color depth or palette affects the cast member itself—not just its appearance on the Stage. You can't undo changes to the color depth and palette. If you want to keep a cast member's original bitmap unchanged but temporarily apply a different palette, use the Member tab in the cast member's Property Inspector. To change the size of only the sprite on the Stage, use the Sprite tab in the sprite's Property Inspector.

You can also remap images to new palettes with an image editing program such as Fireworks.

The Transform Bitmap dialog box displays values for the current selection. If more than one cast member is selected, a blank value indicates that cast members in the selection have different values. To maintain a cast member's original value, leave that value blank in the dialog box.

To use Transform Bitmap:

1   Select the bitmap cast members to change.

2   Choose Modify > Transform Bitmap.

3   To change the size of the bitmap, do one of the following:

   If multiple cast members are selected, you can resize all the cast members to the dimensions you enter.

   • Enter new measurements (in pixels) in the Width and Height fields.

   • Enter a scaling percentage in the Scale box.

   Select Maintain Proportions to keep the width and height of the selected cast member in proportion. If you change the width, the proportional height is automatically entered in the Height field. If you use Transform Bitmap to change several cast members at once, be sure to deselect Maintain Proportions. If you don't, all cast members will be resized to the values in the Width and Height boxes.

4   To change the color depth, choose an option from the Color Depth pop-up menu.

   For more information about the color depth of bitmap cast members, see "Controlling color" on page 220.

5 To change the palette, choose a palette from the Palette pop-up menu and choose one of the following remapping options:

• Remapping replaces the original colors in the graphic with the most similar solid colors in the new palette. This is the preferred option in most cases.

• Dithering blends the colors in the new palette to approximate the original colors in the graphic.

256 grays

Remapped to closest colors in black and white

Dithered in black and white

6 Click Transform to execute the changes.

The settings you choose in Transform Bitmap cannot be undone.

Controlling bitmap images with Lingo

Lingo lets you control bitmap images in two different ways. First, you can perform simple operations that affect the content of entire image cast members. These include changing the background and foreground colors, and switching the image that appears in a specific cast member with that of another cast member. Each of these operations manipulates a property of the entire image cast member.

Second, you can use Lingo to perform fine manipulations of the pixels of an image or to create entirely new images. This allows you to be extremely flexible about which images you display. You can create images based on dynamic information, such as user input, or based on any other factors you wish to include. To perform this kind of image operation, Lingo works with image objects.

To change the image assigned to a bitmap cast member:

• Set the picture cast member property. See picture (cast member property) in the *Lingo Dictionary*.

To specify the background or foreground of a bitmap sprite:

• Set the backColor or foreColor sprite property. See backColor and foreColor in the *Lingo Dictionary*.

To capture the current graphic contents of the Stage:

• Set a bitmap's picture cast member property to the Stage's picture property. See picture (cast member property) in the *Lingo Dictionary*.

For example, the statement member("Archive").picture = (the stage).picture makes the current image of the Stage the image for the bitmap cast member Archive.

Creating image objects

An image object can be either a self-contained set of image data or a reference to the image data of a cast member or of the Stage. If an image object is created by referring to a cast member, the object will contain a reference to the image of the member. The following statement creates an image object containing a reference to the image of the cast member called Boat.

```
myImage = member("Boat").image
```

Because the image object myImage contains a reference to the cast member Boat, any changes you make to the object will be reflected in the cast member. These changes will also be reflected in any sprites made from that cast member.

You can also create an image object containing a reference to the graphic contents of the Stage:

```
myImage = (the stage).image
```

Any changes to this image object will be reflected on the Stage.

To create an image object that is a self-contained set of image data instead of a reference to a cast member, you must tell Lingo what kind of image you want to create. You do this by providing parameters that describe the size and bit depth of the image you are creating.

This statement creates an image object that contains a 640 x 480 pixel, 16-bit image:

```
myImage = image(640, 480, 16)
```

Editing image objects

Once you have created an image object, its data can be edited with a variety of Lingo commands designed to manipulate the pixels of the image. You can crop images, draw new pixels on them, copy sections of them, and work with mask and alpha channel information. For more information, see the individual commands in the *Lingo Dictionary*.

To draw a line on an image object:

Use the draw() command. You must specify both the locations of each end of the line and the line's color.

This statement draws a line on the previously created 640 x 480 image object myImage, running from 20 pixels inside the top left corner to 20 pixels inside the lower right corner, and colors it blue:

```
myImage.draw(20, 20, 620, 460, rgb(0, 0, 255))
```

To draw a rectangle on an image object:

Use the fill() command. You provide the same information as for the draw command, but Director draws a rectangle instead of a line.

This statement draws a red 40 x 40 pixel rectangle near the upper left corner of the image object myImage:

myImage.fill(rect(20, 20, 60, 60), rgb(255, 0, 0))

To determine the color of an individual pixel of an image object or set that pixel's color:

Use getPixel or setPixel.

To copy part or all of an image object into a different image object:

Use copyPixels(). This command requires you to specify the image you are copying from, the rectangle to copy the pixels to, and the rectangle to copy the pixels from in the source image.

This statement copies a 40 x 40 rectangle from the upper left area of the image object myImage and puts the pixels into a 40 x 40 rectangle at the lower right of the 300 x 300 pixel object called myNewImage:

myNewImage.copyPixels(myImage, rect(260, 260, 300, 300), rect(0, 0, 40, 40))

When using copyPixels(), you can specify optional parameters that tell Lingo to modify the pixels you are copying before drawing them into the destination rectangle. You can apply blends and inks, change the foreground or background colors, specify masking operations, and more. You specify these operations by adding a property list at the end of the copyPixels() command.

This statement performs the same operation as the previous example and tells Lingo to use the Reverse ink when rendering the pixels into the destination rectangle:

myNewImage.copyPixels(myImage, rect(260, 260, 300, 300), rect(0, 0, 40, 40), [#ink: #reverse])

To make a new image object from the alpha channel information of a 32-bit image object:

Use extractAlpha(). This can be useful for preserving the alpha channel information of a 32-bit image object that you plan to reduce to a lower bit depth. A reduction in bit depth would otherwise delete the alpha information.

This statement creates a new image object called alphaImage from the alpha channel information of the 32-bit image object called myImage:

alphaImage = myImage.extractAlpha()

There are many more image editing operations available through Lingo. See the categorized section of the *Lingo Dictionary* for a complete list of these commands.

Using gradients

Director can create gradients in the Paint window. You can use gradients with the Brush tool, the Bucket tool, the Text tool, or any of the filled shape tools. Typically, a gradient consists of a foreground color at one side (or the center) of an image and another color, the destination color, at the other side (or outside edge) of the image. Between the foreground and destination colors, Director creates a blend of the two.

To use a gradient:

1 Choose the Brush tool, the Bucket tool, or one of the filled shape tools.

2 Choose the type of gradient from the Gradient pop-up menu.

Gradient
pop-up menu

Choosing a gradient type automatically sets the current Paint window ink to Gradient. You can also choose Gradient ink from the Ink pop-up menu at the bottom left of the Paint window to create a gradient with all the current settings.

To manually specify a gradient, choose Gradient Setting from the pop-up menu. See "Editing gradients" in Director Help.

3 Choose a foreground color from Gradient Colors pop-up menu on the left.

The foreground color is the same color specified for the Paint window.

Foreground
color

Destination
color

4 Choose a destination color from the Gradient Colors pop-up menu on the right.

The destination color is the color of the gradient when it completes the color transition.

5 Use the current tool in the Paint window.

Director uses the gradient you've defined to fill the image.

6 To stop using a gradient, choose Normal from the Ink pop-up menu.

Using patterns

You can choose among three sets of patterns included with Director or create your own custom patterns. The patterns you change or edit in the Paint window do not affect the patterns available for shapes.

To use a pattern:

1 Choose the Brush tool, the Bucket tool, or one of the filled shape tools.

2 Choose the type of pattern from the Patterns pop-up menu.

   To manually specify a pattern, choose Pattern Settings from the pop-up menu. See "Editing patterns" in Director Help.

Creating a custom tile

Custom tiles provide an effective way of filling a large area with interesting content without using a lot of memory or increasing the downloading time. They are especially useful for large movies on the Web. A custom tile uses the same amount of memory no matter what size area it fills.

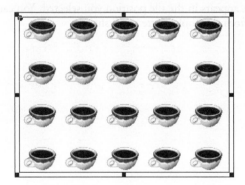

To create a custom tile:

1 Create a bitmap cast member to use as a tile and display it in the Paint window.

2 Click the pattern box in the Paint window and choose Tile Setting from the bottom of the Patterns pop-up menu.

3 Click an existing tile position to edit.

The existing tiles appear next to the Edit label. You have to replace one of the built-in tiles to create a new one. To restore the built-in tile for any tile position, select it and click Built-in.

4 Click Cast Member.

The cast member appears in the box at the lower left. The box at the right shows how the image appears when it is tiled. The dotted rectangle inside the cast member image shows the area of the tile.

To choose a different cast member for the tile, use the arrow buttons to the right of the Cast Member button to move through the movie's cast members.

5 Drag the dotted rectangle to the area of the cast member you want tiled.

6 Use the Width and Height controls to specify the size of the tile.

The new tile appears in the tile position you selected. You can use it in the Paint window or from the Tool palette to fill shapes.

Using bitmap filters

Bitmap filters are plug-in image editors that apply effects to bitmap images. You can install Photoshop-compatible filters to change images within Director.

Original image

Filtered image

To install a filter, place it in the Xtras folder in the Director application folder. See "Installing Xtras" on page 82.

You can apply a filter to a selected portion of a bitmap image, to an entire cast member, or to several cast members at once.

To apply a filter:

1 Open the cast member in the Paint window or select the cast member in the Cast window.

You can apply a filter to several cast members at once by selecting them all in the Cast window. To apply a filter to a selected portion of a cast member, use the Marquee or Lasso tool in the Paint window to select the part you want to change.

2 Choose Xtras > Filter Bitmap.

3 In the Filter Bitmap dialog box, choose a category on the left and a filter on the right.

To view all the filters at once, choose All from the Categories list.

4 Click Filter.

Many filters require you to enter special settings. When you choose one of these filters, a dialog box or other type of control appears after you click Filter. When you finish choosing filter settings and proceed, the filter changes the cast member.

Some filters have no changeable settings. When you choose one of these filters, the cast member changes with no further steps.

Using filters to create animated effects

You can use Auto Filter to create dramatic animated effects with bitmap filters. Auto Filter applies a filter incrementally to a series of cast members. You can use it either to change a range of selected cast members or to generate a series of new filtered cast members based on a single image. When you define a beginning and ending setting for the filter, Auto Filter applies an intermediate filter value to each cast member.

You can tween a bitmap filter with Auto Filter.

Note: Most filters do not support auto filtering. The Auto Filter dialog box lists only those filters that do.

To use Auto Filter:

1 Select a bitmap cast member or a range of cast members and then choose Xtras > Auto Filter.

   If you want to change only a portion of a bitmap cast member, use the Marquee or Lasso tool in the Paint window to select the part you want to change.

2 In the Auto Filter dialog box, select a filter.

3 Click Set Starting Values and use the filter controls to enter filter settings for the first cast member in the sequence.

   When you finish working with the filter controls, the Auto Filter dialog box reappears.

4 Click Set Ending Values and use the filter controls to enter filter settings for the last cast member in the sequence.

5 Enter the number of new cast members you want to create. The box is not available if you have selected a range of cast members.

6 Click Filter to begin the filtering.

   A message appears to show the progress. Some filters are very complex and require extra time for computing.

   Auto Filter generates new cast members and places them in empty cast positions following the cast member you selected. If you selected a range of cast members, no new cast members appear, but the cast members in the range you selected are changed incrementally.

Using onion skinning

Onion skinning derives its name from a technique used by conventional animators, who drew on very thin "onion skin" paper so that they could see through it to one or more of the previous images in the animation.

With onion skinning in Director, you can create or edit animated sequences of cast members in the Paint window using other cast members as a reference. Reference images appear dimmed in the background. While working in the Paint window, you can view not only the current cast member that you're painting but also one or more cast members blended into the image.

You can use onion skinning to do the following:

- To trace over an image or create a series of images all in register (aligned) with a particular image.

- To see previous images in the sequence and use those images as a reference while you are drawing new ones.

- To create a series of images based on another parallel animation. The series of images serves as the background while you paint a series of foreground images.

Onion skinning uses registration points to align the current cast member with the previous ones you have chosen. Be careful not to move registration points for cast members after onion skinning. If you do, the cast members may not line up the way you want them to. See "Changing registration points" on page 315.

You must have created some cast members in order to use onion skinning.

To activate onion skinning:

1 Open the Paint window and choose View > Onion Skin. The Onion Skin toolbar appears.

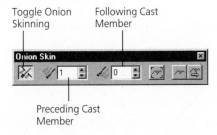

Toggle Onion Skinning   Following Cast Member

Preceding Cast Member

2 Click the Toggle Onion Skinning button at the far left of the toolbar to enable onion skinning.

To define the number of preceding or following cast members to display:

1 Open the Paint window and choose View > Onion Skin. The Onion Skin toolbar appears.

2 If necessary, click the Toggle Onion Skinning button on the Onion Skin toolbar to activate onion skinning.

3 Specify the number of preceding or following cast members you want to display.

- To specify the number of preceding cast members to display, enter a number in the Preceding Cast Members box.

- To specify the number of following cast members to display, enter a number in the Following Cast Members box.

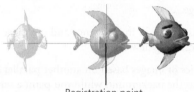

Registration point

Two preceding cast members shown with onion skinning and registration points

The specified number of cast members appear as dimmed images behind the current cast member. The order is determined by the position in the cast.

To create a new cast member by tracing over a single cast member as a background image:

1   Open the Paint window and choose View > Onion Skin. The Onion Skin toolbar appears.

2   In the Paint window, open the cast member that you want to use as the reference image or background.

3   If necessary, click the Toggle Onion Skinning button on the Onion Skin toolbar to activate onion skinning.

4   To set the background image, click the Set Background button on the Onion Skin toolbar.

5   To create a new cast member, click the New Cast Member button in the Paint window.

6   Click the Show Background button on the Onion Skin toolbar.

The original cast member appears as a dimmed image in the Paint window. You can paint on top of the original cast member's image.

7   Paint the new cast member using the background image as a reference.

To use a series of images as a background while painting a series of foreground images:

1 In the Cast window, arrange in consecutive order the series of cast members you want to use as your background.

Cast members in both the foreground and the background series must be adjacent to each other in the cast.

2 Open the Paint window and choose View > Onion Skin. The Onion Skin toolbar appears.

The Onion Skin toolbar appears.

3 If necessary, click the Toggle Onion Skinning button on the Onion Skin toolbar to activate onion skinning.

Make sure all values in the Onion Skin toolbar are set to 0.

 4 Open the cast member you want to use as the first background cast member in the reference series. Click the Set Background button.

 5 Select the position in the cast where you want the first cast member in the foreground series to appear. Click the New Cast Member button in the Paint window to create a new cast member.

The first cast member in the foreground series can be located anywhere in any cast.

 6 Click the Show Background button to reveal a dimmed version of the background image.

 7 Click the Track Background button on the Onion Skin toolbar.

8 Paint the new cast member using the background image as a reference.

9 When you have finished drawing the cast member, click the New Cast Member button again to create the next cast member.

When Track Background is enabled, Director advances to the next background cast member in the series. Its image appears in the background in the Paint window.

10 Repeat step 8 until you have completed drawing all the cast members in the series.

Using shapes

Shape cast members are the same non–anti-aliased shapes that were available in older versions of Director. Similar to vector shapes, they are very memory efficient.

Shapes are images you can create directly on the Stage with the Line, Rectangle, Rounded Rectangle, and Ellipse tools on the Tool palette. You can fill shapes with a color, pattern, or custom tile. Shapes require even less memory than vector shapes, but Director does not anti-alias shapes, so they don't appear as smooth on the Stage as vector shapes. Use shapes for creating simple graphics and backgrounds when you want to keep your movie as small as possible. Shapes are especially useful for filling an area with a custom tile to create an interesting background that downloads quickly from the Internet. See "Creating a custom tile" on page 323.

The Radio Button, Check Box, and Button tools in the Tool palette work create simple buttons. These buttons do not do anything unless you attach a behavior or Lingo script to them.

To create a shape:

1 Select a frame in the Score where you want to draw a shape.

2 Choose color, line thickness, and pattern settings with the controls in the Tool palette. (To open the Tool palette, choose Window > Tool Palette.)

3 Click a tool and then drag on the Stage to draw the shape.

The new shape appears on the Stage and in the Cast window.

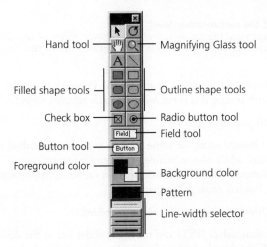

Use the Field button to create field cast members directly on the Stage. Use the Push Button tool to create push button cast members directly on the Stage.

To specify a shape's type with Lingo:

Set the shapeType cast member property. See shapeType in the *Lingo Dictionary*.

To specify a shape's fill with Lingo:

Set the filled and pattern shape cast member properties. See filled and pattern in the *Lingo Dictionary*.

To specify the line size for a shape with Lingo:

Set the lineSize cast member or sprite property. See lineSize in the *Lingo Dictionary*.

Compressing bitmaps

If you plan to distribute your movie over the Internet, you can compress your bitmap images to ensure faster downloading. Director lets you compress images at the movie level and for individual cast members. Bitmap compression set at the cast member level overrides compression settings at the movie level.

In addition to Director standard compression, you can use JPEG compression and specify a range of image quality. If you have Fireworks installed, you can use the Optimize in Fireworks button to launch Fireworks, then dynamically apply compression settings while viewing how your image will look at those settings. When you determine the most suitable compression level, Director will remember the settings you established in Fireworks. For more information, see "Optimizing Bitmaps in Fireworks" in the Director Support Center Web site.

To compress a bitmap at the cast member level:

1   Select bitmap cast members or sprites and click the Bitmap tab of the Property Inspector.

    If you've selected multiple cast members or sprites, the Property Inspector displays the compression setting if it is the same for each selected object.

2   Click the Compression pop-up window.

•   To compress selected bitmaps using the same settings as those established for movie-level compression, select Movie Setting. For more information on setting bitmaps at the movie level, see the information on the Compression tab under "Changing Publish settings" on page 441.

•   To use the standard Director compression, select Standard.

•   To use JPEG compression, select JPEG and move the slider bar to the desired level of compression. Note that the higher the number you specify, the less your bitmap will be compressed (e.g., 100 indicates no compression).

Movie Setting is usually the default compression setting, except under certain conditions when the compression feature is disabled, or when Director controls image compression choices.

For example, when the image is a JPEG, the compression setting defaults to JPEG compression. You cannot select another compression option.

Similarly, the Compression setting defaults to Standard compression, and you cannot change this, when the cast member is any of the following:

- An 8-bit cast member created in the Paint window

- A GIF imported as a bitmap with no alpha channel information

- An 8-bit PNG

- A linked cast member or a cast member created with Lingo

If you open a Director 7 movie in Director 8, bitmap cast members are assigned Movie Setting as the default, and compression settings at the movie level, set in the Publish Settings dialog box, default to the Standard compression setting. This ensures the movie will continue to play as it did in Director 7.

To compress bitmaps at the movie level:

1 Choose File > Publish Settings.

   The Publish Settings dialog box appears.

2 On the Compression tab, make a selection from the Image Compression pop-up menu and click OK.

- To use the standard Director compression, select Standard.

- To use JPEG compression, select JPEG and move the slider bar to the desired level of compression. Note that the higher the number you specify, the less your bitmap will be compressed (e.g., 100 indicates no compression).

Note: Director saves your publish settings when you save your movie.

CHAPTER 13
Text

Director creates text that is editable, anti-aliased, and compact—for fast downloading in any font on any platform. Combine these features with any of Director's animation capabilities, such as rotation, and you can create text effects not possible in any other application.

You can embed fonts in a movie to ensure that text appears in a specific font when a movie is delivered, regardless of which fonts are available on the user's computer.

Because Director renders text in the display font and anti-aliases it as the movie plays, text in Director is very compact and downloads quickly from the Internet. Most of the high-quality text you see in Web browsers is actually a GIF or JPEG graphic, and takes longer to download than Director text.

Director provides many ways to add text to a movie. You can either create new text cast members within Director or import text from an outside source such as a document stored on the Internet. You can import plain text, RTF, or HTML documents. Once text is part of your movie, you can format the text in a variety of ways using Director's formatting tools. Director offers standard professional formatting functions, including alignment, tabs, kerning, spacing, subscripts, superscripts, color, and so on. You can also create hyperlinks for any text.

Text in Director is editable when you are working on your movie and, optionally, while a movie plays.

You can also use Lingo to control text. For example, you can use Lingo to edit the text in existing cast members, specify text formatting such as font and size, and interpret strings that users enter.

To create the smallest possible text cast members, use field text. Field text is standard text controlled by your system software, just like the text you see in dialog boxes and menu bars. Director does not anti-alias field text or support paragraph formatting and tabs for fields. As with regular text, Lingo can control field text and specify whether field text is editable while a movie plays.

Whereas regular text is best suited for large type that you want to look as good as possible, field text is an excellent choice for large blocks of smaller text in standard fonts (such as Times or Helvetica) that do not need to be anti-aliased.

Embedding fonts in movies

Before creating text or field cast members, it's good practice to embed the fonts you want to use in the movie. Embedding fonts makes Director store all font information in the movie file so that a font will display properly even if it is not installed in a user's system. Because embedded fonts are available only to the movie itself, there are no legal obstacles to distributing fonts in Director movies.

Embedded fonts appear in a movie as cast members and work on Windows and Macintosh computers. Director compresses embedded fonts so they usually only add 14 to 25K to a file.

For the best display at smaller sizes, include bitmap versions of a font when you embed a font. For small font sizes, usually from about 7 to 12 points, bitmap fonts often look better than anti-aliased outline fonts. (See "About anti-aliased text" on page 344.) Adding a set of bitmap characters does, however, make the font cast member larger. Examine the text display quality of your movie to find out if this option is worthwhile.

To speed up movie downloading, you can keep file size small by specifying a subset of characters to be included. You can also specify which point sizes to include as bitmaps and which characters to include in the font package. If you do not embed fonts in a movie, Director substitutes available system fonts.

If you create embedded fonts using the original font name followed by an asterisk (for example, Arial* for the Arial font), Director uses the embedded font for all the text in the movie that uses the original font. This saves you the trouble of manually reapplying the font to all the text in existing movies.

Once you embed a font in a movie file, the font appears on all of the movie's font menus, and you can use it as you would any other font.

To embed a font in a movie:

1 Choose Insert > Media Element > Font.

2 From the Original Font pop-up menu, choose a font that is currently installed on your system.

   You cannot embed a font that is not installed on your system.

   In the New Font Name box, the name of the font is followed by an asterisk. This is the name that will appear on all font menus in Director. In most cases, you should not change the name of a font.

3 To include bitmap versions of the font in specified sizes, click the Sizes button for Bitmaps and enter the point sizes you want to include, separated by spaces or commas. For example, you might enter **9, 10, 14**.

4 To include bitmap versions of bold or italic characters with the font, select Bold or Italic.

   This option provides better-looking bold and italic fonts if you are including a bitmap version of the font, but it increases the file size.

5 To specify the characters included in the font, choose an option for Characters.

• Entire Set includes every character (symbols, punctuation, numbers, and so on) with the font.

• Partial Set lets you choose exactly which characters are included. To choose a group of characters, select Punctuation, Numbers, Roman Characters, or Other. If you choose Other, enter the characters to be included in the box on the right. In some double-byte languages, other groups of characters may appear.

To embed a font in a movie with Lingo:

Use the recordFont command. See recordFont in the *Lingo Dictionary*.

Creating text cast members

You can create text within Director or import text from external files.

Creating text in Director

Director provides two ways to create text cast members: directly on the Stage or in the Text window.

To create text cast members directly on the Stage:

 1 Click the Text tool in the Tool palette.

2 Drag the pointer on the Stage to create a text cast member.

You cannot adjust the height of the text object at this point—the height adjusts automatically when you add text.

When you release the mouse button, a text insertion point appears in the area you just defined.

3 Enter text.

The new text cast member appears in the first available position in the current cast; the sprite is placed in the first open cell in the current frame in the Score.

To create text cast members in the Text window:

1 Choose Insert > Media Element > Text.

 If the Text window is already open, click the New Cast Member button to create a new text cast member.

2 Enter text in the Text window.

Text you enter appears in the first available cast position, but it is not automatically placed on the Stage.

3 To change the width of the cast member, drag the bar at the right edge of the cast member.

Drag

Importing text

You can import text from any application that saves text in rich text format (RTF), in plain text (ASCII), or from HTML documents. Use the standard importing procedure with File > Import to import any RTF, ACII, or HTML document. To import an HTML document from the Internet, use the Internet button in the Import dialog box and enter a URL.

Note: Text and RTF files are always imported and stored inside the movie file even if you select Link to External File.

When importing text from an HTML document, Director recognizes most standard tags and parameters, including tables, and approximates the formatting. Director does not recognize embedded objects other than tables, and it does not support nested tables. It also does not recognize APPLET, FORM, FRAME, INPUT, or IMAGE tags.

Director ignores any tags it does not recognize. Be sure to test the importing of any HTML file that is updated frequently to make sure you're satisfied with the formatting.

When importing text from an RTF file, Director recognizes most standard RTF formatting, but it does not import pictures embedded in the file.

The amount of text in a cast member is limited only by the memory available in the playback system.

Importing text with Lingo

Lingo can import text in several ways. See individual entries in the *Lingo Dictionary*.

* To import text from a URL, use the getNetText() function.

* To import text from an external file from a URL or the local computer, select or create a text cast member and set its fileName property to the name of the external file that contains the text. To import text from a file on disk, use the getPref() function. If no setPref command has already written such a file, the getPref() function returns VOID. See getPref() in the *Lingo Dictionary*.

Editing and formatting text

Director offers a number of ways to edit and format text. You can edit text directly on the Stage and format it with the floating Text Inspector, or use the Text window to work in a more traditional text editing environment. Many of the same formatting controls are in the Font and Paragraph dialog boxes as well as in the Text window and the Text Inspector. Choose the most convenient option for your work style.

Selecting and editing text on the Stage

For basic text editing, it's fastest to edit text directly on the Stage.

To edit text on the Stage:

1 Click a text cast member on the Stage to select it as a sprite.

   The text sprite appears as a normal sprite with double borders.

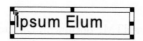

2 Click twice to edit the text.

   An insertion point appears in the text, and you can begin editing.

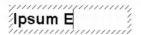

3 Use the Text Inspector to reformat the text.

   You can also use the Modify > Font and Modify > Paragraph commands to reformat selected text.

   When you make a change, Director updates all sprites that display the text cast member.

Note: If you're changing the background color of text, you have two options. To change the background color of the cast member, double-click the text sprite on the Stage and assign a value from the Color box on the Tool palette. You can also tint the sprite's background, which blends the background color of the cast member with the background color of the sprite. To apply this effect, select the sprite and choose a background color on the Sprite tab of the Property Inspector.

To edit text on the Stage during playback:

1 Select a text sprite and click Editable in the Sprite tab of the Property Inspector. See "Displaying and editing sprite properties in the Property Inspector" on page 126.

2 Begin playing back the movie.

3 On the Stage, double-click to edit the text.

Formatting characters

Once you have created text cast members for your movie, you can format them in a variety of ways: you can set the font, style, size, line spacing, and color. The following procedure uses the Font dialog box, but many of the same options are available in the Text Inspector and the Text window.

To format characters:

1 Double-click inside a text sprite.

2 Drag to select the text you want to format.

3 Choose Modify > Font to open the Font dialog box.

4 Choose from the following options in the Font dialog box:

• To specify the font, choose a font from the pop-up menu. Be sure to use embedded fonts for movies you intend to distribute (see "Embedding fonts in movies" on page 336).

• To use bold, italic, underline, superscript, subscript, or strikeout for text, click the appropriate box.

• To change the point size of text, increase or decrease the size with the Size option.

• To change the distance between lines of text, increase or decrease the spacing with the Spacing option.

• To specify kerning between selected characters, use the Kerning option to specify the number of points. This setting supplements the standard kerning applied to the entire cast member in the Text Cast Member Properties dialog box. See "About kerning" on page 345.

• To change the text color, click the color box and choose a color from the Color menu.

Formatting paragraphs

You can specify the alignment, indentation, tabs, and spacing for each paragraph in a text cast member. The following procedure explains how to format paragraphs while you work in the Text window, but many of the same formatting options are available in the Text Inspector and the Paragraph dialog box.

To make formatting changes to a paragraph:

1   Double-click the text cast member in the Score to open the Text window.

2   If the ruler is not visible, choose View > Ruler.

To change the unit of measure on the text ruler, choose File > Preferences > General and select Inches, Centimeters, or Pixels from the Text Units pop-up menu.

3   Place the insertion point in the paragraph you want to change, or select multiple paragraphs.

4   To define tabs, use any of the following options:

• Set tabs by clicking the tab button until the type of tab you want appears. Then click the ruler to place the tab.

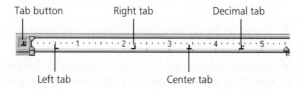

• Move a tab by dragging the tab marker on the ruler.

• Remove a tab by dragging the tab marker up or down off the ruler.

5   To set margins, drag the indent markers on the ruler.

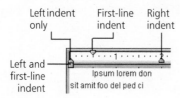

6 To set line spacing, change the setting with the Line Spacing control.

Director adjusts line spacing to match the size of the text you are using.

If you change the line spacing setting, Director stops making automatic adjustments. To resume automatic adjustments of spacing, enter 0 in the Line Spacing box.

7 To set paragraph alignment, click one of the alignment buttons.

8 To change the kerning of selected characters, change the value of the Kerning option.

9 Set spacing before and after paragraphs by choosing Modify > Paragraph and using the Spacing Before and After options.

Formatting entire cast members

Director can apply formatting changes to entire cast members. This process is much faster than manually opening each cast member and applying changes. Any change you apply to a cast member affects all the text within the cast member.

To format text cast members:

1 In a Cast window or on the Stage, select the cast members you want to change.

You can select as many cast members as you want to change.

2 Use the Text Inspector, Modify > Font, or Modify > Paragraph to make formatting changes.

The change affects all text in the selected cast members.

Formatting with the Text Inspector

The Text Inspector provides many of the most useful formatting controls in a compact floating window for use on the Stage or with entire cast members in the Cast window.

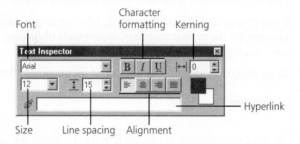

Most of the formatting controls also appear at the top of the Text window and in the Font and Paragraph dialog boxes.

To display the Text Inspector:

Choose Window > Inspector > Text, or press Control+T (Windows) or Command+T (Macintosh).

About anti-aliased text

Anti-aliased text is text that uses color variations to make its jagged angles and curves look smoother. Director activates anti-aliasing by default. You can change this setting in the Text tab of the Property Inspector (see "Setting text or field cast member properties" on page 350.) Anti-aliasing functions the same way for embedded fonts and for system fonts that have not been embedded (see "Embedding fonts in movies" on page 336).

Using anti-aliased text dramatically improves the quality of large text on the Stage, but it can blur or distort smaller text. Experiment with the size settings to get the best results for the font you are using.

Anti-aliasing on
Anti-aliasing on

Anti-aliasing off
Anti-aliasing off

Director can anti-alias all outline (TrueType, PostScript, and embedded) fonts, but not bitmap fonts. When you select a font that cannot be anti-aliased, the message "This font cannot be anti-aliased" appears in the Font dialog box below the font list. (Display the Font dialog box by selecting text or a text sprite and then choosing Modify > Font.)

About kerning

Kerning is a specialized form of spacing between certain pairs of characters that look best when they overlap slightly, such as A and W (AW). Kerning dramatically improves the appearance of large text for headlines, but it often does not improve the appearance of text at small font sizes.

If the Kerning option is on in the Text tab of the Property Inspector, Director kerns all the characters in the cast member according to standard kerning tables (see "Setting text or field cast member properties" on page 350). The setting you enter in the Text window or Font dialog box (see "Formatting characters" on page 341) supplements the standard kerning.

Finding and replacing text

Use the Find > Text command to quickly search for and replace text in the Text, Field, or Script window. All searches start at the insertion point and search forward.

To search and replace text:

1 Choose Window > Text, Window > Field, or Window > Script to open the window in which you want to search.

2 Place the insertion point at the position where you want the search to begin.

3 Choose Edit > Find > Text.

4 Enter the text you want to search for in the Find box.

5 Enter the text you want to use in place of the found text in the Replace box.

6 To specify the cast members in which to search, choose a Search option:

- Cast Member *Name* limits the search to the current cast member.

- Cast *Cast Name* limits the search to cast members in the current cast.

- All Casts extends the search to all cast members in all casts.

7 To set additional search options, select Wrap-Around, Whole Words Only, or Case Sensitive.

- Wrap-Around specifies whether or not Director returns to the beginning of text once it reaches the end. If you select this option but not All Casts, Director continues searching from the top of the current text after it reaches the bottom of the window. If you select both options, Director searches all cast members of the same type (either text, field, or script, depending on where you initiated the search), beginning with the currently selected cast member and returning to the first cast member of that type if necessary.

- Whole Words Only searches only for occurrences of the specified whole word.

- Case Sensitive searches only for text with the same capitalization as the text in the Find box.

Creating a hyperlink

In the Text Inspector, you can turn any selected range of text into a hyperlink that links to a URL or initiates other actions. Director automatically adds standard hyperlink formatting to the selected text so that it initially appears with blue underlining. You can turn off this formatting in the Text tab of the Property Inspector. See "Setting text or field cast member properties" on page 350.

The following procedure describes how to add a hyperlink to selected text. To make a hyperlink actually do something, you need to write an on hyperlinkClicked event handler. See on hyperLinkClicked in the *Lingo Dictionary*.

You can enter any string in the hyperlink box; it does not have to be a URL. The string cannot contain a double quotation mark or the Lingo continuation character.

To define a hyperlink:

1 Select the text you want to define as a hyperlink.

2 Choose Window > Inspector > Text to open the Text Inspector.

3 In the Hyperlink box, enter the URL to which you want to link, or enter any message you want to send to the on hyperlinkClicked handler. Then press Enter (Windows) or Return (Macintosh).

Working with fields

Working with field cast members is similar to working with text. Just as with text cast members, you edit fields on the Stage or in a window and apply formatting with the Text Inspector. Not all text formatting options are available for fields: you cannot apply spacing, tabs, or indents to individual paragraphs within fields. Alignment settings apply to every paragraph in the field.

To create a field cast member:

1 Do one of the following:

• Choose Insert > Control > Field.

• Click the Field tool in the Tool palette and then drag on the Stage to define the area of the field.

 —— Field tool

The field is created and an insertion point is placed at the beginning of the field.

2 Enter the text for the field. When you are finished, click outside the field to exit the field.

To specify field settings:

Choose Window > Field, or double-click a field cast member in the Cast window.

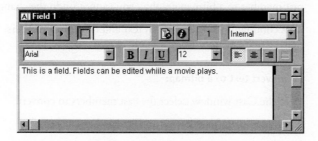

If necessary, use the Previous Cast Member and Next Cast Member buttons to navigate to the field you want to edit. See "Setting text or field cast member properties" on page 350.

Using editable text

Editable text lets users enter text on a Web page, customize a game, and so on. When text is editable, editing the text changes the text cast member and all the text in the sprites where the cast member appears.

You can make text editable and let users tab between editable sprites from the Property Inspector (see "Setting text or field cast member properties" on page 350) or from Lingo.

You can make a text sprite editable in only a certain range of frames in the Score.

To make a text sprite editable in a range of frames:

1 Select a range of frames within a sprite.

   You can select an entire sprite, or Shift-Alt-click (Windows) or Shift-Option-click (Macintosh) to select frames within a sprite.

2 Click the Text or Field tab of the Property Inspector using the Graphical view.

3 Click Editable.

To control whether text is editable with Lingo:

Set the editable property. See editable in the *Lingo Dictionary*.

To have Lingo specify whether pressing Tab opens the next sprite for editing:

Set the autotab property. See autoTab in the *Lingo Dictionary*.

Converting text to a bitmap

Use Convert to Bitmap to change a text or field cast member to a bitmap. The converted graphic can then be edited in the Paint window. Once you convert a cast member to a bitmap graphic, you cannot undo the change.

This command works only with text and field cast members. You can't convert a shape to a bitmap.

To convert text to a bitmap:

1 In the Cast window, select the cast members to convert.

2 Choose Modify > Convert to Bitmap.

   Director converts the cast members to bitmaps.

Mapping fonts between platforms for field cast members

Director uses a file named Fontmap.txt to map fonts in fields between the Windows and Macintosh platforms. When you create a new movie, Director looks for Fontmap.txt in the same folder as the Director application.

The version of Fontmap.txt included with Director assigns fonts as shown in the following table. These settings provide the best equivalents of common system fonts on both platforms.

Windows font	Macintosh font
Arial	Helvetica
Courier	Courier
Courier New	Courier
MS Serif	New York
MS Sans Serif	Geneva
Symbol	Symbol
System	Chicago
Terminal	Monaco
Times New Roman	Times (Because Times New Roman is larger than Times, Fontmap.txt assigns a smaller point size.)

Fontmap.txt also determines the scaling of fonts and how special characters such as bullets and symbols are translated between platforms. Again, the default settings are correct for nearly all applications, but you can edit the settings if necessary.

Setting text or field cast member properties

Use the Property Inspector to view and change settings for selected text cast members. In addition to standard Name and Unload properties, you can specify whether text is editable while the movie plays, improve performance with pre-rendering, and control anti-aliasing and kerning.

To view or change text or field cast member properties:

1 Select a text cast member.

2 To display the Property Inspector, choose Modify > Cast Member > Properties or choose Window > Properties > Inspector.

3 If necessary, click the Member tab using the Graphical view.

   The following noneditable settings are displayed:

- The cast member size in kilobytes

- The cast member creation and edit dates

- The name of the last person who modified the cast member

4 To view or edit the cast member name, use the Name field.

5 To add comments about the cast member, use the Comments field.

6 To specify how Director removes the cast member from memory if memory is low, choose an option from the Unload pop-up menu. See "Controlling cast member unloading" on page 114.

7 To change the text of the cast member, click Edit.

8 Click the Text or Field tab of the Property Inspector using the Graphical view.

9 To determine how Director places text within the boundaries of the cast member, choose a Framing option:

- Adjust to Fit expands the text box vertically when text that is entered extends beyond the current size of the box.

- Scrolling attaches a scroll bar to the right side of the text box. This is useful when there is a large amount of text. Note that the scroll bar will be drawn direct to Stage; this means that even if another cast member is in front of a cast member containing a scroll bar, the scroll bar will appear frontmost.

- Fixed retains the original size of the text box. If you enter text that extends beyond the limits of the box, the text is stored but not displayed. You can set up scrolling with Lingo (see "Controlling scrolling text with Lingo" on page 356).

- Limit to Field Size (available only for field cast members) displays only the amount of text that fits within the field's bounding rectangle.

10 To set editing and display options, choose from the following options:

- Editable makes the cast member editable while the movie plays (see "Using editable text" on page 348).

- Wrap increases the vertical size of the text box or field on the Stage so that all text is visible.

- Tab to Next Editable Item advances the text insertion point to the next editable sprite on the Stage when the user presses Tab.

- Direct to Stage (text cast members only) makes text display more quickly by rendering it directly to the Stage without composing it with other sprites. This prevents other sprites from appearing over the text and limits the ink options to Copy.

- Use Hypertext Styles (text cast members only) makes hypertext links appear as they do in a Web browser, initially using blue underlining, and then red once the link has been visited. (See "Creating a hyperlink" on page 346.)

11 To make text of a text cast member appear on the Stage more quickly, choose a pre-render option. Pre-rendering controls when text buffers will be created.

Without pre-rendering, large amounts of anti-aliased text can take a while to load, causing a noticeable pause on a frame that displays the text for the first time. When a pre-render option is selected, text buffers are created when the current text member is loaded instead of when the member first appears on the Stage.

Select one of the following pre-render options from the Pre-Render pop-up menu:

- None provides no pre-rendering.

- Copy Ink optimizes the pre-rendering for Copy Ink. (This option renders text more quickly than Other Ink.)

- Other Ink pre-renders the text for all other ink types.

If you choose a pre-render option, you can make text appear on the Stage even more quickly by selecting Save Bitmap. See the next section, "Using the Save Bitmap feature for pre-rendered text" on page 352.

12 To control how Director anti-aliases text for a text cast member, choose an Anti-Alias option:

- All Text anti-aliases all the text in the text block.

- Larger Than anti-aliases only text larger than the point size entered in the Points field.

- None turns off anti-aliasing for the current cast member.

Anti-aliasing dramatically improves the appearance of large text, but it can blur or distort smaller text. Experiment with the size setting to get the best results for the font you are using. (See "About anti-aliased text" on page 344.)

13 To control how Director kerns text, choose a Kerning option.

Kerning often does not improve the appearance of text at small point sizes. See "About kerning" on page 345.

- All Text kerns all the text in the cast member according to the standard kerning table.

- Larger Than kerns only text larger than the point size entered in the Points field.

- None turns off kerning for the current cast member.

Using the Save Bitmap feature for pre-rendered text

The Save Bitmap feature works in tandem with pre-render options to display a buffer image of your text while your user waits for the actual text to load. This feature is useful when you're working with a large amount of anti-aliased text. (The Save Bitmap feature is different from the Convert to Bitmap menu command, which converts a text cast member into a bitmap image.)

You can also use the Save Bitmap feature with pre-render options if you're using special text characters for an audience not equipped to display them. For example, using Save Bitmap enables a non-Japanese system to display a text sprite that contains Japanese characters. Note, however, that the Save Bitmap option adds to the file size. The feature works with static text, but not with editable or scrolling text.

To use the Save Bitmap feature for pre-rendered text:

1 Select the text sprite.

2 On the Text tab of the Property Inspector, select from the Pre-Render pop-up menu:

- If the text sprite's ink is Copy Ink, select Copy Ink.

- If the text sprite's ink is any type of ink other than Copy Ink, select Other Ink.

  For this procedure to work, you must make the correct selection from the Pre-Render pop-up menu. You can determine the Sprite's ink on the Sprite tab of the Property Inspector.

3 Select Save Bitmap.

Formatting chunks of text with Lingo

The Director interface lets you format a variety of text characteristics, such as the font, size, style, and line spacing. Using Lingo, you can format text dynamically as the movie plays. You can also use Lingo to rapidly format text during authoring.

Formatting text with Lingo

Lingo can format text in an entire cast member or any specific chunk of text using the following properties. See entries for individual properties in the *Lingo Dictionary*.

* To select or identify a chunk of text in a field cast member, use the selStart and selEnd cast member properties. These properties identify the first and last characters of a text selection.

* To refer to a selected chunk of text, use the selection cast member property.

* To specify the font for a text cast member, field cast member, or chunk expression, set the font cast member property.

* To specify the character size for a text cast member, field cast member, or chunk expression, set the fontSize property.

* To specify the line spacing for a field cast member, set the lineHeight property.

* To specify the style for a text cast member, field cast member, or chunk expression, set the fontStyle property.

* To specify the drop shadow size for the characters in a field cast member, set the boxDropShadow property.

* To specify additional spacing applied to a chunk expression in a text cast member, set the charSpacing property.

* To specify the foreground color for a field cast member, set the foreColor property.

Applying paragraph formats with Lingo

Lingo can control paragraph formatting such as alignment and indenting for a chunk expression. See entries for individual properties in the *Lingo Dictionary*.

- To set text alignment for a text or field cast member, set the alignment property.

- To set line spacing in points for a text cast member, set the fixedLineSpace property.

- To add pixels below paragraphs in a text cast member, set the bottomSpacing property.

- To add pixels above paragraphs in a text cast member, set the topSpacing property.

- To specify line spacing in a field cast member, set the lineHeight property.

- To add pixels to the first indent in a chunk expression in a text cast member, set the firstIndent property.

- To set the left indent (in pixels) of a chunk expression in a text cast member, set the leftIndent property.

- To set the right indent (in pixels) of a chunk expression in a text cast member, set the rightIndent property.

- To specify or obtain a list of tabs that are in a chunk expression in a text cast member, set or test the tabs property.

Formatting text or field cast members with Lingo

In addition to formatting text in any chunk expression, Lingo can specify anti-aliasing and kerning for an entire text cast member and control the appearance of the text's bounding rectangle.

Setting anti-aliasing and kerning with Lingo

Use Lingo to specify anti-aliasing and kerning for a text cast member. See entries for individual properties in the *Lingo Dictionary*.

- To specify whether Director anti-aliases text in a text cast member, set the antiAlias cast member property.

- To specify the size at which anti-aliasing in a text cast member takes effect, set the antiAliasThreshold cast member property.

- To specify automatic kerning for a text cast member, set the kerning cast member property.

- To specify the size at which automatic kerning for a text cast member takes effect, set the kerningThreshold cast member property.

Formatting text boxes with Lingo

Lingo can specify the type of box that surrounds a text or field cast member. For field cast members, Lingo can also specify box characteristics such as borders, margins, drop shadows, and height. See entries for individual properties in the *Lingo Dictionary*.

- To specify the type of box around a text or field, set the boxType cast member property.

- To specify the size of the border around a field, set the border field cast member property.

- To specify the size of the margin inside a field's box, set the margin field cast member property.

- To specify the size of the drop shadow for a field's box, set the boxDropShadow field cast member property.

- To specify the height of a field's box on the Stage, set the pageHeight field cast member property.

Setting text autotabbing and wrapping with Lingo

Lingo can set text autotabbing and wrapping. See entries for individual properties in the *Lingo Dictionary*.

- To specify autotabbing for text or field cast members, set the autoTab cast member property.

- To specify whether lines wrap in a field cast member, set the wordWrap cast member property.

Controlling scrolling text with Lingo

Lingo can scroll text and determine the location of specific text within the text box for text and field cast members. For example, this statement sets the scrollTop value for the text cast member called Discussion to 0, which makes its first line appear at the top of its scrolling field:

```
(member "Discussion").scrollTop = 0
```

This procedure can be useful for making a scrolling field automatically scroll back to the top. For more information on the following properties, see individual entries in the *Lingo Dictionary*.

- To scroll up or down by a specific number of pages in a text or field cast member, use the scrollByPage command.

- To scroll up or down by a specific number of lines in a text or field cast member, use the scrollByLine command.

- To determine the number of lines that appear in a field cast member on the Stage, set the lineCount cast member property. (This property doesn't apply to text cast members.)

- To determine a line's distance from the top edge of a text or field cast member, use the linePosToLocV() function.

- To determine the number of the line that appears at a specific vertical position in a text or field cast member, use the locVToLinePos() function. (This measures the distance from the top of the cast member, not what appears on the Stage.)

- To determine the point in a text or field cast member that is closest to a specific character, use the charPosToLoc() function.

- To determine the character that is closest to a specific point in a text or field cast member, use the locToCharPos() function.

- To check or set the distance from the top of the line that is currently visible to the top of the box for a scrolling field or text cast member, test or set the scrollTop cast member property.

Checking for specific text with Lingo

The Lingo operators contains and equals (=) are useful for checking strings. The contains operator compares two strings to see whether one string contains the other. The equals operator can determine whether a string is exactly the same as the contents of a field cast member. Use these operators to check whether a specified string is in a field cast member. See contains in the *Lingo Dictionary*.

You can also use Lingo to evaluate strings returned by the text property of a text or field cast member. See text in the *Lingo Dictionary*.

Modifying strings with Lingo

As time passes or other conditions change, you may want to update and change text. For example, you may want to frequently update a text sprite that displays the user's name or a description of a musical selection that the user is currently streaming from a Web site. See individual entries in the *Lingo Dictionary*.

- To set the entire content of a text or field cast member, set the text cast member property to a new chunk of text. The chunk can be a string or another text cast member.

- To combine character strings, use the & and && operators. The & operator attaches the second string to the end of the first string. The && operator includes a space between two strings when they are combined.

- To insert a string of characters into another string, use the put...after, put...into, or put...before command. The put...before command places the string at the beginning of another string. The put...into command replaces a specified chunk expression with another chunk expression. The put...after command places the string at the end of another string.

- To delete a chunk expression from a string of text, use the delete command.

CHAPTER 14
Sound, Video, and Synchronization

You can give your movie added appeal by including a soundtrack, a voice-over, ambient noises, or other sounds. Adding digital video to your movie creates even more interest. Digital video not only offers high-quality real-time image animation and sound but also supports new types of media such as QuickTime VR.

With Director, you have control over when sounds start and stop, how long they last, their quality and volume, and a number of other effects. Using Shockwave Audio, you can compress sounds for easier distribution and stream them from an Internet source.

Director supports QuickTime video for Windows and Macintosh, and Video for Windows (AVI). QuickTime is a multimedia format in its own right. It offers sophisticated sound features and can include graphics in many formats, including basic navigation of QuickTime VR2 files. For a list of supported QuickTime formats, see Apple Computer's Web site at www.apple.com. To use QuickTime, you must also obtain QuickTime 3 or later from Apple.

Director's media synchronization features let you synchronize events in a movie to precise cue points embedded in sound and digital video.

Sound and video make significant demands on a computer's processing power, so you may need to manage them carefully to make sure they do not adversely affect your movie's performance.

Lingo gives Director more flexibility when playing sound and digital video and can help overcome performance concerns. You can use it to play sound and digital video in ways not possible with the Score alone. Using Lingo, you can do the following:

- Turn sound on and off in response to movie events.

- Control sound volume.

- Control the pan of a sound relative to the pan of a QuickTime VR movie.

- Preload sound into memory, queue multiple sounds, and define precise loops.

- Precisely synchronize sound, digital video, and animation.

- Turn digital video on and off on demand and control individual video tracks.

- Control QuickTime VR.

Note: You can export movies or portions of movies as QuickTime or AVI videos. See "Exporting digital video and frame-by-frame bitmaps" on page 454.

Importing internal and linked sounds

Director handles sounds as either internal or linked. You can determine whether a sound is internal or linked when you import it. Each type of sound has advantages for different situations.

Director stores all the sound data for an internal sound cast member in a movie or cast file and loads the sound completely into RAM before playing it. After an internal sound is loaded, it plays very quickly. This makes internal sound best for short sounds, such as beeps or clicks, that recur frequently in your movie. For the same reason, making a large sound file an internal sound is not a good choice, since the sound may use too much memory.

Director does not store sound data in a linked sound cast member. Instead, it keeps a reference to a sound file's location and imports the sound data each time the sound begins playing. Because the sound is never entirely loaded into RAM, the movie uses memory more efficiently.

Also, Director streams many sounds, which means it begins playing the sound while the rest of the sound continues to load from its source, whether on disk or over the Internet. This can dramatically improve the downloading performance of large sounds. Linked sounds are best for longer sounds such as voice-overs or nonrepeating music.

Director can stream the following sounds:

- QuickTime, Shockwave Audio, and MP3 sounds that are linked via a URL

- QuickTime, Shockwave Audio, MP3, AIFF, and WAV sounds that are linked to a local file

Director imports AIFF and WAV sounds (both compressed and uncompressed), AU, Shockwave Audio, MP3, and Macintosh System 7 sounds. For best results, use sounds that have 8- or 16-bit depth and a sampling rate of 44.1, 22.050, or 11.025 kHz.

To import a sound:

1 Choose File > Import.

2 Choose sound files to import.

3 To determine whether the imported sounds will be internal or linked sounds, choose a Media option:

- Standard Import makes all the selected sounds internal sound cast members.

- Link to External File makes all the selected sounds linked.

4 Click Import.

Note: If you're authoring on a Macintosh computer that has an audio input or microphone attached, you can record sounds directly into a movie's cast by choosing Insert > Media Element > Sound. The Sound command opens the Macintosh sound recording dialog box. Director for Windows has no equivalent feature.

Setting sound cast member properties

You can use sound cast member properties to make a sound loop, change its name, change the external sound file it's linked to (if it's a linked sound), and set its unload priority.

To set sound cast member properties:

1 Select a sound cast member.

2 Click the Sound tab of the Property Inspector.

There are several noneditable options in the Sound tab of the Property Inspector:

- The duration of the sound

- The sample rate, sample size, and channels

3 To make the sound play continuously, click Loop. See "Looping a sound" on page 364.

4 To play the sound, click the Play button.

5 Click the Member tab in the Property Inspector.

The following noneditable settings are displayed:

- The cast member size in kilobytes

- The cast member creation and edit dates

- The name of the last person who modified the cast member

6 Use the Name field to view or edit the cast member name.

7 To change the external sound file to which the cast member is linked (if it is a linked sound), enter a new path and file in the Filename field. You can also use the Browse button to select a new file.

8 To specify how Director removes the cast member from memory if memory is low, choose an option from the Unload pop-up menu. See "Controlling cast member unloading" on page 114.

Controlling sound in the Score

You control sounds in the Score in much the same way that you control sprites. You place sounds in one of the two sound channels at the top of the Score and extend the sounds through as many frames as required.

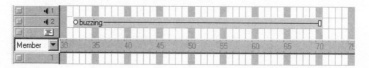

Unless you use a behavior or other Lingo to override the Score's sound channels, sounds play only as long as the playback head is in the frames that contain the sound. After a sound begins playing, it plays at its own speed. Director cannot speed up or slow down sounds. If a sound is not set to loop, it stops playing at the end, even if the sprite specifies a longer duration. See "Looping a sound" on page 364.

Note: You can speed up or slow down a sound by converting it to a sound-only QuickTime movie and using the movieRate sprite property.

In addition to the two sound channels in the Score, Director can use up to six additional sound channels simultaneously. However, the additional channels are accessible only from Lingo or from behaviors. Available RAM and the computer's speed are the real constraints on the number of sounds Director can use effectively.

To place a sound in the Score:

1 If the sound channels are not visible, click the Hide/Show Effects Channels button at the top right side of the Score.

2 Do any of the following:

- Drag a sound cast member from a Cast window to a frame in one of the sound channels.

- Double-click a frame in the sound channel and then choose a sound from the Frame Properties: Sound dialog box. You can also preview any sound cast member in the movie from this dialog box.

- Drag a sound to the Stage to place it into the first available sound channel in the current frame of the Score.

3 Extend the sound through as many frames as necessary.

New sounds are assigned the same number of frames as set for sprites in the Sprite Preferences dialog box. You may need to adjust the number of frames to make the sound play completely or change a tempo setting to make the playback head wait for the sound to finish. See "Synchronizing media" on page 384.

Note: Sound in the last frame of a movie continues to play (but not loop) until the next movie begins or you exit from the application. This sound can provide a useful transition while Director loads the next movie. You can stop the sound using the puppetSound command.

Looping a sound

You may find that you want to play a sound over and over to create a continuous sound effect, such as the sound of a person walking. A looped sound repeats as long as the playback head is in a frame where the sound is set. See "Importing internal and linked sounds" on page 360.

To make a sound loop:

1 Select a sound cast member.

2 On the Property Inspector's Sound tab, select the Loop option.

You can also loop sounds with Lingo. See "Playing sounds with Lingo" on page 365.

Using sound in Windows

The following issues are specific to managing sound for Windows:

- In Windows, a sound that is already playing in either sound channel overrides the sound in a QuickTime or AVI video or a Flash movie. It also prevents the video sound from playing even after the sound in the sound channel has stopped. Once the sound in a digital video has started, however, it overrides a sound in either sound channel.

- To mix QuickTime audio tracks with internal Director sounds, use the soundDevice system property to specify QT3Mix or install the Microsoft DirectSound sound driver software version 5.0 or higher (available from www.microsoft.com), and use the soundDevice property to specify DirectSound..See soundDevice in the *Lingo Dictionary.* (Note that Windows NT4 does not support DirectSound 5.) Check the Director Support Center Web site for the latest developments related to this issue.

- The default number of sounds that Director can mix in Windows is eight. This number can be decreased by modifying the value for MixMaxChannels in the Director.ini file in the Director folder.

Playing sounds with Lingo

Lingo lets you play and control sounds regardless of the settings in the Score. You can use Lingo to play sounds, turn them on and off, and play external sounds that aren't cast members. Using Lingo to play sounds lets you control the exact timing of when sounds start and stop. Lingo also allows you to play only part of a sound cast member or play several sounds in succession without interruption.

Sounds played by Director play at the volume set in the computer's sound level control. You can use Lingo to modify the computer's sound level to suit the needs of your movie, or to modify the volume of the sound channel itself.

You can also use Lingo to control and stream Shockwave Audio. See "Playing Shockwave Audio and MP3 audio with Lingo" on page 370.

Playing sound cast members

Once a sound has been imported as a cast member, you can control many aspects of how the sound is played.

To play sound cast members regardless of the settings in the Score:

Use the queue() and play() functions. The queue() function loads the sound into Director's RAM buffer so that it can be played immediately when called for. The play() command starts the sound playing. If you omit the queue() function, the sound may not play immediately when called for. See queue() and play() in the *Lingo Dictionary*.

The following statements load the sound called Siren into RAM and start it playing in sound channel 1:

```
sound(1).queue(member("Siren"))
sound(1).play()
```

To queue more than one sound to play in succession:

Use the queue() function to list each sound in the order you want them to play. If you queue them before they are played, Director plays the sounds with no pauses between the sounds. Once the sounds are queued, only one play() command is needed.

These statements queue the sound members Explosion and Siren and play them in succession in sound channel 2:

```
sound(2).queue(member("Explosion"))
sound(2).queue(member("Siren"))
sound(2).play()
```

To control how a queued sound plays:

Include optional parameters in a property list within the queue() function. See queue() in the *Lingo Dictionary.*

When setPlayList() is used, any previously set queue of sounds will be replaced by the new playlist.

Once sounds are queued, you can still control whether the queue is obeyed. You can choose to interrupt loops with the breakLoop() command, or to pause playback with the pause() function. The playNext() command lets you skip immediately to the next sound in the queue. See the *Lingo Dictionary* for details on these and other sound commands.

Playing external sound files

To play external sound files that aren't cast members:

Use the sound playFile command. See sound playFile in the *Lingo Dictionary.*

Playing external sound files from disk minimizes the amount of RAM used to play sounds. However, since the computer can read only one item from disk at a time, loading cast members or playing more than one sound from disk can cause unacceptable pauses when you use the sound playFile command.

Controlling sound channels

You can use Lingo to make actions in a movie dependent on whether a sound is playing. Lingo lets you determine whether a sound is playing in a particular sound channel and control how a channel plays sound. See the *Lingo Dictionary* for more information.

- To determine whether a specific channel is playing a sound, use the isBusy() function.

- To turn off the current sound in a specific channel, use the setPlayList() command with [ ] as the new play list. This will delete the entire sound queue and leave the current sound playing. Use the stop() command to stop the currently playing sound.

- To fade a specific channel's sound in and out, use the fadeTo() function.

- To control a specific sound channel's volume, specify the volume property.

- To control the left-to-right panning of a sound, specify the pan property.

About Shockwave Audio

Shockwave Audio is a technology that makes sounds smaller and plays them faster from disk or over the Internet.

Shockwave Audio can compress the size of sounds by a ratio of up to 176:1 and is streamable, which means Director doesn't have to load the entire sound into RAM before it begins playing. Director starts to play the beginning of the sound while the rest of the sound is still streaming from its source, whether coming from disk or over the Internet. When used properly, the Shockwave Audio compression and streaming features provide fast playback of high-quality audio, even for users with relatively slow modem connections to the Internet.

Compression quality in Shockwave Audio

Although Shockwave Audio uses advanced compression technology that alters original sounds as little as possible, the more a sound is compressed the more it is changed.

Set the amount of compression by choosing a bit rate setting in any of the Shockwave Audio Xtras. The bit rate is not related to sampling rates you may have used in other audio programs. Try compressing the same sound at several different bit rates to see how the sound changes.

Choose the bit rate appropriate for the intended delivery system (modem, ISDN, CD-ROM, hard disk, and so on), the type of movie, and the nature of the sound itself. Voice-over sound quality, for example, may not need to be as high as that of music. Test the sound on several systems to find the right balance between quality and performance.

The more compressed a sound is, the faster it streams. If you choose to use a high quality and low degree of compression, a slow delivery system may not be able to send the data fast enough, resulting in gaps during playback. Most developers choose 16 Kbps for the best results over the Internet.

The following table suggests some general guidelines for setting the bit rate for different delivery systems. It also provides a rough estimate of perceived quality for different rates of compression. Note that real transmission times may be slower than the times shown in this table, depending on network traffic and server load.

Delivery	Bit rate	Quality
T1	64 to 128 Kbps	Equal to source material
ISDN or CD-ROM	32 to 56 Kbps	FM stereo to CD
28.8 modem	16 Kbps	FM monaural or good-quality AM
14.4 modem	8 Kbps	Telephone

Note: Any sound compressed at less than 48 Kbps is converted to monaural.

Compressing internal sounds with Shockwave Audio

Shockwave Audio can compress any internal sounds in a movie. Although internal sounds are not streamed, compressing them with Shockwave Audio dramatically decreases the size of the sound data in a movie, shortens the download time from the Internet, and saves disk space.

You can use Shockwave Audio settings to specify compression settings for internal sound cast members. The compression settings you choose apply to all internal sound cast members. You cannot specify different settings for different cast members.

You can choose compression settings at any time, but compression occurs only when the Director movie is compressed with the Create Projector, Save as Shockwave Movie, or Update Movies commands. When creating a projector, Director compresses sounds only if the Compressed option is turned on in the Projector Options dialog box. Compressing sounds can substantially increase the time required to compress a Director movie. See "Creating projectors" on page 449.

Note: Shockwave Audio does not compress SWA or MP3 audio sounds.

When you distribute a movie that contains sounds compressed with Shockwave Audio, the SWA Decompression Xtra is already included in the Shockwave player. If you compress sounds in Shockwave format in a projector, you must provide the SWA Decompression Xtra for the projector.

To have Director compress internal sound cast members when you create a projector, save a movie as Shockwave, or update the movie:

1 Choose File > Publish Settings.

2 Select the Compression tab.

3 Select Compression Enabled to turn on compression.

4 Choose a setting from the kBits/second pop-up menu.

5 Select Convert Stereo to Mono if you want to convert a stereo file to monaural.

At rates lower than 48 Kbps, all sounds are converted to monaural.

6 Click OK.

Streaming linked Shockwave Audio and MP3 audio files

Director streams sounds that have been compressed with Shockwave Audio as well as MP3 audio files, from either a local disk or a URL. Before you can set up a streaming Shockwave Audio cast member, you must create a Shockwave Audio or MP3 file.

To create external Shockwave Audio files, do one of the following:

* In Windows, choose Xtras > Convert WAV to SWA and choose the WAV files to convert.

* On the Macintosh, use the Peak LE 2 software to export Shockwave Audio sounds.

For both methods, the audio settings are similar to those for using Shockwave Audio to compress internal sounds. See "Compressing internal sounds with Shockwave Audio" on page 368.

Note: Converting WAV to SWA does not compress IMA compressed sounds.

To stream a linked Shockwave Audio or MP3 sound:

1 Choose Insert > Media Element > Shockwave Audio.

  This creates a cast member that controls the streaming Shockwave Audio.

2 In the SWA Cast Member Properties dialog box that appears, click Browse and choose a Shockwave Audio file on a local disk, or enter a URL in the Link Address box.

  Unless you choose a file in the same folder as the movie, the movie always links to the exact location you specify. Be sure to link to the correct location.

3 Set the remaining cast member properties in the Property Inspector as follows:

- To set the volume of the sound, use the Volume slider in the SWA tab of the Property Inspector.

- To choose the sound channel for the sound, choose a number from the Channel pop-up menu in the SWA tab. To avoid potential conflicts, choose Any. This will cause the sound to play in the highest numbered available sound channel.

- To specify the size of the stream buffer, use the Preload option in the SWA tab. Director attempts to load enough sound data to play for the specified time in seconds. This prevents gaps in sounds played over slow or interruption-prone Internet connections.

4 Drag the Shockwave Audio cast member to a sprite channel (*not* one of the sound channels) to create a sprite. Extend the sprite through all frames in which the sound should play, or use the tempo channel to make the movie wait for the end of the sound. See "Synchronizing media" on page 384.

You cannot place streaming audio cast members in the sound channels. The sound streams from the source location when the movie plays.

Playing Shockwave Audio and MP3 audio with Lingo

Use SWA Lingo to preload and control SWA and MP3 sounds, and to determine how much of the sound has streamed over the Internet.

Lingo that controls other types of sounds can also control streaming SWA and MP3 sounds by controlling the sound channel that the sound plays in. See the *Lingo Dictionary* for more information on each of these commands.

- To preload part of a streaming sound file into memory, use the preLoadBuffer member command.

- To specify the amount of a streaming cast member to download before playback begins, set the preLoadTime cast member property.

- To determine what percentage of a streaming sound file has actually played, test the percentPlayed cast member property.

- To determine the percent of a streaming file that is already streamed from an Internet server, test the percentStreamed cast member property.

- To specify the sound channel in which a streaming sound plays, set the soundChannel property.

- To begin playback of a streaming cast member, use the play member command.

- To pause a streaming sound file, use the pause member command.

- To stop a streaming sound file, use the stop member command.

- To determine the state of a streaming sound file, test the state cast member property.

- To determine whether an error occurred when streaming a sound file, use the getError() function.

- To obtain a string describing an error that occurred when streaming a sound file, use the getErrorString() function.

- To determine the length of a streaming sound file, use the duration cast member command.

- To determine the bit rate of a streaming sound cast member, test the bitRate cast member property.

- To determine the original bit depth of a streaming sound, test the bitsPerSample property.

- To determine the sample rate of the original sound used for a streaming cast member, test the sampleRate cast member property.

- To determine the number of channels in a streaming sound, test the numChannels streaming cast member property.

- To specify a streaming sound's volume, specify the volume streaming cast member property.

- To specify a streaming sound file's URL, set the URL cast member property.

- To obtain or set the copyright text in a streaming sound file, test or set the copyrightInfo cast member property.

Importing digital video

When you import QuickTime or AVI digital video, the cast members you create always remain linked to the original external file, even if you choose the Standard Import option. When you distribute a movie, you must always include all digital video files along with the movie.

QuickTime must be installed on a computer in order to author or play back a movie that contains QuickTime digital video.

Director converts an AVI video to QuickTime when it plays one on a Macintosh.

For security reasons, Shockwave will link to media on a local disk only if it is in a folder named dswmedia. To test movies in a browser locally before uploading them to your Web server, place the movie, linked casts, and linked media in folders within a dswmedia folder, and use relative links to refer to them. In order for them to be accessible from your server, you must use file and folder names that do not have spaces or capital letters, and that have recognized file extensions like .dcr and .gif. For more information, see the Director Support Center Web site.

To import a digital video:

1 Choose File > Import.

2 Choose QuickTime or AVI (Windows only) from the Files of Type pop-up menu.

3 Choose digital video files to import.

 Because digital video is always imported as linked, you do not have to select an option in the Media pop-up menu.

4 Click Import.

5 Select QuickTime or AVI as the import format.

 If you choose QuickTime, Director imports the video as a QuickTime Asset Xtra, which provides additional playback options. See "Setting digital video cast member properties" on page 373.

Using the Video window

Whether a digital video is a cast member or a sprite on the Stage, you can preview it in the Video window. There is a different version of the window for QuickTime and AVI movies.

To open the Video window, do either of the following:

- Double-click a digital video cast member.
- Choose Window > QuickTime or Window > AVI.

The Video window appears.

If you are working with a QuickTime digital video, a video controller bar appears, and you can start and stop the movie as you want. With AVI, you can click the movie to start and stop it.

Setting digital video cast member properties

Use cast member properties to control the media in a digital video, specify how it is framed and whether it plays direct-to-Stage, and set other important options.

To set digital video cast member properties:

1 Select a digital video cast member in the cast.

2 Click the Member tab of the Property Inspector.

There are several noneditable options in the Member tab of the Property Inspector:

- The cast member size in kilobytes
- The cast member creation and edit dates
- The name of the last person who modified the cast member

3 Use the Name field to view or edit the cast member name.

4 To change the external file to which the cast member is linked, enter a new path and file in the Filename field. You can also use the Browse button to select a new file.

5 To specify how Director removes the cast member from memory if memory is low, choose an option from the Unload pop-up menu. See "Controlling cast member unloading" on page 114.

6 Click the QuickTime or AVI tab to set the remaining properties.

7 To determine how a movie image appears within the sprite bounding rectangle when the movie is rotated, scaled, or offset, set Framing options:

- Crop displays the movie image at its default size. Any portions that extend beyond the sprite's rectangle are not visible. For more information, see "Cropping digital video" on page 382.

- Center is available only if Crop is selected. It determines whether transformations occur with the cast member centered within the sprite or with the cast member's upper left corner aligned with the sprite's upper left corner.

- Scale fits the movie inside the bounding rectangle.

8 To determine how the video plays back, set options in the bottom portion of the window:

- Show Video displays the video portion of the digital video. If this option is turned off, the video portion does not play. Deselect this option and select Sound if you want to play only the audio portion of a movie.

- Play Sound plays the sound portion of the digital video.

- Direct to Stage allows QuickTime or AVI drivers installed on the computer to completely control the video playback. For more information, see "Playing digital video direct-to-Stage" on page 375.

- (QuickTime only) Show Controller displays a controller bar at the bottom of the video if Direct to Stage is selected.

- Paused stops the digital video when it first appears on the Stage (while playing the Director movie).

- Loop replays the digital video continuously from the beginning to the end and back to the beginning.

- Preload loads the cast member into memory when the movie starts. For more information, see "Preloading digital video" on page 384.

- (QuickTime only) Streaming begins playing the video while the rest of the video continues to load from its source.

9 If Direct to Stage is selected, choose a Playback option in the top portion of the window to specify how to synchronize the video to its soundtrack.

- Sync to Sound makes the digital video skip frames (if necessary) to keep up with its soundtrack. The digital video may also take less time to play.

- Play Every Frame (No Sound) makes every frame of the digital video appear but does not play the soundtrack, since the video cannot play the soundtrack asynchronously while the video portion plays frame by frame. Depending on the data rate of the digital video, the sprite may play more smoothly with this option selected, but this is not a certainty. In addition, playing every frame may cause the digital video to take more time to play.

10 If Play Every Frame (No Sound) is selected, choose options from the Rate pop-up menu to set the rate at which a digital video plays:

- Normal plays each frame at its normal rate, and no frames are skipped.

- Maximum plays the movie as fast as possible while still displaying each frame.

- Fixed plays the movie using a specific frame rate. Enter the number of frames per second in the field at the right. Use this option only for digital videos that use the same frame rate for each frame of the movie.

Playing digital video direct-to-Stage

Director can play digital video using a feature called Direct to Stage. Direct to Stage allows QuickTime or AVI drivers installed on the computer to completely control the video playback.

Direct to Stage often provides the best performance from a digital video, but there are two disadvantages to using it:

- The digital video always appears in front of all other sprites on the Stage, no matter which channel contains the sprite.

- Ink effects do not work, so it is difficult to conceal the video's bounding rectangle with Background Transparent ink.

When Direct to Stage is off, Director layers a digital video on the Stage exactly like other sprites, and Background Transparent ink works normally. (Matte ink does not work for digital videos.)

To set Direct to Stage options:

1 Select a digital video cast member.

2 Click the QuickTime or AVI tab in the Property Inspector.

3 Select or deselect Direct to Stage.

4 If Direct to Stage is selected, choose a Playback option:

- Sync to Soundtrack makes the digital video skip frames (if necessary) to keep up with its soundtrack. The digital video may also take less time to play.

- Play Every Frame makes every frame of the digital video appear but does not play the soundtrack, since the video cannot play the soundtrack asynchronously while the video portion plays frame by frame. Depending on the data rate of the digital video, the sprite may play more smoothly with this option selected, but this is not a certainty. In addition, playing every frame may cause the digital video to take more time to play.

5 (QuickTime only) If Direct to Stage is on, select Show Controller to display a controller bar below the movie to allow the user to start, stop, and step through the movie.

Controlling digital video in the Score

Add a digital video cast member to a movie just as you would add any other sprite. Digital videos begin playing when the playback head reaches the frame containing the video sprite. Use the QuickTime or AVI tab of the Property Inspector to make the movie pause or loop. See "Setting digital video cast member properties" on page 373.

If there's a white bounding rectangle around the video, use the Background Transparent ink to remove it. Inks don't work if Direct to Stage is turned on (see "Playing digital video direct-to-Stage" on page 375). Matte ink does not work for any type of digital video.

To create a digital video sprite:

1 Drag a digital video cast member to any sprite channel in the Score.

2 Extend the sprite through as many frames as necessary.

Playing complete digital videos

A digital video, like a sound, is a time-based cast member. If you place a video in just a single frame of the Score, the playback head moves to the next frame before Director has time to play more than a brief instant of the video.

To make sure that Director plays an entire digital video, do one of the following:

- Create a tempo setting in the tempo channel using the Wait for Cue Point option in the Frame Properties: Tempo dialog box. This option keeps the playback head from moving to the next frame until a cue point in the video has passed or, if there are no cue points, until the end of the video is reached. For more information, see "Synchronizing media" on page 384.

- Use Lingo or behaviors to make the playback head stay in a frame until the end of the video or until a certain cue point passes. See "Synchronizing media with Lingo" on page 385.

- Extend the video through enough frames to give it time to play all the way through.

QuickTime VR

You can use a QuickTime VR movie in a Director movie by inserting it as you would any other QuickTime cast member. To get the best performance, turn on Direct to Stage (see "Playing digital video direct-to-Stage" on page 375).

Playing digital video with Lingo

Lingo can take advantage of the most important and powerful features of digital video. Besides playing digital video linearly, Lingo can pause, stop, and rewind a video. These abilities are useful for jumping to segments within a digital video and for emulating a typical digital video control panel. This last feature is especially useful for AVI digital video, which has no control panel of its own.

Lingo also lets you work with individual tracks in a digital video by determining the tracks' content and position and turning these tracks on and off.

Controlling digital video playback with Lingo

The following are ways you can control digital video with Lingo. See the *Lingo Dictionary* for more information.

- To turn on looping in a digital video cast member, set the digital video's loop cast member property to TRUE.

- To determine the current time of a digital video sprite, check the sprite's currentTime property.

- To pause a digital video sprite, set the sprite's movieRate property to 0.

- To start a paused digital video sprite, set the sprite's movieRate property to 1.

- To play a digital video sprite in reverse, set the sprite's movieRate property to -1.

- To rewind a digital video sprite to the beginning, set the sprite's movieTime property to 0.

- To control a digital video sprite's playback rate, set the sprite's movieRate property to the desired rate.

- To mix QuickTime audio tracks with internal Director sounds (necessary only in Windows), use the soundDevice system property to specify QT3Mix.

Determining digital video content with Lingo

The following are ways that Lingo can determine a digital video's content. See the *Lingo Dictionary* for more information.

- To determine the time units a digital video cast member uses, check the video's timeScale cast member property.

- To determine whether a digital video is QuickTime or AVI, check the digital video's digitalVideoType cast member property.

- To determine the number of tracks in a digital video sprite or cast member, check the digital video's trackCount sprite or cast member property.

- To determine which type of media a digital video track contains, check the digital video's trackType sprite or cast member property.

- To determine the start time of a track in a digital video sprite or cast member, check the digital video's trackStartTime sprite or cast member property.

- To determine the stop time of a track in a digital video sprite or cast member, check the digital video's trackStopTime sprite or cast member property.

- To determine whether a sprite's track is enabled to play, check the digital video's trackEnabled sprite property.

- To obtain the text at the current time from a text track in a digital video sprite, check the digital video's trackText sprite property.

- To determine the time of the track just before the current time in a digital video, check the digital video's trackPreviousSampleTime cast member property and trackPreviousKeyTime sprite property.

- To determine the time of the next sample after the current time in a digital video, check the digital video's trackNextSampleTime cast member property and trackNextKeyTime sprite property.

Turning on and off digital video tracks with Lingo

By turning a digital video's soundtracks on or off, you can play just the animation or control which sounds play.

To control whether individual digital video tracks play:

Use the setTrackEnabled command. See setTrackEnabled in the *Lingo Dictionary*.

Controlling QuickTime with Lingo

Lingo can control QuickTime in ways that aren't available for AVI. You can use Lingo to control a QuickTime video's appearance and sound volume. For QuickTime VR, you can use Lingo to pan a QuickTime VR digital video and specify what happens when the user clicks or rolls over portions of the video.

You can set the rotation, scale, and translation properties for either a QuickTime cast member or a sprite. See the *Lingo Dictionary* for more information.

- To determine whether a cast member or sprite is a QuickTime VR digital video, test the isVRMovie property.

- To obtain a floating-point value that identifies which version of QuickTime is installed on the local computer, use the quickTimeVersion() function.

- To control a QuickTime sprite's sound volume, set the volume sprite property.

- To set the internal loop points for a QuickTime cast member or sprite, set the loopBounds sprite property.

Applying masks for QuickTime

Director provides specific Lingo properties for applying masks to QuickTime digital videos. See the *Lingo Dictionary* for more information.

- To use a black-and-white cast member as a mask for QuickTime media rendered direct-to-Stage, set the mask cast member property.

- To control the way Director interprets a QuickTime video's mask cast member property, set the invertMask property.

Responding to user interaction

Lingo lets you control how QuickTime VR responds when the user clicks a QuickTime VR sprite. Use Lingo to specify how Director handles image quality, clicks and rollovers on a QuickTime VR sprite, clicks on hotspots, and interactions with QuickTime VR nodes. See the *Lingo Dictionary* for more information.

- To set the codec quality to use when the user drags on a QuickTime VR sprite, set the motionQuality sprite property.

- To specify the codec quality to use when a QuickTime VR panorama image is static, set the staticQuality sprite property.

- To enable or disable the specified hotspot for a QuickTime VR sprite, use the enableHotSpot command.

- To control how Director passes mouse clicks on a QuickTime sprite, set the mouseLevel sprite property.

- To find the approximate bounding rectangle for a specific hotspot in a QuickTime VR sprite, use the getHotSpotRect() function.

- To specify the name of the handler that runs when the pointer enters a QuickTime VR hotspot that is visible on the Stage, set the hotSpotEnterCallback QuickTime VR sprite property.

- To find the ID of the hotspot, if any, at a specific point on the Stage, use the ptToHotSpotID() function. .

- To specify the name of the handler that runs when the user clicks a hotspot in a QuickTime VR sprite, set the triggerCallback sprite property.

- To determine the name of the handler that runs when the pointer leaves a QuickTime VR hotspot that is visible on the Stage, set the hotSpotExitCallback property.

- To specify the ID of the current node that a QuickTime VR sprite displays, set the node QuickTime VR sprite property.

- To specify the name of the handler that runs after the QuickTime VR sprite switches to a new active node on the Stage, set the nodeEnterCallback QuickTime VR sprite property.

- To specify the name of the handler that runs when a QuickTime VR sprite is about to switch to a new active node on the Stage, set the nodeExitCallback QuickTime VR sprite property.

- To determine the type of node that is currently on the Stage, test the nodeType QuickTime VR sprite property.

Rotating and scaling QuickTime video

Lingo can rotate and scale QuickTime videos. See the *Lingo Dictionary* for more information.

- To control the rotation of a QuickTime sprite, set the rotation QuickTime sprite property.

- To control the scaling of a QuickTime sprite, set the scale QuickTime sprite property.

Panning QuickTime VR

Use Lingo to pan a QuickTime VR digital video without the user dragging the image. See the *Lingo Dictionary* for more information.

- To set the current pan of the QuickTime VR sprite, set the pan QuickTime VR sprite property.

- To nudge a QuickTime VR sprite in a specific direction, use the nudge command.

Displaying QuickTime video

Lingo can control how a movie displays QuickTime videos. See the *Lingo Dictionary* for more information.

- To specify the type of warping performed on the panorama of a QuickTime VR sprite, set the warpMode QuickTime VR sprite property.

- To specify a QuickTime VR sprite's current field of view, set the fieldOfView QuickTime VR sprite property.

- To swing a QuickTime VR sprite to a specific pan, tilt, or field of view, set the swing function.

Cropping digital video

Cropping a digital video means trimming the edges off the top or sides of the movie image. Cropping doesn't permanently remove the portions you crop; it just hides them.

To crop a digital video:

1 Select the cast member in the Cast window.

2 Click the QuickTime or AVI tab in the Property Inspector.

3 Select Crop.

Director retains the movie's original size if you resize the bounding rectangle; however, the edges of the movie will be clipped if you make the bounding rectangle too small.

4 Select Center, if you wish.

Director centers the movie when you resize the bounding rectangle. If Center is not selected, the movie maintains its original position when you resize its bounding rectangle. Center is available only if Crop is selected.

5 Click OK.

6 Select the video in the Score.

7 Go to the Stage and drag any of the handles that appear on the selection rectangle that surrounds the video image.

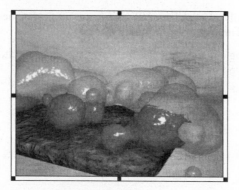

Director displays only as much of the movie image as will fit in the area defined by the selection rectangle.

If you would rather scale the movie than resize it, select Scale instead of Crop in the QuickTime tab of the Property Inspector. Director scales the movie if you resize the bounding rectangle.

To use Lingo to move the image of a QuickTime video around within the sprite's bounding rectangle:

Set the digital video's translation QuickTime sprite or cast member property.See translation in the *Lingo Dictionary*.

About using digital video on the Internet

In both stand-alone projectors and movies playing in Web browsers, Director can handle digital video the same way it handles all other media, or it can stream the digital video using QuickTime 4. You can link the digital video to a URL, and the movie begins to download and play the digital video when its sprite first appears on the Stage.

In order for the digital video member to stream, you must set its streaming di property to TRUE. QuickTime 4 must be installed to enable streaming.

If a streaming QuickTime file contains cue points you wish to use, you must set the text track to be preloaded (use a QuickTime editor such as MoviePlayerPro to do this). If you do not preload the text track, Director will disable the cue points so it can stream the file without entirely downloading it first.

You can also import an RTSP (Real Time Streaming Protocol) stream as a QuickTime cast member. The rtsp:// URL must end with the file name extension .mov so that Director knows it should be treated as a QuickTime stream.

When using streaming digital video in a movie distributed on the Internet, keep these points in mind:

- The video begins to play immediately unless the member's pausedAtStart property is set to TRUE or the controller member property is set to TRUE.

- Once a digital video begins to download, the download continues until it is finished, even if the sprite no longer appears on the Stage. Use the percentStreamed member property to test how much of the media has been downloaded.The feature works with QuickTime videos only. See percentStreamed in the *Lingo Dictionary*.

Preloading digital video

You can eliminate the delay caused by loading a digital video from disk during a Director movie by loading it at the beginning of the movie. You can preload an entire digital video (or as much of the video as will fit into available memory) using the Property Inspector.

To preload a digital video:

1 Select a digital video cast member in the Cast window.

2 Click the QuickTime or AVI tab in the Property Inspector.

3 Select Preload.

This option uses the preLoad or preLoadMember command. If there is not enough memory to load the entire movie, Director loads only what will fit into memory. If this option is turned off, Director does not load the movie into memory and instead plays it from disk. This results in slower animation speeds, since each frame must be retrieved from disk before it is played.

Synchronizing media

To pause the playback head until a specified cue point in a sound or digital video is reached, you can use the Wait for Cue Point option in the Tempo dialog box. You can also use this function to wait for the end of the sound or digital video, even if it has no cue points. Cue points can also be used to trigger events that will be interpreted by Lingo. See "Synchronizing media with Lingo" on page 385.

For example, you can use cue points to make text appear in time with narration. First, use a program such as Peak LE 2 to place cue points in the sound file that correspond to the times when you want the text to appear on stage. In Director, use the Tempo dialog box to pause the playback head at the frame where the corresponding text appears until the voice-over reaches the proper cue point.

In Windows, use Sound Forge 4.0 or later or Cool Edit 96 or later to define cue points (called markers or regions within these programs). (See the Readme Windows Sound Loop-Cue.txt file in the Director application folder for instructions on doing this.)

On the Macintosh, use Sound Edit 16 2.07 or later, or Peak LE 2 or later, to define cue points in AIFF and Shockwave Audio sounds, and in QuickTime digital videos.

Note: You can insert cue points into QuickTime files only on the Macintosh; however, the cue points can be used on both platforms.

AVI digital video does not support cue points.

To use cue points:

1 Place cue points in a sound file or (on the Macintosh only) in a QuickTime file.

Use an audio editing program to define cue points in both sounds and digital videos.

2 Import the sound or digital video into Director.

Note: Digital video is always linked, whether you choose the Standard Import option or the Link to External File option in the Import dialog box.

3 Place the sound or digital video in a channel in the Score and extend it through all the frames in which you want it to play.

4 Double-click the frame in the tempo channel where you want the playback head to wait for a cue point.

5 In the Tempo dialog box, choose Wait for Cue Point.

6 Select the sound or digital video from the Channel pop-up menu.

7 Choose the cue point to wait for from the Cue pop-up menu.

Select the End or Next cue point or any named or numbered cue point in the sound or digital video. Director recognizes the end of a sound regardless of whether you've defined cue points ahead of time.

When the movie plays, the playback head pauses at the frame until the cue point passes.

Synchronizing media with Lingo

By writing Lingo that performs an action when a cue point is reached in a sound or QuickTime file, you can synchronize a movie with sound or digital video. See individual properties and functions in the *Lingo Dictionary*.

- To set up Lingo that runs when the movie reaches a cue point in a sound or QuickTime file, put the Lingo in an on cuePassed handler.

- To determine whether a sound or QuickTime file has passed a specific cue point, use the isPastCuePoint() function.

- To find the ordinal number of the last cue point passed in a sound or QuickTime file, use the mostRecentCuePoint function.

- To obtain a list of names for the cue points in a specific sound or QuickTime file, test the cuePointNames property.

- To obtain a list of times for cue points in a specific sound or QuickTime file, test the cuePointTimes property.

CHAPTER 15
Using Interactive Media Types

To add complex media and new capabilities to your movie, you can use Flash movies, other Director movies, PowerPoint presentations, and ActiveX controls. Each of these multimedia formats has interactive capabilities that are preserved by Director.

A Flash movie in a Director movie provides a vector-based, scalable, interactive animation that is optimized for use on the Web.

Director movies within other Director movies simplify complex productions. A linked movie appears within another movie as a single cast member, saving you the trouble of managing extra cast members and Score data. Using discrete movies also helps you manage file size for easier downloading.

A PowerPoint presentation can be a starting point for a Director movie. Director converts the entire presentation into a movie file that works almost exactly like the original presentation. Director converts all the presentation media into cast members, lays them out on the Stage, and generates Score data to control events.

ActiveX controls in Director can manage ActiveX application resources from within a movie. ActiveX controls provide a variety of features, including Web browsing, spreadsheet functions, and database management. ActiveX controls function as normal sprites in a movie. ActiveX controls work only in Director for Windows.

Using Flash Movies

You can incorporate Flash vector-based animation in your Director movies, projectors, and Shockwave movies for the Web simply by importing a Flash movie into Director and using it like any other cast member. Effects that once required multiple versions of a bitmap cast member—such as blending one shape into another—can now be accomplished with a single, small Flash movie.

Director can import Flash 2.0 or later. It supports new features of Flash 4, including editable text.

In Director, you can control nearly every Flash movie property—including playing, rewinding, and stepping forward and backward through any Flash movie, adjusting quality settings, and turning sound on or off—using Lingo commands.

In Flash, you can create cross-platform Windows and Macintosh movies and then play or manipulate them in Director. You can create Flash movies that communicate with your Director movie by sending events that Director scripts can capture and process. You can store entire Flash movies in the Director cast file, or you can link to external Flash movies. Director automatically loads the Flash movie it encounters in the Score into memory from disk, from a network drive, or from anywhere on the Internet.

Flash movies are particularly effective for use in Shockwave movies because, as vector-based media, they are extremely small and therefore load much more quickly than most other media types. Because Flash movies are vector-based, you can scale and rotate them while still maintaining their sharpness. For example, you can create splash screens for your Director Shockwave movies that load with lightning speed and entertain your users while the rest of the Director movie streams into memory, or you can create interactive maps in Flash that users can pan across or zoom in on to reveal details with vector-based precision.

Adding a Flash movie cast member

All Flash cast members added to a Director movie must have been created with Flash 2.0 or later and saved in Flash format (SWF).

The following procedure explains how to create a Flash cast member and set properties for it at the same time. You can also import a cast member by using File > Import or by dragging and dropping.

To add a Flash movie as a cast member:

1 Choose Insert > Media Element > Flash Movie.

2 In the Flash Asset Properties dialog box, select the Flash movie (SWF) file you want to add to your Director cast.

- To add a file from your computer or from a network drive, click Browse, select the file, and click Open.

- To add a file from a location on the Internet, click Internet, type the URL of the file, and click OK.

- Type the pathname or the URL of the file in the Link File box.

3 Set Media options:

- Select Linked to leave the actual media of the Flash movie stored in an external file. When a sprite created with this cast member appears on the stage in a Director movie, Director will automatically load the file into memory by looking in the location specified in the Link File box. Deselect Linked to have Director copy the Flash movie into the cast.

- Select Preload to require Director to load the entire Flash movie into memory before playing the movie's first frame. Deselect Preload to have Director start playing the movie immediately while continuing to stream the cast member into memory. This option is available if you selected Linked.

4 Select Playback options to control how a Flash movie sprite plays in a Director projector, in a Shockwave Director movie, and while you are authoring in Director:

- Image displays images from the Flash movie when it plays. When Image is deselected, the images are invisible.

- Sound enables any sound in the Flash movie to play. When Sound is deselected, the movie plays without sound.

- Paused displays only the first frame of the movie without playing the movie. When Paused is deselected, the movie begins playing immediately when it appears on the Director Stage.

- Loop makes the movie play again from frame 1 once it finishes. When Loop is deselected, the movie plays once and stops.

- Direct to Stage displays the movie when it appears on the stage with the fastest, smoothest playback. Deselect Direct to Stage to have Director draw the entire sprite first in memory with other sprites and apply ink effects before actually displaying it. The disadvantage of Direct to Stage is that the movie always appears on top of other sprites, regardless of the channel in which it appears in the Score, and ink effects don't work.

5 Specify a Scale value by typing the percentage to scale the cast member.

6 Specify a Quality value:

- Select a high-quality setting to have the Flash movie play with anti-aliasing turned on, which slows down performance; choose Auto-High to have Director start playing the movie with anti-aliasing on but turn it off if it can't play the movie at the required frame rate.

- Select a low-quality setting to turn off anti-aliasing but speed up performance; choose Auto-Low to have Director start playing the movie without anti-aliasing but turn on anti-aliasing if it can do so and continue playing the movie at the required frame rate.

7 Select a Scale Mode value to control how the Flash movie's sprites are scaled on Stage:

- Show All maintains the movie's aspect ratio and, if necessary, fills in any gaps along the horizontal or vertical dimension using the movie's background color.

- No Border maintains the movie's aspect ratio by cropping the horizontal or vertical dimension as necessary without leaving a border.

- Exact Fit stretches the movie to fit the sprite exactly, disregarding the aspect ratio.

- Auto-Size adjusts the sprite's bounding rectangle to fit the movie when it is rotated, skewed, or flipped. This option always sets the scale to 100% in the Director score.

- No Scale places the movie on the Stage with no scaling. The movie stays the same size no matter how you resize the sprite, even if it means cropping the movie.

8 Select a Rate value to control the tempo at which Director tries to play the Flash movie:

- Normal plays the Flash movie at the tempo stored in the Flash movie.

- Fixed plays the movie at a rate you specify by typing a value in the entry box.

- Lock-Step plays a frame of the Flash movie for each Director frame.

Note: A Flash movie will not play faster than the frame rate set in the Director movie.

9 When you have finished selecting options, click OK.

Director adds the Flash movie to the cast.

Note: You can also use Lingo extensions to adjust these and other properties of the Flash movie. See "Controlling a Flash movie with Lingo" on page 391.

About using a Flash movie in a Director movie

Once you have added a Flash movie to the Director cast, using it in your movie is as simple as dragging it to the stage and positioning it where you want it. You can then use the Flash movie sprite in much the same way that you use other sprites.

When working with a Flash movie on the Stage, keep these points in mind:

- A Flash movie's animation plays only as long as the Flash movie's sprite is actually on the Stage. (Flash movies resemble digital video and sound sprites in this regard.)

- Because a Flash movie uses a vector format, you can stretch the movie's sprite without loss of the movie's clarity.

- You can rotate, skew, scale, or flip a Flash movie just as you would a vector shape or bitmap.

- If the movie is set up to play direct-to-Stage, the movie will always appear on top of other sprites, regardless of the channel in which it is placed, and ink effects will be ignored.

- Only the Copy, Transparent, Background Transparent, and Blend ink effects work with Flash movies.

- Blend and color settings are supported for Flash sprites just as they are for vector shapes.

Controlling a Flash movie with Lingo

Lingo gives you precise control over the way Director streams and displays a Flash movie. You can use Lingo to check and control member streaming, zoom and colorize the Flash asset, and pan the Flash image.

When a movie is playing, Lingo can change the Flash cast member's properties. Some cast member properties, such as the flashRect and frameRate cast member properties, are valid only after the Flash movie's header has streamed into memory.

Director provides the following Lingo that lets you manage how Director uses a Flash movie. See the *Lingo Dictionary* for more information.

- To control whether changes to a Flash movie cast member immediately appear in sprites that use the cast member, set the cast member's broadcastProps property.

- To control whether a Flash movie is stored in an external file, set the linked property.

- To control which frame of a Flash movie Director uses for the Flash movie's thumbnail image, set the posterFrame property.

- To display a list of a Flash movie's current property settings in the Message window, use the showProps command.

Controlling a Flash movies's appearance with Lingo

Lingo can control how a Flash movie appears on the Stage and which part of the Flash movie appears in its sprite's bounding rectangle. Lingo can also skew, rotate, scale, and flip the Flash movie.

Director supports only the Copy, Transparent, Background Transparent, and Blend inks for Flash sprites.

Flipping, rotating, and skewing Flash sprites

Lingo can flip, rotate, and skew Flash sprites as the movie plays. See the *Lingo Dictionary* for more information.

- To flip a Flash sprite, set the flipH and flipV sprite properties.

- To skew a Flash sprite, set the skew sprite property.

- To rotate a Flash sprite, set the rotation property. Set the obeyScoreRotation property to specify whether a Flash sprite obeys the rotation specified in the Score.

    If obeyScoreRotation is set to TRUE, Director ignores the cast member's rotation property and obeys the Score rotation settings instead.

Colorizing and blending Flash sprites

You can use Lingo to change a sprite's color and blend as the Director movie plays. See the *Lingo Dictionary* for more information.

To specify the color of a Flash sprite:

Set the color sprite property.

To specify the blend for a Flash sprite:

Set the blend sprite property.

Scaling Flash movies

You can use Lingo to scale Flash cast members and sprites. See the *Lingo Dictionary* for more information.

To control the scaling of a Flash movie:

Set the scale and scaleMode properties.

To set the scale percentage of a Flash movie within its sprite's bounding rectangle:

Set the viewScale property.

Controlling a Flash movie's bounding rectangle and registration points

You can use to Lingo to control a Flash movie's bounding rectangle and to set a Flash movie's registration points. See the *Lingo Dictionary* for more information.

- To control which part of a Flash movie appears within its sprite's bounding rectangle, set the viewH, viewpoint, viewScale, and viewV properties.

- To control the default size for all new Flash sprites, set the defaultRect property. Use the defaultRectMode property to control how the default size is set.

- To determine the original size of a Flash cast member, test the flashRect property.

- To specify a Flash movie's registration point around which scaling and rotation occurs, set the originH, originMode, originPoint, and originV properties.

- To recenter a Flash cast member's registration point after resizing the cast member, set the centerRegPoint property to TRUE.

Placing Flash movies on the Stage

Lingo can set whether a Flash movie appears at the front of the Stage and whether specific areas of a Flash movie and the Stage overlap. See the *Lingo Dictionary* for more information.

- To determine whether a Flash movie plays in front of all other layers on the Stage and whether ink effects work, set the directToStage property.

- To determine which Stage coordinate coincides with a specified coordinate in a Flash movie, use the flashToStage() function.

- To determine which Flash movie coordinate coincides with a specified coordinate on the Director Stage, use the stageToFlash function.

- To improve performance for a Director movie that uses a static (not animated) Flash movie, set the static property.

- To control whether a Flash movie's graphics are visible, set the imageEnabled property.

- To control whether a Flash movie plays sounds, set the sound property.

- To control whether Director uses anti-aliasing to render a Flash movie, set the quality property.

Streaming Flash movies with Lingo

In addition to the Lingo that lets you stream many of Director's media types, Director offers Lingo that specifically lets you control and monitor streaming Flash movies. For general information about using Lingo to stream media in Director, see Chapter 16, "Playing Movies over the Internet." See the *Lingo Dictionary* for more information on specific Lingo functions and commands.

- To specify whether a linked movie streams or not, set the preLoad property.

- To specify how much of a Flash cast member streams into memory at one time, set the bufferSize cast member property.

- To check how many bytes of a Flash movie have streamed into memory, test the bytesStreamed property.

- To determine how much of a Flash movie is currently streamed, test the percentStreamed property or check the streamSize function.

- To set when Director attempts to stream part of a Flash movie, set the streamMode property.

- To clear an error setting for a streaming Flash movie, use the clearError command.

- To determine whether an error occurred while streaming a Flash movie, use the getError() function.

- To check the current state of a streaming file, test the state property.

- To attempt to forcibly stream a specified number of bytes of a Flash movie, use the stream command.

Playing back Flash movies with Lingo

Lingo lets you control how a Flash movie plays back and whether the Flash movie retains its interactivity.

Controlling Flash movie playback with Lingo

You can use Lingo to control a Flash movie's tempo, to specify which frame plays, and to start, stop, pause, and rewind the Flash movie. See the *Lingo Dictionary* for more information.

- To control the tempo of a Flash movie, set the fixedRate and playBackMode properties.

- To determine the original frame rate of a Flash movie, test the frameRate property.

- To determine the number of frames in a Flash movie, test the frameCount property.

- To determine the frame number associated with a label in a Flash movie, use the findLabel() function.

- To play a Flash movie starting from a specified frame, set the frame property or use the goToFrame command.

- To set whether a Flash movie starts playing immediately when the Flash sprite appears on the Stage, set the pausedAtStart property.

- To check whether a Flash movie is playing or paused, test the playing property.

- To rewind a Flash movie to frame 1, use the rewind sprite command.

- To stop a Flash movie at its current frame, use the stop command. .

- To stop a Flash movie at its current frame but let any audio continue to play, use the hold command.

Controlling Flash movie interactivity with Lingo

Lingo can control whether a Flash movie remains interactive. See the *Lingo Dictionary* for more information.

- To control whether the actions in a Flash movie are active, set the actionsEnabled property to TRUE.

- To control whether buttons in a Flash movie are active, set the buttonsEnabled property.

- To control when a Flash movie detects mouse clicks or rollovers, set the clickMode property.

- To control whether clicking a button in a Flash movie sends events to sprite scripts, set the eventPassMode property.

- To determine which part of a Flash movie is directly over a specific point on the Stage, use the hitTest function.

- To check whether the mouse pointer is over a button in a Flash movie, test the mouseOverButton property.

Sending Lingo from Flash movies

A Flash 3 or 4 movie can send Lingo instructions to a Director movie. (Flash 2 movies do not support this feature.) The Lingo determines how the movie responds when the user clicks a button or the Flash movie enters a frame. In Flash, you can send a string to Lingo with a Flash on getURL handler. The string can be an event message or a complete Lingo statement.

In Flash, you create a button or frame and then assign it a Get URL action in which you specify the Lingo that the Flash cast member sends.

To set up a Flash movie to generate an event:

1 In Flash, select a button.

2 Choose Modify > Instance. In the Instance Properties dialog box, click the Actions tab and select Get URL from the Action menu.

   Do not specify anything for the Target Window option. (Director ignores this field.)

3 In the URL field, enter the Lingo that you want Flash to send to the movie.

• To specify a string to pass to an on getURL handler in the Director movie, enter the string. In Director, include an on getURL handler that receives the string from the Flash movie and reads the string as a parameter.

   For example, in Flash, you can specify this in the Network URL field:

   Dali

   In Director, you can write this handler:

   on getURL me stringFromFlash
        go to frame stringFromFlash
   end

   When the on getURL handler receives the text string, it reads the string and then jumps to the frame labeled Dali in the Director Score.

• To specify an event message, specify the word event followed by a colon, the name of a handler you will write in Director, and a parameter (if any) to pass along with the event.

   For example, in Flash, you can specify this in the Network URL field:

   event: FlashMouseUp "Dali"

   In Director, you write this handler:

   on FlashMouseUp me whichFrame
        go to frame whichFrame
   end

   When the Director script receives the FlashMouseUp message and the parameter, the movie jumps to the frame specified by the parameter.

- To specify a Lingo statement, specify the word lingo, followed by a colon, followed by the Lingo statement that you want Director to execute.

For example, in Flash, you can specify this in the Network URL field:

lingo: go to frame "Dali"

When Director receives the getURL message from the Flash movie, the movie immediately executes the Lingo statement.

You can place handlers to capture events from Flash movies in a Flash sprite or cast member script or in a frame or movie script. The event follows the normal Director message hierarchy.

Using Lingo to set and test Flash 4 variables

Two new sprite functions have been added to support variables in Flash 4 sprites: getVariable() and setVariable(). Also, a return value has been added to the hitTest() function. See the *Lingo Dictionary* for more information.

To return a string that contains the current value of a Flash sprite variable, use the following statement:

getVariable(sprite X, variableName)

To set the current value of a Flash sprite variable to a specified string, use the following statement:

setVariable(sprite X, variableName, newValue)

Note: Be sure to pass the Flash variable's name as a string in both the getVariable and setVariable functions. Failure to do so will result in script errors being produced when the functions are executed.

To return the type of object within the Flash sprite that is currently over the specified stage location, use the following statement:

hitTest(sprite X, somePointLocation)

In previous versions of Director, there were only three possible return values for this function: #background, #normal, and #button. With the new Flash Asset Xtra, there is a fourth return value possible: #editText. This value indicates that an editable text field within the Flash sprite is over the specified location.

Playback performance tips for Flash movies

Performance of Flash movies can vary greatly, depending on the options in effect and the playback environment. Following are tips for getting optimal playback performance from Flash:

- If adequate for your needs, use the Low quality setting rather than High. Using Low turns off anti-aliasing, which speeds up Flash animation rendering. A handy technique is to switch the quality of the sprite to Low while displaying a fast-moving animation sequence (such as a spinning logo), and then switch the quality back to High on the fly as the animation slows down or comes to a stop. This way, performance can be improved during the part of the sequence where it would be more difficult to perceive the improved quality anyway, without sacrificing quality in the end result.

- Experiment with different system color depths to see what provides the best performance. Some display drivers are still optimized for 8 bits, so performance can be faster when running in this mode. Some graphics, such as gradients, display faster at 16 bits.

- Use Copy ink if possible. Transparency, using Background Transparent ink, requires much more processing time. If your Flash sprite is in the background (no other Director sprites are behind it), use Copy instead of Background Transparent, and author your Flash movie in such a way that its background color is the same as the background color you chose for your Director Stage.

- Use Direct to Stage if possible. Layering and transparency are not supported in this mode; however, if you just want to play a Flash movie within a box with the best performance possible, this may be the way to go.

- Make sure that the Director movie tempo is set high enough. Unless you're using Direct to Stage, your Flash movie will not play faster than the Director movie frame rate, regardless of the frameRate or fixedRate setting. For smoothest playback, set the Director frame rate to at least 30 frames per second (fps).

- Use Lock-Step or Fixed playback mode to adjust the Flash movie frame rate. Lock-Step gives the best performance, because playback of the Flash movie is synchronized to the Director movie frame for frame.

- Set the static property of the sprite to TRUE if your sprite contains no animation (such as a static block of text) and doesn't overlap other moving Director sprites. This keeps Director from redrawing the sprite every frame unless it moves or changes size.

- When modifying Flash properties using Lingo, set the properties for the sprite rather than for the cast member. Setting the properties for the cast member modifies values at the cast member level and broadcasts the change to all sprites on the Stage. This overhead can affect performance. If you have only a single sprite for the cast member, modify the sprite property directly.

- Limit the amount of Lingo that executes while the Flash movie plays. Avoid tight repeat loops between frames. The usual Director performance optimizations apply when using Flash movies.

Using Director movies within Director movies

You can import a Director movie into another movie as an internal or linked cast member, with the Import command. As with other media types, you can link to an external movie file or import the file so that it becomes internal media. The way you choose to import a movie affects its properties.

- For linked movies, cast member scripts and behaviors (sprite scripts) work as before; select Enable Scripts in the Linked Movie tab of the Property Inspector. Frame and movie scripts do not work. As with other types of linked media, the external movie file must be present on the system when the host movie plays.

- For movies imported as internal media, the movie appears as a film loop.

For both types of imported movies, the host movie controls the tempo settings, palette settings, and transitions. Settings for these functions in the imported movie are ignored.

Once it is imported, the movie appears as a cast member in the Cast window. The cast members of a movie imported as internal media also appear in the Cast window. You can animate the cast member just as you would any graphic cast member, film loop, or digital video.

To import a Director movie:

1 Choose File > Import.

2 From the Files of Type pop-up menu, choose Director Movie.

3 Select a Director movie.

4 To determine whether the movie is imported into the current movie file or linked externally, choose a Media option.

- Standard Import imports all the movie's cast members into the current cast and creates a film loop that contains the Score data.

- Link to External File creates a cast member that references the external movie file. A linked movie appears as a single cast member

5 Click Import.

To place a Director movie cast member in the current movie:

1 Do one of the following:

- For an internal movie, drag the film loop cast member to the Stage or Score.

- For a linked external movie, drag the movie cast member to the Stage or Score.

2 Extend the sprite through all the frames in which you want it to appear.

3 To change any of the movie's properties, use the Movie tab of the Property Inspector.

See "Setting linked Director movie properties" in Director Help.

Using PowerPoint presentations

You can import Microsoft PowerPoint 4 presentations into Director and then play your presentations as they are, or you can use them as a starting point for creating rich multimedia projects in Director. You can save your Director project as a stand-alone projector or as a movie for the Web. For example, you can animate your presentation by adding bars or lines one at a time, or you can synchronize music, sounds, or video to action in your movie—such as a self-running presentation with voice-over narration—or advance a presentation to the next slide after the narration on the current slide finishes.

Importing your PowerPoint presentations into Director imports the artwork, text, and transitions as individual cast members into your Director cast, converts each PowerPoint slide into a Score section, and assembles the Score for you—complete with build effects and tempo settings that pause the action when necessary. You can use Director to add sophisticated interactivity, sounds, and animations.

Lingo can add more interactivity, such as letting users decide the order in which to view slides in a kiosk, track the slides visited, and list the slides still to be viewed.

Importing a presentation into Director creates a copy of the presentation file. Because the presentation you play in Director is a copy, not the original PowerPoint file, you can enhance your presentation in Director without affecting the PowerPoint original. In most cases, the Director movie will look and act almost exactly like the PowerPoint presentation. For a list of differences, see "Comparison of PowerPoint and Director features" on page 402.

Importing a PowerPoint presentation into Director

Director can import presentations from PowerPoint 4 or later. If necessary, open the presentation in PowerPoint and use the File > Save As command to save the presentation in the PowerPoint 4 format.

Presentations that contain OLE objects or large or numerous bitmaps may require additional memory. If you run out of memory while importing a presentation, try saving the presentation as two or more files. Import those files into Director movie files and then recombine the Director movie files by cutting and pasting.

To import a PowerPoint presentation:

1 Create a new movie by choosing File > New > Movie.

You cannot import a presentation into an existing Director movie.

2 Choose Xtras > Import PowerPoint File and choose a PowerPoint presentation.

Director opens the PowerPoint Import Options dialog box.

3 Set up the way you want to import the presentation.

- For Slide Spacing, enter the number of blank frames that you want between each slide in the Score.

- For Minimum Slide Duration, enter the minimum number of frames a slide will take up in the Score.

- For Item Spacing, if the presentation contains build effects (other than fly effects), enter the number of frames used for each item before the next item appears on the Stage.

- For Fly Transition Item Spacing, specify the number of frames to the next keyframe, where the item is in full view. Fly transitions are imported as a Score animation. In the first frame in which the item appears, the item is positioned offstage. In general, the larger the number of frames, the smoother the fly effect will be, and the longer it will take to appear on screen.

For more information on how Director assembles the Score, see "Using PowerPoint presentations" on page 400.

4 Click Import.

When the presentation has been imported, save your movie.

Comparison of PowerPoint and Director features

In cases where there is no exact match for a PowerPoint feature in Director, Director uses the closest matching feature. The following tables summarize how Director handles nonmatching PowerPoint features as well as other issues that occur when importing presentations.

PowerPoint text	Director equivalent
Text Tool objects on the Slide Master	Text Tool objects on the Slide Master aren't placed in the Score. Cast members are created, but you must manually add them to the Score.
Bold or italic text	Depending on the font used, text wrap and character spacing may differ in Director.
Embossed text font effect and shadow font effect	Text appears as regular text. As a workaround, in PowerPoint you can use the Format > Shadow command to add a shadow effect to the entire text block.
Rotated text	Text is not rotated.
Text that uses unavailable fonts	Text uses the nearest matching font. Text spacing and wrapping may change as a result.
Text using non-anti-aliased fonts and italic style	Cast members are inverted (reading left to right).
Text with text wrap turned off	Text wrapping is turned on.
Colored text in Microsoft Word tables within a presentation	Text appears as black text.
Multiple line spacing settings or line spacing in text objects that use multiple fonts	One line spacing setting is used per object.

PowerPoint lines and fills	Director equivalent
Dotted and dashed lines	Solid lines are used.
Medium dashed lines	Lines are not imported. Change the line weight in PowerPoint before importing.
Lines with arrowheads	Lines don't have arrowheads.
Lines with blunt ends	Line ends are tapered or rounded, depending on the line type.
Pattern fills	The object appears as a solid object.
Arcs with fills that end flush with their fills	Arcs with fills extend beyond their fills.
Semitransparent AutoShape fills	No fill is used. It is recommended that you set the blend of the Director sprite to 50%.
From Title shading	From Center radial gradient is used.

PowerPoint bulleted lists	Director equivalent
Backgrounds for bulleted text blocks using build effects	The background appears on the Stage in the same frame in which the first bulleted item appears. If necessary, extend the background sprite's duration to an earlier frame in the Score.
Bullet builds	Bullets always build one bullet item at a time, regardless of their level.
Bulleted items with the Random Effects build effect	A single transition, selected at random, is assigned to each bullet in the text block.
Dimming of previous bulleted items	Dimming is achieved by setting the cast member to a 50% blend. The dimming color is not used.
Text with a text anchor set to top centered, middle centered, or bottom centered	The vertical anchor setting is preserved. All items in a bulleted list must have consistent settings for the centered anchor setting to be preserved.

PowerPoint transitions	Director equivalent
CheckerBoard Across transition	CheckerBoard Down transition
Fade Through Black transition	No transition
Cut and Cut Through transitions	No transition

PowerPoint objects and bitmaps	Director equivalent
Bitmaps saved in a Macintosh presentation and imported into Director for Windows, or bitmaps saved in a Windows presentation and imported into Director for Macintosh	Cross-platform bitmaps are not imported. Before importing, open the presentation on the same platform you will use for Director and save the presentation. For example, before importing into Director for Windows, first open the Macintosh presentation file in PowerPoint for Windows and save the file.
Color depth of graphics	Director creates bitmaps for all graphics in the current monitor depth when importing. For a different color depth, change the monitor setting before importing or use the Modify > Transform Bitmap command to modify the bitmap cast members.
Bitmaps with white extending beyond colored borders	Director strips white space from the outer edges of bitmaps. This may lead to differences in alignment of objects on the Stage, or objects may be stretched to fill the space.
EPS format graphics	There may be some distortion of graphics in this format when it is re-created in Director.
8-bit graphics	On occasion, some colors may not import correctly in 8-bit displays. If this occurs, set the display to a higher color depth before you import.
OLE objects (such as a Microsoft Excel chart or Microsoft Word table)	These objects are imported as bitmaps.
Solid-color shadows on clip art and charts	Solid-color shadows are reproduced as duplicates of the object and are offset by the number of pixels specified for the shadow.
Objects using shading that are created in PowerPoint on the Macintosh and imported into Director on Windows	In rare cases, Director may re-create the shaded objects in different colors.

PowerPoint objects and bitmaps	Director equivalent
Page numbers	Page numbers inserted on the SlideMaster using PowerPoint 4 are not imported. However, page numbers inserted into the master slide footer using PowerPoint 95 or PowerPoint 97 are imported properly after they are saved in PowerPoint 4 format.
Hidden slides	If the last slide of your PowerPoint presentation is hidden, Director will display the slide and play it back. Either remove the slide from the Score or move the end marker and script one frame to the left.
Notes pages	Objects on the Notes pages aren't placed in the Score. Bitmap cast members are created for objects such as pictures, clip art, and tables. However, text is ignored.
Rotated shapes	Changing and saving shapes several times may obscure rotation data in Director. Shapes may be imported with rotation off by 180°. Try copying the shapes to a new PPT file and saving them.
Files edited and saved using multiple versions of PowerPoint	If items are not imported as expected, or if bullet builds do not occur, saving the PPT file in multiple PPT formats may have obscured the data to Director. Try copying the slides to a new PPT file and saving.

Using ActiveX controls

In Director for Windows, you can embed ActiveX controls that let you take advantage of the technology and adapt ActiveX controls (formerly known as OLE/OCX controls) to make them function as sprites in Director. You can use ActiveX controls to manage application resources for the hosted ActiveX control—for instance, to manage properties, events, and windows and filing properties. You can also manage resources used by the ActiveX control within the Director movie.

The range of uses for ActiveX in Director is as limitless as the variety of ActiveX controls available. Using the Microsoft Web Browser control (installed with Microsoft Internet Explorer 3.0 or higher), you can browse the Internet from within a multimedia production; using the FarPoint Spreadsheet control, you can create and access spreadsheets; using the InterVista VRML control, you can explore virtual worlds; using MicroHelp's extensive library of Windows widget controls, you can build and simulate complete Windows applications.

Note: Not all ActiveX controls expose their methods and properties in all hosts. Test the controls you want to use to see how they work in Director.

Inserting an ActiveX control

You can place ActiveX controls in a Director movie and have them function as sprites. Note that this procedure is designed only for Director for Windows.

To insert an ActiveX control on the Stage:

1 Make sure that the ActiveX control you want to use in Director is installed on your system.

   Most controls have their own installation utilities provided by the manufacturer of the control.

2 Choose Insert > Control > ActiveX.

3 In the dialog box that appears, select the desired ActiveX control and then click OK. The ActiveX Control Properties dialog box appears.

   (If the desired ActiveX control does not appear in the list, it may not have been installed properly by the system. You can attempt to verify this by viewing the list of ActiveX controls in another application such as Visual Basic.)

   The ActiveX Control Properties dialog box lets you edit each ActiveX control and view information regarding each method the control supports and each event the control can generate.

4 Set the values for each property in the ActiveX control and then click OK. The ActiveX control now appears in the cast.

5 Drag the ActiveX control from the Cast to the Stage.

   Once the ActiveX control appears on the Stage, it can be repositioned and resized just like any other sprite Xtra. When you pause the movie, the ActiveX control stays in authoring mode and does not react to mouse or keyboard events. When you play the movie, the control responds to user input.

Setting ActiveX control properties

An ActiveX control describes its information using properties—named characteristics or values such as color, text, font, and so on. Properties can include not only visual aspects but also behavioral ones. For example, a button might have a property that indicates whether the button is momentary or push-on/push-off. An ActiveX control's properties define its state—some or all of which properties may persist. Although the control can change its own properties, it is also possible that the container holding the control might change a property, in response to which the control would change its state, user interface, and so on.

When an ActiveX control is inserted into a Director movie, the properties that the control exposes can be viewed and edited by clicking the Properties tab of the Control Properties dialog box for the ActiveX Xtra. Each property exported by the ActiveX control is identified along with the current value of the property. The user edits a property value by simply clicking over the existing value with the mouse. For most properties, such as numeric or string values, the new value can be directly entered into the list using the keyboard.

In Director, all properties that an ActiveX control exports are properties of the corresponding sprite. This is the generic Lingo syntax for setting an ActiveX control property:

set the PropertyName of sprite X to Value

The generic Lingo syntax for getting an ActiveX control property is as follows:

put the PropertyName of sprite X into Value

As an example, if the Microsoft Access Calendar control is inserted into a Director movie as the second sprite on the score, the following Lingo code sets the Year property of the Calendar control to a specific year:

set the Year of sprite 2 to 1995

To get the Year property from the same Calendar control and place it into a Lingo variable named CalendarYear, you can use this Lingo code:

put the Year of sprite 2 into CalendarYear

Some ActiveX control properties are read-only, and trying to set a property for such a control will cause an error in Director.

Using ActiveX control methods

An ActiveX control describes its functionality using methods. Methods are simply functions implemented in the control that Director can call to perform some action. For example, an edit or other text-oriented control supports methods that let Director retrieve or modify the current text, perhaps performing such operations as copy and paste.

When you insert an ActiveX control in a Director movie, you can view the methods exposed by the control by clicking the Methods tab of the Control Properties dialog box for the ActiveX control. The dialog box displays each method supported by the ActiveX control and a description of the parameters for each method.

In Director, all methods that an ActiveX control supports are functions for the corresponding sprite. The generic Lingo syntax for calling an ActiveX control method is as follows:

put MethodName (sprite N, param1, param2, ...) into RetValue

As an example, if the Microsoft Access Calendar control is inserted into a Director movie as the second sprite on the Score, the following Lingo code would increment the year displayed within the Calendar control:

NextYear (sprite 2)

For the same Calendar control, the following Lingo code would decrement the year displayed by the Calendar control:

PrevYear (sprite 2)

Parameters passed to the ActiveX control are automatically converted from their Director data types to equivalent ActiveX data types. Likewise, the return value is automatically converted from an ActiveX data type to an equivalent Director data type.

Using ActiveX control events

Each ActiveX control typically generates a variety of events. For example, a button ActiveX control may generate a click event when the button is pressed, and a calendar ActiveX control may generate a dateChanged event when the date within the calendar is changed. Director converts any event generated by the ActiveX control to a sprite event that it can handle. A list of the control's events appears in the Events tab of the ActiveX Control Properties window.

To respond to an event generated by the ActiveX control, you must write an event handler to capture the event. You can place these event handlers in movie scripts, sprite behaviors, scripts assigned to cast members, or frame behaviors. However, you normally place the handler in the behavior attached to the sprite for the ActiveX control.

As an example, if the Microsoft Access Calendar control is inserted into a Director movie as a sprite on the score, the following Lingo code would capture the click event from the Calendar control:

```
on click
    -- Do something interesting here.
    beep 2
end
```

A sprite behavior is a good location for this handler.

16

CHAPTER 16
Playing Movies over the Internet
. . . .

A Director movie can use the Internet in various ways: hosting multiuser sessions such as chats and games, streaming movies and sounds, retrieving data from the network, and interacting with a browser. Whether it is distributed on disk or downloaded from the Internet, a movie can use an active network connection to retrieve linked files, send information, open Web pages, and perform many other network activities.

To make a movie appear in a user's browser, you can save it as a Shockwave movie and embed it in an HTML document. The movie can play from a local disk or an Internet server. When the user opens the HTML document stored on an Internet server, the movie begins streaming to the user's system, and usually begins playing after the first frame's content has been downloaded.

You can also distribute a movie over the Internet as a projector—a packaged movie that the user downloads and executes. A projector plays in a stand-alone application, not in a browser. See "About distribution formats" on page 438.

While authoring a movie, consider how the movie will be distributed and played on users' systems. If the movie will stream from an Internet source, you may need to modify the movie for the best streaming performance, and to use Director's built-in behaviors to make the movie wait while certain cast members download. Controls and Lingo commands offer methods for sending and retrieving media and other information, interacting with a browser, and monitoring downloading.

About streaming movies

When you distribute a movie on the Internet, streaming provides an immediate and satisfying experience for your users. If you do not specify streaming, your user must wait for the entire movie to download before it begins to play. A streaming movie begins playing as soon as a specified amount of content reaches the user's system. As the movie plays, the remaining content downloads in the background and appears when it is needed. Streaming can dramatically decrease the perceived downloading time.

When Director streams a movie over the Internet, it first downloads the Score data and other nonmedia information such as scripts and the size of each cast member's bounding rectangle. This data is usually quite small compared to the size of the movie's media—usually only a few kilobytes. Before starting the movie, Director then downloads the internal and linked cast members required for the first frame of the movie (or more frames if you have increased the number in the Movie Playback dialog box). After the movie starts, Director continues to download cast members (along with any associated linked media) in the background, in the order the cast members appear in the Score.

If the movie jumps ahead in the Score or uses cast members referenced only by Lingo scripts, the required cast member may not be available when necessary. If cast members are not available, the movie will either ignore them or display a placeholder, depending on how you set the streaming options in the Movie Playback Properties dialog box.

A challenge of authoring for Internet streaming is ensuring all cast members have been downloaded by the time the movie needs them. To avoid missing cast members, make sure that all the cast members required for a particular scene have been downloaded before beginning the scene. You can use Director's behaviors to wait for media in certain frames, or for particular cast members. See "About streaming with the Score and behaviors" on page 423. You can also write your own Lingo code to do the same thing. See "Checking whether media elements are loaded with Lingo" on page 424.

Director movies stream unless you turn off streaming. In addition to turning streaming off and on, you can specify that the media elements for a certain number of frames must finish downloading before the movie starts playing.

You control streaming movies by arranging sprites in the Score and controlling the movement of the playback head either with Director's behaviors or with Lingo. You can also use Lingo to specify when externally linked files are downloaded.

About network operations

Director allows a network operation to begin even though a previous network operation isn't complete. This capability, often referred to as background loading, allows Director to perform multiple operations while loading files. Because something else is happening while files are loading, the user doesn't perceive the wait.

Note: Loading data from a network is different from loading cast members in Director. Loading from a network loads data to the local disk. Loading cast members in Director means loading cast members into memory.

It's a good idea to author a Shockwave movie so that it performs other tasks while data is loading in the background. Because Internet operations require background loading, Lingo for the Internet behaves differently than Lingo commands that run within one movie. See "Using Lingo in different Internet environments" on page 428.

Setting movie playback options

To change basic streaming settings for a movie, you use the Movie Playback Properties dialog box. You can turn streaming off and on, specify a number of frames to download before playing the movie, and make Director display placeholders if cast members haven't been downloaded yet. The Movie Playback Properties dialog box also includes options for locking the current tempo and pausing the movie when the window is deactivated.

Turning off streaming makes sense for some types of movies. For example, a game that requires all cast members to be available at once might not be suitable for streaming. Other movies work best if the media for a certain number of frames downloads before the movie begins playing. This option is especially useful for streaming movies that were not originally designed for streaming.

Placeholders are rectangles that appear in place of media elements for cast members that have not yet been downloaded. Placeholders are useful when testing to note missing media.

You can specify streaming options any time before saving a movie as a Shockwave movie.

Note: If you want to test how a movie will stream from a server before you save the movie as a Shockwave movie, first use File > Save and Compact to make sure the data in the movie is properly ordered and that redundant data is removed.

To set movie playback options:

1 Choose Modify > Movie > Playback to define streaming options.

2 To stop the movie from streaming, deselect Play While Downloading Movie.

3 To make the movie wait for all media elements (internal and linked) for a specified range of frames, enter the number of frames in Download __ Frames Before Playing.

   By default, movies download the first frame only. Adjust this setting to the number of frames that is best for your movie.

4 To make the movie display placeholders for media elements that have not been downloaded, select Show Placeholders.

   The placeholders appear as rectangles when the movie plays.

5 To lock the movie to its current tempo settings, select Lock Frame Durations. See "Locking frame durations" on page 235.

6 To make the movie pause when its window is deactivated, turn on Pause When Window Inactive.

To set Shockwave playback options, see the next section.

Setting Shockwave playback options

To view Shockwave movies, your users must have the Shockwave player, which comes preinstalled on many computer systems. The player is also available for free downloading from Macromedia's Web site.

The Shockwave player includes a volume control and a standard context menu that appears when a user right-clicks (Windows) or Control-clicks (Macintosh) a movie. You can select specific playback options to include for your users when you save your movie as a Shockwave movie.

Shockwave movies loop by default. To cause a Shockwave movie to play only once, add the Hold on Current Frame behavior to the last frame of the movie.

To set Shockwave playback options:

1 Choose File > Publish Settings.

The Publish Settings dialog box appears.

2 On the Shockwave tab, select the options you want your users to have:

- Volume Control lets users adjust the volume of the movie's soundtrack.

- Transport Control provides controls for rewinding, stopping, and stepping through the movie in Shockmachine.

- Zooming determines if stretchable Shockwave is allowed. You can disable zooming with Lingo by setting the allowZooming property. For more information, see the *Lingo Dictionary*.

- Save Local lets users save movies on their local computers for playback in Shockmachine.

- Display Progress Bar and Display Logo determine if the progress bar and logo appear while the movie loads in the browser.

About creating multiuser applications

The Shockwave Multiuser Server and Xtra let two or more users exchange information over the Internet or smaller networks. Director users rely on multiuser functionality for a wide variety of purposes, including the following:

• Creating a chat movie that allows real-time conversation

• Adding human interaction between an e-commerce site and its customers for technical support and customer service

• Conducting an online meeting with a shared "whiteboard" that each participant can write on

• Running a multiplayer interactive game

Director includes the Multiuser Xtra and a 50-user version of the server application as part of the default installation. You can modify the Multiuser.cfg file to enable 1000 users to connect to the server. For more information, see"Enabling 1000 connections to the Multiuser Server" on page 419.

The Library palette contains multiuser behaviors that add commonly used multiuser functionality to a movie, such as connecting to the Multiuser Server.

Using the Multiuser Xtra

The Multiuser Xtra takes messages sent from movies and checks them for errors. The Xtra then prepares the messages for transmission over a network. Movies that use the Multiuser Xtra can exchange information in three ways:

• By sending it to the Shockwave Multiuser Server, which then sends it to the intended movie or movies

• By establishing peer-to-peer connections directly with other movies, bypassing the Shockwave Multiuser Server

• By connecting to a text-based server such as a standard mail server or Internet relay chat server

The Multiuser Xtra extends Lingo by adding new commands and other elements to the Lingo vocabulary. You can use the Xtra with multiuser behaviors, or with other Lingo scripts.

In addition to Director, the Shockwave Player also includes the multiuser Xtra. If you're creating a projector, however, you must add the Multiuser Xtra to the movie's Xtras list. See "About Xtras" on page 435.

Using the Shockwave Multiuser Server

The Multiuser Server is a separate application from the Multiuser Xtra. The server typically runs on a separate computer from the computer running your Director movie, but it can also run on the same computer as your Director movie. After determining who should receive a message, the server sends it to the recipient. The recipient's Multiuser Xtra then receives the message from the network.

When using the server, movies can communicate with other instances of the same movie (such as when two people are using two instances of the same movie to play chess together) or with different movies (such as when chess players use a chess movie to chat with other game players running a different movie in a virtual game room).

The messages your movie sends depend on how the movie is designed. Movies can share all the types of data that Lingo supports.

In addition to simply passing information from movie to movie, the Shockwave Multiuser Server also provides functions that make it easy to create a complex multiuser movie in which you can do the following:

* Store and retrieve information such as user names or profiles in databases.

* Create groups to organize users logically, such as by teams.

* Assign attributes to groups, such as a team's score.

* Send messages directly to the server to retrieve information about it and other movies connected to the server.

Installing the Multiuser Server application

The Multiuser Server is part of the default installation that automatically occurs when you install Director.

You'll find the server application in your Director 8 application folder, in a subfolder named Shockwave Multiuser Server 2.1.

To install the Multiuser Server on a computer other than the one on which you're installing Director:

1 Use your Director 8 CD to run the Installer.

2 After you accept the legal agreement, when the dialog box with installation options appears, select Custom Install from the Install pop-up menu and select Shockwave Multiuser Server.

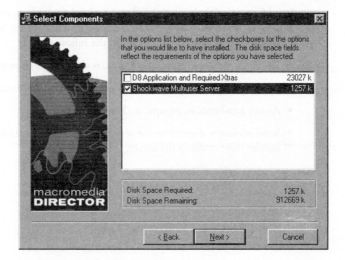

The Director application does not need to be installed on the computer where you install the server.

3 To specify where the server application will install, click the Install Location pop-up menu, select or browse to a location, and then click Install.

Note: You can also copy the Shockwave Multiuser Server folder from one location to another.

Enabling 1000 connections to the Multiuser Server

The Multiuser Server, by default, allows 50 users to connect. You can enable 1000 simultaneous connections to the server by modifying the multiuser.cfg file.

To enable 1000 connections to the server:

1 In the Multiuser Server 2.1 subfolder of your Director 8 application folder, locate the Multiuser.cfg file and open it as a text file.

2 In the Director users licensing information section, find the line that asks for the ServerOwnerName. Delete the pound sign at the beginning of the line and replace the Enter Your Name Here text with your name.

3 On the next line, delete the pound sign and replace the serial number with a valid serial number, and then save and close the file.

```
#=================================================================
# Director users licensing information
#
# If you have purchased a copy of Director 8, uncomment the
# following two entries and enter your serial number
# and name below.  This will allow the server to accept
# up to 1000 incoming connections.
#
# For some Windows computers, you may need to reconfigure the
# system to allow more connections.  Read TechNote #14107 on
# http://www.macromedia.com/support/director for more information.
#=================================================================
# ServerOwnerName = "Enter Your Name Here"
# ServerSerialNumber = DRW800-12345-12345-12345
```

Delete the pound signs

Type your serial number here

Type your name here

Launching the Shockwave Multiuser Server

You launch the Multiuser Server using the subfolder where the server was automatically installed.

To launch the Multiuser Server:

1 In the Multiuser Server 2.1 subfolder of your Director 8 application folder, double-click the MultiuserServer icon to launch the server.

2 To determine the server's IP address and see additional information about the server, choose Status > Server.

3 Write down the server IP address or copy it to the clipboard.

You add the IP address to the IP Address field in the Connect to Server behavior's Parameters dialog box. See "Connecting users to the Multiuser Server" on page 421.

Using multiuser behaviors

The Library palette includes eight Multiuser behaviors that assist you in creating multiuser applications. To access the Multiuser behaviors from the Library List, choose Internet > Multiuser.

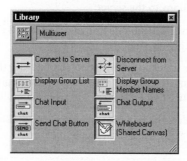

Director Multiuser behaviors include the following:

- Connect to Server connects your user to the Shockwave Multiuser Server. You drag the Connect to Server behavior to the sprite your user will click to establish a server connection. You can attach this behavior to any type of sprite; it's usually attached to a button or bitmap. For additional information, see the next section.

- Disconnect From Server lets your user disconnect from the Shockwave Multiuser Server on MouseUp. In the behavior parameters, you can specify a marker in the Score to go to after your user disconnects. You can attach the Disconnect from Server behavior to any type of sprite.

- You attach the Send Chat Button behavior to the sprite that your user will click to send information to the Multiuser Server. You can attach the Send Chat Button behavior to any type of sprite. In the behavior parameters, you select the sprite that contains the information to send.

- Whiteboard (Shared Canvas) is a behavior that works with the Canvas behavior and with other paintbox behaviors. You can attach the Whiteboard (Shared Canvas) behavior only to a bitmap sprite.

- You attach the Chat Output behavior to the field or text sprite that displays text that other chat members send. Behavior parameters include the ability to add a welcome message and the ability to specify the total number of text lines that will appear in the text output area.

- Chat Input is the behavior you attach to the text or field sprite in which your user enters information.

- You can attach the Display Group Member Names behavior to a sprite to display a list of group members. You can attach this behavior to a field or text sprite.

- By attaching the Display Group List behavior to a sprite, you're including functionality that displays a list of groups, and the members within the group. You can attach this behavior to a field or text sprite.

For more information on using behaviors, see Chapter 5, "Behaviors."

Connecting users to the Multiuser Server

To let your users connect to the Multiuser Server, you can use the multiuser behavior included in the Library palette. You can also write Lingo scripts that configure the Multiuser Xtra and establish communication with the server. For more information about writing Lingo for multiuser applications, see "Using the Shockwave Multiuser Sever" on the Director Support Center.

Before using the Connect to Server behavior, you should have markers in the Score that your users will go to under different circumstances. For example, you may want the playback head to loop at a Waiting marker while a connection is attempted, then advance to a Mainchat marker when the connection is established.

Your Director movie should also contain the cast members your multiuser movie requires, such as the fields and graphics for the Connect and Disconnect buttons, and the cast members that will contain the input and output information.

To use a behavior that connects users to the server:

1 If the Library palette is not open, choose Window > Library Palette.

2 In the Library palette, click the Library List menu and choose Internet > Multiuser.

3 Drag the Connect to Server behavior to the sprite on the Stage that your user will click to establish a server connection.

4 In the Parameters dialog box, use the three Which Member pop-up menus to select cast members that will contain the user name, contain the user password, and display errors.

5 Use the three Which Marker pop-up menus to select the markers in the Score that your users will go to while connecting, when connected, and if the connection fails.

6 In the Server Address field, enter the server IP address. See "Launching the Shockwave Multiuser Server" on page 419.

Note: You can also connect to the server that Macromedia hosts, which allows 16 simultaneous connections, by typing trialserver.macromedia.com in the Server Address field.

7 Verify that the Server Port Number field contains 1626 as the default.

8 Either accept the default name for your movie in the Movie ID String field, or enter a new name.

9 To specify encryption during your user's login, select Encryption and enter the encryption key string in the next field. (You must also enter the encryption key string in the Multiuser Server config file.)

10 When you finish setting the parameters, click OK.

About streaming with the Score and behaviors

The easiest way to create a movie that streams well is to arrange the Score properly and use behaviors to control the playback head. Director downloads cast members in the order in which they appear in the Score. Try to arrange the Score so that events don't make the playback head jump far ahead in the Score, where cast members have not yet been downloaded. For example, if you place a menu in the first frame of a movie and a user chooses an option that sends the playback head to frame 400, the cast members for frame 400 probably won't be available right away.

To avoid this problem, begin a movie with a simple introductory scene containing a few small cast members, preferably vector shapes. You can use a streaming behavior from the Library palette to make the introduction loop until the cast members required for the next scene have been downloaded in the background.

Several behaviors included with Director control the playback head or a progress bar while media elements are downloading. These behaviors make it easy to allow enough time for downloading to catch up with action in the Score.

Looping behaviors

Looping behaviors make the playback head return (loop) to a frame or stay on the current frame until specified media elements have been downloaded, and then continue to the next frame. Attach a looping behavior to a frame in the script channel, not to a sprite.

Loop until Next Frame is Available loops the playback head to a specified frame until all the media elements required for the next frame have been downloaded.

Loop until Member is Available loops the playback head to a specified frame until a certain cast member has been downloaded.

Loop until Media at Marker is Available loops the playback head to a specified frame until all the media elements for the frame at the specified marker have been downloaded.

Loop until Media in Frame is Available loops the playback head to a specified frame until all the media elements required for a certain frame have been downloaded.

Jumping behaviors

Jumping behaviors make the playback head skip to a specified frame or marker once certain media elements have been downloaded. Attach a jumping behavior to a frame in the script channel, not to a sprite.

Jump When Member is Available moves the playback head to the specified frame once a certain cast member has been downloaded.

Jump When Media in Frame is Available moves the playback head to the specified frame once the media elements for a particular frame have been downloaded.

Jump When Media in Marker is Available moves the playback head to the specified frame once the media elements for the frame at a particular marker have been downloaded.

Checking whether media elements are loaded with Lingo

Director has several options that let an initial portion of a movie start playing as soon as the required data and cast members are available. You can use Lingo to check whether media elements have been downloaded from a network by testing the following:

- Whether a specific cast member is loaded before the movie proceeds

- Whether the cast members used in a specific frame are loaded before the frame plays

Checking whether a cast member or sprite is loaded

To determine whether a specified cast member is available locally, you use the mediaReady cast member or sprite property. You can check for a specific cast member or the cast member assigned to a specific sprite. When mediaReady returns TRUE, the cast member is available. See mediaReady in the *Lingo Dictionary*.

This property always returns TRUE for local files. It is useful only for movies that stream from a remote server. Since playback can begin before the entire movie has been downloaded, you must make sure that the needed media elements have been downloaded as the movie plays.

Checking whether a frame's contents are loaded

Use the frameReady() function to determine whether all the media elements that the specified frame requires are available locally. See frameReady() in the *Lingo Dictionary*.

Downloading files from the Internet with Lingo

Lingo uses the Internet's resources by obtaining files from the Internet. The data is copied to the local disk or cache. After data is available on the local computer, use Lingo to retrieve the data for the movie. See "Retrieving network operation results with Lingo" on page 427.

For a movie or projector playing outside a browser, background loading isn't required. However, preloading is a good idea because it improves playback performance.

All network Lingo operations that obtain data from the network begin downloading the data and return a network ID. The data isn't immediately available.

An unlimited number of network Lingo operations can take place at once. When multiple network Lingo operations run simultaneously, rely on the network ID that the function returns to distinguish which operation is complete. Be aware that running more than four operations at once usually adversely affects performance.

When using network Lingo, the current handler must finish before an operation's result is returned. For best results, place Lingo that initiates a network operation and Lingo that uses the operation's result in different handlers. An on exitFrame handler is a good location for checking whether an operation is complete.

To execute a network Lingo operation:

1 Start the operation.

   For example, this statement initiates a text downloading operation and assigns the network ID returned by the getNetText() operation to the variable theNetID:

   ```
   set theNetID = getNetText("http://www.thenews.com")
   ```

2 Make sure the operation finishes.

   To check an operation's status regularly until the function indicates that the operation is complete, use the netDone() function. See netDone() in the *Lingo Dictionary*.

   For example, this statement loops in the current frame until the download operation is complete:

   ```
   if not netDone(theNetID) then go to the frame
   ```

3 Check whether the operation was successful by using the netError() function. See netError() in the *Lingo Dictionary*.

4 Obtain the results if the operation is complete.

To cancel a network operation in progress:

Use the netAbort command to cancel a network operation without waiting for a result. This frees up capacity for Internet access, which allows other network operations to finish faster. See netAbort in the *Lingo Dictionary*.

To retrieve a file as text:

1 Use the getNetText() function or the postNetText command to start retrieving text. See getNetText() or postNetText in the *Lingo Dictionary*.

2 Use netTextResult to return the text you retrieved with getNetText or postNetText. See netTextResult in the *Lingo Dictionary*.

To retrieve and play a new Shockwave movie from the network:

Use the gotoNetMovie command. See gotoNetMovie in the *Lingo Dictionary*.

The current movie continues to run until the new movie is ready to play. After the new movie is ready, the player quits the current movie without warning and plays the new movie in the same display area as the calling movie.

To open a URL in the user's browser:

Use the gotoNetPage command. This command works whether the URL refers to a Shockwave Director movie, HTML, or another MIME type. See gotoNetPage in the *Lingo Dictionary*.

You can specify that this command replace a page's content or open a new page. If the browser isn't open, the command launches the browser. If the gotoNetPage command replaces the page that the movie is playing in, the movie keeps playing until the browser replaces the page.

The gotoNetPage command is similar to Director's open command. It doesn't return a value.

To preload a file from the server into the cache:

Use the preloadNetThing() function. See preLoadNetThing() in the *Lingo Dictionary*.

The preloadNetThing() function initiates downloading a linked movie asset into the cache, where it is available for later use. Director can later preload the asset into memory without a download delay.

The current movie continues playing while preloading takes place.

To test whether getNetText(), preloadNetThing, or gotoNetMovie operations are complete:

Use the netDone() function. See netDone() in the *Lingo Dictionary*.

To post information to a server and retrieve a response:

Use the postNetText command. See postNetText in the *Lingo Dictionary*.

Retrieving network operation results with Lingo

Lingo can retrieve network operation results, such as a text result, a unique identifier for a network operation, a file's MIME type, and the date an HTTP item was last modified.

A returned network ID is for the network operation whose results are being retrieved.

To retrieve the text result of a network operation:

Use the netTextResult() function. See netTextResult() in the *Lingo Dictionary*.

To retrieve the "date last modified" string from the HTTP header for a specific item:

Use the netLastModDate() function. See netLastModDate() in the *Lingo Dictionary*.

To obtain the MIME type of the HTTP item:

Use the netMIME() function. See netMIME() in the *Lingo Dictionary*.

To conserve memory, Director discards the results of the netTextResult(), netDone(), netError(), netMIME(), and netLastModDate() functions within a short time after the operation completes successfully.

- For netTextResult(), Director discards the results when the next operation starts.

- For the other functions, Director retains the results through seven subsequent network operations.

To determine the state of a network operation that retrieves data:

Use the getStreamStatus() function or the on streamStatus event handler. See getStreamStatus() or on streamStatus() in the *Lingo Dictionary*.

Using Lingo in different Internet environments

Some Lingo features behave differently depending on whether the movie is playing back in a browser, as a projector, or within the authoring environment.

Using Lingo with Internet security restrictions

Because of security issues for movies that play back in browsers, the following Lingo features are unsupported for Shockwave movies playing in a browser. Many of these restrictions are imposed by the Internet environment. For details about security concerns when playing a movie on the Internet, see "Director and Internet Security" on the Director Support Center Web site.

In general, the following Lingo features are unsupported because of Internet security concerns:

* Setting colorDepth for the user's monitor

* Saving a movie by using the saveMovie command

* Printing by using the printFrom command

* Opening an application by using the open command

* Stopping an application or the user's computer by using the quit, restart, or shutDown command

* Opening a local file that isn't in the dswmedia folder or a subfolder of the dswmedia folder

* Pasting content from the Clipboard by using the pasteClipBoardInto command

* Searching for files on a user's system with getNthFileNameInFolder(), searchCurrentFolder, or searchPath

Using URLs with Lingo

In addition to the Lingo explicitly intended for use with network operations, some Lingo elements can use URLs as references to external files.

These Lingo elements can use URLs as file references in all circumstances:

* moviePath

* pathName

* unloadMovie

The following Lingo supports URLs as references to external files. If you use this Lingo in projectors or during authoring, you can avoid pauses while the file is being downloaded by first using preloadNetThing to download the file. After the file has been downloaded, you can use these Lingo elements with the file's URL without a delay.

When the following Lingo is used in a browser, however, you must first download the file by using the preloadNetThing command. If you do not, the Lingo fails.

- Using a go to movie statement
- Using an importFileInto command
- Using a preLoadMovie command
- Using a play movie command
- Using an open window command (disabled in browsers)

These Lingo elements can use URLs to SWA sound files as file references:

- streamName
- URL cast member property

These Lingo elements can use URLs as file references only during authoring or in projectors:

- getNthFileNameInFolder()
- searchCurrentFolder

These elements don't work in Shockwave movies because Shockwave doesn't support movies in windows (MIAWs):

- open window
- forget window
- close window

Differences in scripting Lingo for browsers

There are some general differences in the way to script Lingo for a movie that plays over the Internet, depending on whether the movie is in a browser.

- For a movie playing in a browser, it is best to use preloadNetThing to load media elements into the browser's cache first. If the media elements aren't preloaded using preloadNetThing, linked media elements may not be present when they are needed.

- Avoid using long repeat loops in browsers; such repeat loops can make the computer appear unresponsive. As an alternative, you can split long operations into sections and execute them over a series of frames or check for user actions in an on exitFrame handler.

- Do not use a repeat while loop to check whether a network operation is complete.

Lingo that is unsupported in browsers

The following Lingo features are unsupported for movies that play back in browsers:

- Creating and managing a movie in a window (MIAW)
- Installing and managing custom menus

Interacting with browsers

Lingo lets you write and read a Prefs file within the dswmedia folder and display a string in a browser's status area.

To write to a Prefs file on a local disk:

Use the setPref command. See setPref in the *Lingo Dictionary*.

After the command runs, a folder named Prefs is created inside the Shockwave player folder (in the same location as the Xtras folder). The setPref command can write only to that folder. The default folder locations for Windows and Macintosh are as follows:

- Windows—the \Macromed\Shockwave 8 subfolder of the system folder; the system folder is typically c:\winnt\system32 or c:\windows\system
- Macintosh—the System Folder:Extensions:Macromedia:Shockwave 8 folder

The setPref command can't write to a file that is on a CD.

For more information, see "Director and Internet Security" on the Director Support Center Web site.

To return the content of a file that was written by a previous setPref command:

Use the getPref() function. If no setPref command has already written such a file, the getPref() function returns VOID. See getPref() in the *Lingo Dictionary*.

To specify text in a browser's status area:

Use the netStatus() function. See netStatus() in the *Lingo Dictionary*.

Note: Some browsers do not support this function.

Testing your movie

However you choose to create your movie, test it thoroughly before releasing it to the public. Make sure you test on systems with all common types of Internet connections, especially on slow modems and at busy times of day. Here is a list of things you might want to check before distributing your movie over the Internet; remember, however, that each movie has its own special needs:

- Compare a streaming version of the movie to a nonstreaming version to see if the performance is different. Some smaller movies may work better without streaming playback.

- Verify that all linked media elements appear correctly. To see if the movie correctly handles an error, try forcing the linked media elements to fail.

- Run the movie on all systems your users are likely to have. For the general public, this includes Windows 95, 98, and NT and Mac OS 8.x and 9.

- Run the movie on very slow modem connections and on fast T3 connections; problems can arise from fast as well as slow connections.

- Check for display problems on systems set to 8-, 16-, 24-, and 32-bit color. Also test as many types of monitors and display adapters as you can.

- Check for font mapping problems in your movie. If your movie uses nonstandard fonts, use embedded fonts. See "Embedding fonts in movies" on page 336.

- Check for sound problems, particularly if you stream sounds with Shockwave Audio.

About downloading speed

Developers distributing multimedia over the Internet usually limit file size, primarily because most users connect at relatively slow speeds. At 28,800 bps, it takes 30 seconds to 1 minute to download a 60K file. Using streaming playback can help you avoid some of the delays caused when downloading large files.

Movies and streaming Shockwave Audio (SWA) sounds always compete for control of the network. This can cause a noticeable problem on slower connections.

If there is heavy traffic at the Internet access point or on the Internet host, or if there is network congestion, the rate drops even lower—to as low as a few hundred bytes per second. In general, it is a good idea to assume your movies will download at about 2K per second.

The following chart shows theoretical throughput times for modems of different speeds. The speeds 14,400 and 28,800 bps are common for modems; 64 Kbps and 128 Kbps are the throughput of an ISDN line; 1.5 Mbps is the throughput of a standard high-speed Internet connection (T1).

Content	14.4 Kbps	28.8 Kbps	64 Kbps	1.5 Mbps
Small graphics and animation, 30K	30 sec	10 sec	6 sec	1 sec
Small complete movie, 100 to 200K	100 to 200 sec	50 to 100 sec	20 to 40 sec	1 sec
500K movie	500 sec	120 to 240 sec	90 sec	3 sec
1 MB movie	--	--	180 sec	6 sec

CHAPTER 17
Packaging Movies for Distribution

When you finish authoring your movie, you have several choices regarding the way to prepare it for distribution. You can distribute a movie in the Shockwave format that plays in a browser or as a stand-alone projector. Stand-alone projectors can include the software necessary to play the movie, or they can use an installed Shockwave player to play the movie independent of a browser. You can also export a movie as a Java applet or as a digital video. For additional information about saving a movie as Java, visit the Director Support Center.

You can use several Director features to prepare movies for distribution. These features include determining Publish settings and deciding which Xtras to include or download. You can also preview your movie in a browser and batch-process movie files to compact them and protect them from being edited.

Shockwave browser compatibility

Shockwave works with Netscape Navigator as a plug-in, with Microsoft Internet Explorer for Windows 95 and NT as an ActiveX control, and with Microsoft Internet Explorer for Mac OS as a plug-in. Shockwave can play Director movies in the following browsers:

Browser	Version	Platform
Netscape Navigator	3.0 or later	Windows and Macintosh
Microsoft Internet Explorer	3.0 or later	Windows
Microsoft Internet Explorer	4.01 or later	Macintosh

Shockwave also works with browsers that are compatible with the plug-in architecture of Netscape Navigator 3.0, including America Online.

When it first encounters an HTML page that references Shockwave, Internet Explorer for Windows 95, 98, and NT asks the user for permission to download the Shockwave ActiveX control if it is not already installed. If the user approves, it downloads and installs the control.

Previewing a movie in a browser

You can preview a movie in a browser on your local computer to view JPEG-compressed bitmaps, and to check the movie design, Lingo, and any other performance issues related to playing a movie in a browser. Previewing a movie creates temporary Shockwave (DCR) and HTML files that open in a browser.

Note: When you use the Publish command rather than the Preview in Browser command, you can create permanent DCR and HTML files that let you view the movie in a browser.

You may notice that linked media does not work as expected when you preview a movie in a browser. Because of security restrictions, movies playing in browsers cannot read files from a local disk unless they are in the dswmedia folder (also called the support folder), which is a subfolder of the folder containing the Shockwave player.

Therefore, to preview a movie that uses linked media, you need to put the movie and all of its linked media in the dswmedia folder. The movie can open a file in a subfolder of dswmedia provided the relative paths have not changed. If you move the movie and its media to another server, the linked media will continue to work if you preserve the same folder structure. For details about security issues when playing a movie in a browser, see "Director and Internet Security" in the Director Support Center.

To specify the browser to use for previewing:

1 Choose File > Preferences > Network.

2 In the Preferred Browser box, enter the path to the browser application file.

To preview a movie in a browser:

Choose File > Preview in Browser or press F12.

About Xtras

All Xtras a movie requires must be installed on your user's system when the movie runs. When you distribute a movie, you must either include these Xtras or provide the user with the means to download them. Using the Movie Xtras dialog box, you can specify the Xtras to include in a projector and whether Xtras should download for use with Shockwave movies. The Movie Xtras dialog box contains a list of the most commonly used Xtras. Including all these Xtras ensures that your movie will work in most cases but makes the projector much larger. You may want to remove Xtras you know you aren't using.

Each time you create a sprite that requires an Xtra, Director adds the Xtra to the list of required Xtras in the Movie Xtras dialog box. If you remove the sprite, Director does not remove the Xtra from the list, in case you later re-create the sprite. Director cannot detect Xtras required in Lingo code. You must manually add any Xtras required by your Lingo code to the list in the Movie Xtras dialog box. See "Managing Xtras for distributed movies" on page 437.

Managing Xtras controls the size and capabilities of the movie you distribute. Many important features in Director, such as text and vector shapes, are controlled by Xtras, as is the ability to import all types of linked media. If you don't use a feature or import a media type that is controlled by an Xtra, you should not distribute the related Xtra with your movie. This is especially true for movies distributed on the Internet.

The Shockwave player includes the Xtras that support the most common features and media types. These include text; vector shapes; Flash; BMP, PICT, JPEG, and GIF file importing; sound management; and Shockwave Audio.

Xtras not included with the Shockwave player must be installed in a user's system before the movie plays. Use the Download If Needed option in the Movie Xtras dialog box to make the movie prompt the user to download the Xtra. Director downloads Xtras from the URL specified in the Xtrainfo.txt file in the Director application folder.

Xtras downloading from projectors requires use of Lingo. See gotonetmovie in the *Lingo Dictionary*.

Xtrainfo.txt includes URLs for all Macromedia Xtras included with Director, but you may need to manually edit Xtrainfo.txt to add the URL for third-party Xtras or Macromedia Xtras not included with Director. Xtrainfo.txt includes a description of how to enter this information. Xtra developers may also provide installation programs or other means of modifying Xtrainfo.txt automatically.

If a user chooses to download an Xtra, Director retrieves the Xtra from the URL specified in Xtrainfo.txt using the Verisign download security system. Verisign is a standard means of downloading software from secure sources. For more information on making Xtras secure for download, see "Using the Xtra Packaging Kit" in the Xtras Support Center of the Macromedia Web site.

You can also include Xtras in projector files. Select the Include in Projector option in the Movie Xtras dialog box for any Xtra you want to include.

Xtras usually required for the movie to play back correctly include the following:

- Xtras that create cast members (text, Flash, vector shapes, QuickTime, and so on)

- Shockwave Audio Xtras (if the movie uses files in the SWA format)

- Transition Xtras (if the movie uses third-party transitions)

- Import Xtras, if the movie uses nonstandard types of linked external cast members

- Network Xtras required for a movie to access the Internet

- Lingo Xtras (if the movie uses any special Lingo that requires Xtras)

Managing Xtras for distributed movies

You can manage Xtras for your movie using the Modify menu.

To manage Xtras for the current movie:

1 Choose Modify > Movie > Xtras.

2 To add or remove Xtras, do any of the following:

- To add the Xtras required to connect a projector to the Internet, click Add Network.

- To restore the list of default Xtras, click Add Defaults.

- To manually add an Xtra to the list (which you would do, for example, if you've used Lingo code that requires Xtras), click Add and choose from the list of Xtras installed in your system.

- To delete an Xtra from the list, highlight the Xtra and click Remove.

3 To change settings for Xtras in the list, select an Xtra and select either of the following options:

- Include in Projector makes Director include the selected Xtra in any projector that includes the current movie.

- Download If Needed makes the movie prompt the user to download a required Xtra if it is not installed in the user's system. The Xtra is downloaded from the location specified in the Xtrainfo.txt file and permanently installed in the user's system.

4 To get information about a selected Xtra, click Info.

The information comes from an Internet source. Not all Xtras include information. Third-party Xtras often include some explanations and information about the developers.

Note: Another way to include Xtras with a movie is to create an Xtras folder containing all required Xtras in the same folder as a projector file. This allows you to see which Xtras are included without opening the movie. If you use this method, you cannot include Xtras in the projector file because the movie will fail to initialize.

About distribution formats

Before deciding how to distribute a movie, it helps to understand how Director plays movies. Director movies play either with the Shockwave player or through a projector player. The Shockwave player is a system component that plays movies in Web browsers and also outside browsers as stand-alone applications. A projector player can only play movies independent of a Web browser.

You can distribute movies as Shockwave movies (with the DCR extension), projectors, protected movies (DXRs), or Java applets. You should not distribute source movies (DIRs) unless you want your users to be able to change the movie in the Director authoring environment.

- A Shockwave movie is a compressed version of a movie's data and does not include a player. Shockwave movies are created primarily to distribute over the Internet for playback in a Web browser. Another reason to create a Shockwave movie is to compress it for distribution on a disk when the movie is contained in a projector. In addition to compressing the data, saving a movie in the Shockwave format removes all information necessary to edit the movie.

- A projector is a movie intended for play outside of a Web browser. A projector can include a player (called the Standard player), Xtras, multiple casts, and linked media in a single file. A projector can also include several different movie files. Configured in this way, a projector can be a completely stand-alone application.

You can use the Shockwave player projector option to make a much smaller projector. A Shockwave projector uses an installed Shockwave player on the user's system to play a movie instead of including the player code in the projector itself. If no Shockwave player is installed on the user's system, the user must download a copy. A Shockwave projector is excellent for distributing movies on the Internet that you don't want to play in a Web browser.

You can also reduce the file size of a projector by turning on projector options that compress the movie data, the player code, or both. In Windows, compressing the player code reduces the minimum projector size from approximately 2.1 MB to 1.1 MB for a projector, and to about 60K for a Shockwave projector.

On the Macintosh, compressing the player code reduces the minimum projector size from approximately 2.5 MB to 1.2 MB for a projector, and to approximately 12K for a Shockwave projector.

- Protected movies (DXRs) are uncompressed movies that users can't open for editing. These can be useful when you want to distribute uncompressed movies on a disk, but you don't want users to edit the source file. Protected movies may play faster than Shockwave movies from a disk because they do not need to be decompressed. These movies are preferable if disk space isn't limited. Like Shockwave movies, protected movies do not include the information necessary to edit the movie or the software that plays the movie. They can be played only by a projector, a movie in a window, or the Shockwave player.

- A Java applet created by Director is a movie converted to Java. Java applets do not require the Shockwave player and provide an alternative for playing simple movies at Web sites where plug-ins are not allowed. Not all Director features are available when saving as Java; you have a number of authoring issues to consider when converting a movie to Java. For a complete description of Java authoring issues, see "Save as Java" in the Director Support Center. You cannot include Java applets in a projector or play them as a movie in a window.

Note: To edit a movie packaged for distribution, you must edit the source file (DIR) and create a new movie in one of the distribution formats. Always save your source files.

Using linked media on the Internet

When you distribute a movie on the Internet for playback in a Web browser, the linked media must be at the specified URL when the movie plays. Otherwise, the user will receive an error message.

Distributing movies on a disk

Whenever a movie plays from a disk, it accesses all external linked files the same way that it did in the authoring environment. All linked media—bitmaps, sounds, digital videos, and so on—must be in the same relative location as they were when you created the movie. To make sure you don't forget any linked media when you distribute a movie on a disk, place linked files in the same folder as the projector or in a folder inside the Projector folder.

If your movie includes Xtras, you must include the Xtras in the projector. If a movie distributed on a disk connects to the Internet in any way, be sure to click the Add Network button in the Movie Xtras dialog box.

Distributing movies on a local network

If you plan to place a movie on a local area network (LAN), all files must be set to read-only, and users must have read/write access to their system folders. Otherwise, the requirements are the same as for normal disk-based distribution.

Creating Shockwave movies

You save your work as a Shockwave (DCR) movie to prepare it for playback in a Shockwave-enabled Web browser, or to make disk-based movies smaller. Using a Shockwave movie also prevents your users from editing the movie if they own Director.

If the Shockwave movie you're creating will be distributed on the Internet and requires any Xtras, make sure the Xtras are listed in the Movie Xtras dialog box and that Download If Needed is selected for each required Xtra. See "Managing Xtras for distributed movies" on page 437.

Note: Use Update Movies to convert several movies at once to the Shockwave format. For more information, see "Processing movies with Update Movies" on page 453.

Using Publish default settings

To create a Shockwave movie, you use the Publish command. The default settings create a DCR file and an HTML file with all of the tags necessary to display your DCR movie.

If you use the default Publish settings, Director will do the following:

- Create a DCR and HTML file in the same directory as your Director (DIR) movie.

Note: Director creates a CCT file for each external cast and, by default, saves the CCT file in the same folder as the DCR file. To specify a different file location, hold Alt (Windows) or Option (Macintosh) when you choose File > Publish. Continue to hold the key for access to dialog boxes that let you specify new paths for both your DCR and CCT files.

- Give both your DCR and HTML files the same name as your DIR file, with the appropriate extensions (e.g., MyMovie.dcr and MyMovie.html).

- Set the DCR movie's width and height to match the dimensions of the DIR movie.

- Configure the DCR movie and HTML file so that if your users resize their browsers, the DCR movie remains the same size as the original DIR movie.

- Use the same background color while loading your DCR movie as your movie Stage color.

- Compress bitmap images and sound using JPEG compression. Note that if you've compressed images for individual cast members, those settings will override compression set at the movie level in Publish settings.

If you change the default Publish settings, Director saves those changes when you save your movie. For more on changing Publish settings, see the next section.

To create a Shockwave movie:

1 Save your movie.

2 Choose File > Publish.

Director creates a Shockwave version of your movie, and an HTML file if you selected a template, based on your Publish settings. Your default browser launches with the HTML page you just created.

Note: Your default browser is specified in your Network Preferences dialog box. To change your default browser, choose File > Preferences > Network.

Changing Publish settings

You can change Publish settings by using the Publish Settings dialog box.

To change Publish settings:

Choose File > Publish Settings.

The Publish Settings dialog box appears with some or all of the following tabs, depending on the HTML template you select. The Image tab, for example, appears only if you select the Shockwave with Image HTML template.

- Formats
- General
- Shockwave
- Compression
- Shockwave Save
- Image

To use the Formats tab:

- To select an HTML template, or to create a Shockwave file without an HTML template, you use the HTML Template pop-up menu.

  To create a Shockwave file without an HTML file, select no HTML Template.

  To use OBJECT and EMBED parameters in the HTML file to display the Shockwave file, use the Shockwave Default template.

  When you select the Detect Shockwave template, JavaScript and VB Script determine if the correct version of the Shockwave plug-in or ActiveX is on your user's computer. If not, a message tells your user to update Shockwave.

  To expand the Shockwave file to fill the entire browser window, select Fill Browser Window.

  To display a Java applet created using the Save as Java functionality, select Java.

  To play a loader movie while the Shockwave file downloads, select Loader Movie.

  To display a game with a progress bar while the Shockwave file loads, select Loader Game.

  To display a progress bar and image while the Shockwave file downloads, select Progress Bar with Image.

  If you select the Shockwave with Image template, the template automatically detects the Shockwave player or Active X control on your user's browser and uses it to display your movie. If Shockwave is not found and the user's browser is Internet Explorer on Windows 95 or NT, the browser automatically installs the Active X control. In all other cases, the image that you specify on the Publish Settings Image tab is displayed. The Image tab is available only when you select the Shockwave with Image template.

  To display a progress bar while the Shockwave file downloads, select Simple Progress Bar.

  To center the Shockwave movie in the browser, select Center Shockwave.

- The HTML File and Shockwave File fields indicate where Director will save your HTML and DCR files, respectively. To specify another path, edit the path in the field, or click the field's Browse button and choose a new path.

- If you select the Java template, the Formats tab includes a Java Class File field. This field points to the Director movie that you saved as Java.

- To launch your movie in a browser automatically when you execute the Publish command, select Output: View in Browser.

To use the General tab:

- To make the DCR movie match the dimensions of your DIR movie, select Match Movie in the Dimensions field.

- If you use the default Match Movie setting in the Dimensions field, values in the OBJECT and EMBED tags in the HTML file are set to the exact dimension of your movie. To change the dimensions, select either Pixels or Percent of Browser Window, and type the new dimensions in the Width and Height fields. Your movie will resize to fit the new rectangle only if you have not selected No Stretching in the Stretch Style pop-up menu on the Shockwave tab.

- To change the background color of your HTML file, either click the Page Background color box and select a color, or enter a value in the hexadecimal field.

  The Page Background setting is different from Background Color, which you specify on the Shockwave tab. Background Color lets you determine the color that appears, while the DCR is downloading, in the rectangle where your DCR movie will play. Another background color option, Stage Fill Color, which you set on the Movie tab of the Property Inspector, defines the color of the Stage.

To use the Shockwave tab:

Select Shockwave playback options to enable the following features for your user:

- Volume Control lets users adjust the volume of the movie's soundtrack.

- Transport Control provides controls for rewinding, stopping, and stepping through the movie in Shockmachine.

- Zooming determines if stretchable Shockwave is allowed. You can disable zooming with Lingo by setting the allowZooming property. For more information, see the Lingo Dictionary.

- Save Local determines if the movie can be saved to Shockmachine.

- Display Progress Bar and Display Logo determine if the progress bar and logo, respectively, appear while the movie loads in the browser.

For more information, see "Setting Shockwave playback options" on page 415.

- To specify how your movie behaves when the width and height values in the HTML file are a different size than the movie, select from the Stretch Style pop-up menu.

  If the HTML height and width values have been set to a percentage on the General tab, the movie will resize as the browser window resizes. The way in which the movie resizes varies according to the stretch style selected.

  No Stretching, the default, means the movie plays at its original size.

  Preserve Proportions keeps the same aspect ratio of your original Director movie no matter what size the user makes the browser. The movie stretches to fill the height and width values specified in the HTML file or those determined by the percentage and size of your browser window.

  Stretch to Fill stretches the movie to fill the height and width values in the HTML file. If the aspect ratio of the movie changes, sprites on the Stage could appear distorted.

  Expand Stage Size lets users resize the Stage, but the sprites on the Stage remain the same size. The setting expands the Stage size to the size of the height and width values in the HTML file.

  Note: If, on the General tab, you're using the default Match Movie Dimension setting, the stretch style settings will not affect the way your movie responds to browser resizing.

- You can use the Stretch Position Horizontal Align and Vertical Align selections to determine how your movie will line up within the OBJECT or EMBED values in the HTML file.

  For more information about using stretch styles, see the procedure under "Setting movie options for browser resizing" on page 447.

- To change the background color that displays while your DCR file is downloading, either click the Background Color box and select a color, or enter a value in the hexadecimal field.

- If you use Lingo to call JavaScript in your movie, you must select Movie Uses Browser Scripting. This creates a flag for Netscape to start Java when the movie loads.

To use the Compression tab:

The Compression tab sets bitmap compression for all cast members in a movie. (You can set the compression quality for individual bitmap cast members on the Bitmap tab of the Property Inspector.)

- To apply compression techniques used by Director in versions 4 through 7, select Standard. This setting is suitable for graphics with few colors.

- To use JPEG compression, click JPEG and specify the image quality setting by moving the slider to a value between 0 and 100 percent. The higher the percentage, the less the image is compressed.

- To compress the sound in your movie, select Compression Enabled and select the level of compression from the kBits/second pop-up menu. For more information about sound compression, see "Compressing internal sounds with Shockwave Audio" on page 368.

- You can convert stereo sounds to monaural by selecting Convert Stereo to Mono.

- If you entered text in the Comments field of the Property Inspector for your cast members, you can include those comments in your DCR file by selecting Include Cast Member Comments. You can then use Lingo to access the comments in the DCR file.

To use the Shockwave Save tab:

To save your Shockwave file for playback with Macromedia Shockmachine, you use fields on the Shockwave Save tab:

- To display the standard Shockwave context menu when your user right clicks (Windows) or Control-Clicks (Macintosh) your DCR file playing in the browser, select Context Menu.

- To suggest a Shockmachine category, such as "games," enter a description in the Suggested Category field.

- You can enter a title for the user interface in the Shockwave Title field. The title can include spaces.

- The Send URL field lets you specify and override the URL that the Shockmachine detects. You can use frame-based targets, encode form data, or include other information in the URL. If the URL is not specified, the movie uses the URL for the page that contains the movie, if the URL is available.

- You can use the Icon File field to specify the path to a BMP file.

- The Package File field lets you enter a fully qualified or relative URL to a package text file. This text file, in XML, provides a list of URLs with support files to download for a complete save of the current project.

- For content with packages, you can use the Total File Size field to specify the size, in bytes, of all content that needs to download for the movie to save successfully.

For more information about the Shockwave Save fields, and for detailed instructions on developing for Shockmachine, visit www.shockwave.com to access the Shock Remote and Shock Machine Development Guide.

To use the Image tab:

If you selected the Shockwave with Image HTML template on the Formats tab, the Image tab appears on the Publish Settings dialog box.

You can specify the image that should appear if the user doesn't have Shockwave or the ActiveX control.

- In the Poster Frame field, enter the frame number from your movie's Score that you want to appear as a JPEG image for users who are unable to view your movie.

- To specify compression for the image, move the Quality slider to the desired compression setting. The higher the percentage, the less the image is compressed.

- To specify that the image download as a progressive JPEG, select Progressive. The JPEG will then display at low resolution and increase in quality as it continues to download. Making a JPEG progressive also reduces its file size.

Setting movie options for browser resizing

If users view your movie in browsers, chances are they will resize their browsers. How your movie behaves when the browser size changes depends on what you select in the Publish Settings dialog box.

To set movie options for browser resizing:

1 Choose File > Publish Settings.

2 On the General tab of the Publish Settings dialog box, select from the Dimensions pop-up menu. Note that when you make a selection, the width and height values default to the movie size.

• To create an HTML file with parameters that match the height and width of the movie, select Match Movie.

• To specify height and width values in the HTML file in pixels, select Pixels.

• You can select Percentage of Browser Window, and specify a percentage in the Width and Height fields. (To make browser resizing affect the size of the DCR movie, you must specify percentages and select either Preserve Proportions, Stretch to Fill, or Expand Stage Size on the Shockwave tab of the Publish Settings dialog box.)

3 On the Shockwave tab, select an option from the Stretch Style pop-up menu.

• To specify that your movie not resize at all, select No Stretching.

• To maintain the same aspect ratio of your original Director movie no matter what size the user makes the browser, select Preserve Proportions. The movie will fit within the width and height parameters, as much as possible, while preserving the movie's aspect ratio. The movie aligns within the window based on the align tags that you specify in step 4.

- To change the size of the movie to fit the size of the browser, select Stretch to Fill. Any browser resizing stretches the movie to fill the width and height parameters. Note, however, that if the aspect ratio of the movie changes, sprites on the Stage could appear distorted. If you select Stretch to Fill, Director ignores the align tags that you specify in step 4.

To let users resize the Stage without resizing the sprites, select Expand Stage Size. The movie is aligned within the browser based on the align tags that you specify in step 4.

4 To specify align tags for your movie, use the Horizontal Align and Vertical Align pop-up menus. You can select left, center, or right horizontal alignment, and top, center, or bottom vertical alignment.

About projectors

To create projectors for any version of Windows, you must use the Windows version of Director; likewise, you can create Macintosh projectors only with the Macintosh version of Director.

Projectors require certain Xtras to use text, use Flash movies, connect to the Internet, and use certain other features. Director includes the most common required Xtras by default. You can include or exclude Xtras for each movie using the Include in Projector option in the Movie Xtras dialog box. You can also add Xtras to a projector manually the same way you select movie files. (See the next section.)

In addition to the standard projector, you can create a fast-start projector, which typically launches faster. A fast-start projector doesn't include Xtras inside the projector itself, so there's nothing to unpack.

Creating projectors

When creating a projector, place the starting movie at the top of the list of files in the Create Projector dialog box. If the Play Every Movie option is selected in the Projector Options dialog box, movies play in the order they appear in the list. If this option is off, only the first movie plays. If your movie contains Lingo that switches between movies, the order of the other movies may not be important.

You can include only Director 8 movies in projectors. Use the Update Movies command to convert older movies to the latest version of Director. For more information, see "Processing movies with Update Movies" on page 453.

To create a standard projector:

1 Choose File > Create Projector.

2 Double-click the movies and external casts to include in the projector. Click Add All to include all the movies in the open folder.

   Director transfers the name of the movies or casts to the file list.

3 Use the Move Up and Move Down buttons to arrange the movies in the proper order.

4 Click Options.

   Director retains the options settings once you define them; you don't have to set them every time.

5   To control how movies interact with the user's system, select Playback options:

- Play Every Movie specifies that the projector play all movies in the play list. Otherwise, the projector plays only the first movie in the play list (unless other movies are called by Lingo from the first movie). In a projector with Play Every Movie selected, pressing Control + period (Windows) or Command + period (Macintosh) will branch to the next movie, and Control + Q (Windows) or Command + Q (Macintosh) will quit.

- Animate in Background allows the movie to continue playing if a user switches to another application. This is useful if you want the movie to continue running in the background when its window is not active. If this option is not selected, the movie pauses when the user switches to another application and resumes when the user switches back.

- Reset Monitor to Match Movie's Color Depth (Macintosh only) automatically changes the color depth of your monitor to the color depth of each movie in the projector play list. For example, if you are working on a color monitor set to 256 colors and a movie in the play list was created in thousands of colors, the monitor will automatically switch to thousands of colors.

6   To determine how the projector appears on the screen, make an Options selection:

- Full Screen displays the movie in the entire screen, placing the menu bar (if there is one) at the top of the screen and hiding all of the desktop. If there's a menu, it overlays the top of the Stage.

- In a Window displays the movie in a normal window, without taking over the screen. The window cannot be resized.

- Show Title Bar is available only if In a Window is selected. If this option is selected, the window where the movie appears has a title bar. The window can be moved only if it has a title bar.

7   To specify how the Stage size of multiple movies in the projector can be adjusted, choose a Stage Size option:

- Use Movie Settings uses the Stage size of the new movie or matches the size of the current movie.

- Match First Movie repositions and resizes the movie based on the first movie in the projector.

- Center centers the Stage on the screen, which is useful if the Stage size is smaller than the screen size. Otherwise, the movie plays using its original Stage position. In Windows, projectors are always centered.

8   To compress the projector's movie data in the Shockwave format, choose Compress (Shockwave Format).

This makes the projector smaller, but it may increase the load time as the movies are decompressed.

9 To determine how the player code is included in the projector, choose an option for Player.

For more about these options, see "About distribution formats" on page 438.

- Standard includes the uncompressed player code in the projector file. This option starts the movie faster than other options but creates the largest projector file.

- Compressed includes a compressed version of the player code in the projector file. This substantially reduces the projector file size, but decompressing the player code adds a few seconds to the startup time of a movie.

- Shockwave makes the projector use the Shockwave player installed in a user's system instead of including the player code in the projector file. If the Shockwave player is not available when the movie runs, the movie prompts the user to download it.

10 (Macintosh only) To make Director use available system memory when its own partition is full, choose Use System Temporary Memory.

11 Once all projector options are set, click OK.

12 Click Create in the Projector dialog box and then enter a name and location for the projector.

To avoid problems with linked media, create the new projector in its final folder location and do not move it to a different folder.

Director turns the movies, casts, and included Xtras into a single projector.

To create a fast-start projector:

1 Create a new folder on your computer desktop.

It does not matter what you name the folder.

2 In Director, choose Modify > Movie: Xtras.

The Xtras dialog box appears.

3 Select the name of each Xtra and deselect Include in Projector for each, then click OK.

4 Choose File > Save and Compact.

If you are adding multiple movies to the package, repeat steps 2 through 4 for each of the movies.

5 Choose File > Create Projector.

6 In the Create Projector dialog box, select the movies to include in the projector and click Add.

7 Click Options and do one of the following:

- Select Shockwave (Windows) and click OK.

- Select Standard (Macintosh) and click OK.

8 In the Create Projector dialog box, click Create.

9 In the dialog box that appears, type a name for the projector. If necessary, use the pop-up menu to browse to the desktop folder you created in step 1, and then click Save.

10 Exit Director and return to your computer desktop.

11 Open the folder you created in step 1. Create a subfolder within this folder and name it Xtras.

12 In your Director application folder, copy the Xtras required to play your movie into the Xtras folder you just created.

You must also include external movies, external casts, and linked media with your projector. If the external files are in the folder that contains the projector, the projector can automatically link to the files.

13 (Windows only) In your Director application folder, copy the files dirapi.dll, iml32.dll, proj.dll, and msvcrt.dll into the Xtras folder.

14 Launch your projector to see it open quickly and play your movies.

For more information about creating a fast-start projector, visit the Director Support Center.

Processing movies with Update Movies

Use the Update Movies command on the Xtras menu to do the following:

- Update movies and casts from older version of Director to the latest file format.
- Compress movies for faster downloading from the Internet.
- Remove redundant and fragmented data in movie and cast files. The Save and Compact and Save As commands do this as well.
- Prevent users from opening movie and cast files.
- Batch-process movie and cast files in large projects.

When beginning a project, use Update Movies to convert Director 6 and 7 files to the latest file format.

At the end of a project, use Update Movies to compress all your movies and casts at once.

To update and compress movies and casts:

1   Choose Xtras > Update Movies.

The Update Movies dialog box appears.

2   Select one of the Action options:

- Update converts movies from Director 5 or later versions to the latest file format. As it updates movies, Director consolidates and removes fragmented data, just as when you use Save As. (To update movies from older versions, you must first convert them to the Director 5 file format.)
- Protect removes all the data required to edit the movie, but it does not compress the movies further. It adds the DXR extension to movies, and CXT to casts. Protect also flags the movie so it can't be opened in the authoring environment.
- Convert to Shockwave Movie(s) rewrites movies and casts in the compressed Shockwave file format and adds the DCR extension to movies and CCT to casts. This options also prevents users from opening the movie or cast and making changes. Once a movie is compressed, there is no way to it to recover an editable file, so be sure to keep the original movie.

3   Select one of the Original Files options:

- Back Up into Folder specifies that the original files go in a selected folder. Click Browse to select the folder for the original files. To avoid overwriting old backups, you should choose a new folder each time you run Update Movies.
- Delete specifies that the newly updated files overwrite the original files. Be very careful when using this option. Once a file is protected or compressed, you cannot open it again in Director.

4 Click OK.

A dialog box appears from which you select the files to change.

5 Select the movies and casts you want to change and click Add.

- Click Add All to add all the movies in the current folder. The items you select appear in the file list at the bottom of the dialog box. You can update movies in different folders at the same time.

- Select Add All Includes Folders before you click the Add All button to include any movies or casts inside folders appearing in the upper list. This option is useful for updating large projects with several levels of folders.

6 Click Update.

Director saves new versions of the selected movies with the same names and locations as the original movies. This ensures that all links and references to other files continue to work properly. Director copies the original movies to the folder you specified, re-creating their original folder structure. If you didn't specify a folder for the original movies, Director prompts you to select one.

Director adds the DCR extension to Shockwave movies and the CCT extension to external casts in the Shockwave format. Protected movies have the DXR extension, and protected casts have the CXT extension.

Exporting digital video and frame-by-frame bitmaps

You can export all or part of a movie as a digital video. You can use this digital video in other applications or import it back into Director. Any interactivity in the movie is lost when it is exported as a digital video. You can also export a movie or a part of a movie as a series of bitmaps: BMP in Windows, and PICS, PICT, or Scrapbook on the Macintosh.

You can export QuickTime digital video from either the Windows or the Macintosh version of Director. QuickTime must be installed on the system to export as QuickTime (version 4 or later required for Windows, version 3 or later required for Macintosh). You can export the Video for Windows (AVI) format only using the Windows version of Director. When you export to AVI, all sounds are lost.

When Director exports animation as a video or bitmaps, it takes snapshots of the Stage moment by moment and turns each snapshot into a frame in the video or a bitmap file. Sprites animated solely by Lingo are not exported.

When Director exports video or bitmaps, it always uses the entire Stage.

To export to digital video or bitmaps:

1 Choose File > Export.

The Export dialog box appears.

2 Select the range of frames you want from the Export options at the top of the dialog box:

- Current Frame exports the current frame on the Stage. This is the default.

- Selected Frames exports the selected frames in the Score.

- All Frames exports all frames.

- Frame Range exports only the range of frames that begin and end with the frame numbers you enter in the Begin and End boxes.

3 If you choose Selected Frames, All Frames, or Frame Range as the Export option, select one of the following options.

These options do not work with digital video.

- Every Frame exports all frames in the selected range.

- One in Every _ Frames exports only the frames at the interval you specify in the box.

- Frames with Markers exports frames with markers set in the Score window.

- Frames with Artwork Changes in Channel exports frames only when a cast member changes in the channel you specify in the box.

4 From the Format pop-up menu at the bottom of the dialog box, choose Video for Windows (AVI), BMP (Windows), QuickTime Movie, PICT (Macintosh), Scrapbook (Macintosh), or PICS (Macintosh).

BMP is the standard format for a Windows bitmap series. PICT, Scrapbook, and PICS are all Macintosh bitmap file formats.

5 If you are exporting in PICS format, click Use Frame Differencing to create smaller files.

This option is dimmed unless you choose PICS from the Format pop-up menu.

6 If you are exporting video, click the Options button.

The Video for Windows or QuickTime Options dialog box appears.

7 Select the options you want to use and then click OK.

For AVI movies, enter a number of frames per second for Frame Rate.

For information about the QuickTime options, see "Setting QuickTime export options" on page 456.

The Export dialog box reappears when you click OK.

8 Click Export.

A dialog box appears, prompting you to save the movie.

9 Name the file and then click Save.

When you click Export, a dialog box appears allowing you to name the file. If you are saving in video, PICS, or Scrapbook format, only one file will be created. If you are saving in BMP or PICT format, Director automatically creates one file for each frame, attaching the corresponding frame number to each file. For example, if the name of the exported file is Myfile, frame 1 will be exported to a file named Myfile0001.

Setting QuickTime export options

You use the QuickTime Options dialog box to specify options for exporting a movie as a QuickTime digital video. This dialog box appears when you click the Options button in the Export dialog box and QuickTime is the specified format.

To set QuickTime export options:

1 Choose File > Export.

2 Choose QuickTime Movie from the Format pop-up menu.

3 Click Options.

4 To set the speed the video will play, choose a Frame Rate option:

• Tempo Settings exports the settings in the tempo channel to the QuickTime movie. This setting lets you create a QuickTime movie at any tempo, even if Director is not capable of playing the movie at that tempo in real time.

The size of an exported QuickTime movie is influenced by the tempo settings, transitions, and palette transitions in the Director movie. Fast tempos, certain transitions, and palette transitions all increase the size of the QuickTime movie. The tempo settings determine the number of QuickTime frames per second and the number of frames per transition. The faster the tempo, the more frames per second.

A movie that would work well with Tempo Settings as the Frame Rate option is one in which the tempos have been carefully timed. For instance, some frames could be set to a tempo of 10 frames per second, and their QuickTime frame durations would be exactly one-tenth of a second. Other frames later in the movie could be set to a tempo of 1 frame per second; when the movie is exported, these slower frames would each last precisely 1 second in the QuickTime movie.

- Real Time lets you export a QuickTime movie that matches the performance of the Director movie as it plays on your system. (You should always play the entire movie with Lingo disabled before using this feature.)

  When you export a movie with Real Time selected, each Director frame becomes a QuickTime frame. Each frame in the QuickTime movie will match the duration of the same frame in the Director movie.

  Director will generate as many frames as required to duplicate each transition, up to 30 frames per second. To increase the number of frames created for any transition, reduce the smoothness of the transition.

  This option causes Director to use the actual durations that were stored the last time you played the entire movie, regardless of the actual tempo settings of the movie.

5 To reduce the file size of a QuickTime movie at the expense of quality, choose an option from the Compressor pop-up menu. Different options appear on the Compressor pop-up menu depending on the video hardware and software available in your system. Consult your QuickTime documentation.

- Animation compression is for simple animations.

- Cinepak compresses 16-bit and 24-bit video for playback from CD-ROMs.

- Component Video is usually used when capturing from a live video feed.

- Graphics compression is for exporting single frames of computer graphics.

- None exports with no compression.

- Photo-JPEG compression is good for scanned or digitized continuous-tone still images.

- Video compression is for exporting video clips.

6 To determine the compression quality and resulting file size when using the chosen compressor, use the Quality slider. A higher-quality setting preserves the appearance of the images and motion but increases the size of the file. A lower-quality setting results in poorer image quality but decreases the size of the file.

7 To determine the color depth (the number of colors) of your artwork, choose a setting from the Color Depth pop-up menu. The compression method you choose determines the color depth options available to you in this pop-up menu.

8 To determine the method by which the exported QuickTime movie is resized, choose values for Scale. You can choose a percentage from the Scale pop-up menu, or you can type pixel dimensions in the fields. By entering the number of pixels, you can stretch a movie so that it plays in a rectangle that does not adhere to the original aspect ratio.

9 To choose which soundtracks are exported with your movie, choose Channel 1 or Channel 2. A checked box indicates that the associated sound channel in the score is exported with your QuickTime file.

External sounds (sounds you imported as linked cast members) are not exported when you export a digital video. To include sound when you export a digital video movie, you must import the sounds as cast members instead of linking to them.

Looped sounds don't loop in a movie that you have exported as a digital video. To loop a sound in a movie that you plan to export as a digital video, you must trigger the sound by alternating it between the two sound channels.

About organizing movie files

In most cases, you should divide a large production into a series of smaller movies. You can combine as many movies as you want in a projector, but larger files take longer to save and are cumbersome to work with. Also, movies are easier to edit if they are organized in discrete sections.

The best way to organize a large production is to create a small projector file that launches the movie and then branches to Shockwave or protected movies. This saves you the trouble of re-creating the projector every time you change one part of a movie.

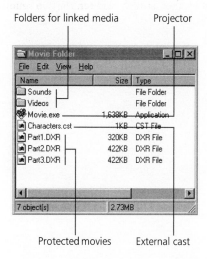

A typical file organization for a distributed movie

This approach also makes sense for movies on the Internet, but for different reasons. If the first movie is small, users don't have to wait as long for something to happen. Branching to a series of smaller movies also enables users to avoid downloading time for parts of the movie they do not use.

The size of your movie may be less of an issue if you use streaming Shockwave. For more information, see "Setting movie playback options" on page 414.

INDEX

Symbols

& operator 357
&& operator 357
¬ (continuation symbol). *See* continuation symbol

Numerics

5.x movies, updating 75
6.x movies, updating 75

A

abbreviating Lingo statements 185
accelerating sprites 243
accelerator keys. *See* keyboard shortcuts
actions, behavior inspector
    Beep 166
    Change Cast Member 166
    Change Cursor 166
    Change Ink 166
    Change Location 166
    Change Palette 166
    Change Tempo 166
    Go to Frame 165
    Go to Marker 165
    Go to Movie 165
    Go to Net Page 165
    New Action 166
    Perform Transition 166
    Play Cast Member 166
    Play External File 166
    Restore Cursor 166
    Set Volume 166
    Wait for Time Duration 166
    Wait on Current Frame 165
    Wait Until Click 166
    Wait Until Key Press 166
ActiveX 88, 405
actorList properties 288
Add ink 154
Add Pin ink 154
Air Brush tool (Paint window) 306, 309

Allow Colored Cells option 70
Allow Drag and Drop option 70
alpha channel, mask effects 151
ancestor
    property 175
    scripts 281
ancestors, in behaviors 175
Animate in Background option 76
Animate in Background projector option 450
animated cursors
    creating 268
    using 266
animated GIFs 303
    tempo 303
animating
    multiple sprites 253
    using multiple cast members 252
animation
    animated color cursors 266
    Cast to Time command 252
    defined 239
    exchanging cast members 249
    film loops 255
    frame-by-frame 249
    onion skinning 327
    with Lingo 256
anti-aliased text, definition 344
anti-aliasing
    setting with Lingo 354
    text 344
arguments
    definition of 182
    for handlers 191
arithmetic operators 208
Arrange menu 125
arrays, *See* lists 194
ASCII characters 349
attaching behaviors 158
audio compression. *See* Shockwave Audio
audio. *See* sound

P

vector shapes *(continued)*
    setting attributes with Lingo 297
    setting gradient for with Lingo 301
verbose syntax in Lingo 186
Verisign Xtra downloading 435
vertex
    defined 293
    selecting 295
Video for Windows (AVI). *See* digital video
video. *See* digital video
Video window 373
View menu, Display commands 131
Volume Control ShockMachine option 415, 443

W

Wait for Cue Point tempo option 234
Wait for Mouse Click tempo option 234
Wait for Time Duration action 166
Wait on Current Frame action 165
Wait Until Click action 166
Wait Until Key Press action 166
Warp button (Paint window) 313
Web216 color palette 225, 231
Width of Score Window sprite preference 121
windows
    AVI 373
    Field window 347
    Marker window 71
    Paint window 304
    Quicktime 373
    Text 338
    Video 373
    Video window 373
Windows operating system, sound issues 364
wipe. *See* transitions

X

Xtras
    about distributing with projectors 83
    Auto Filter command 326
    bitmap filters 325
    cast member 81
    description of 81
    displaying list of 214
    displaying methods 214
    download properties 435
    Filter Bitmap command 325
    importing 81
    installing 82
    managing for distributed movies 435
    Scripting 82
    tool 82
    transition 82, 236, 238
    viewing properties 103, 104
Xtras Cast Member Properties dialog box 117

Z

zero point, moving for paint rulers 309
Zoom pop-up menu, in Score 68
zooming
    Paint window 310
    Stage 63
    Vector Shape window 294
Zooming ShockMachine option 415, 443